Bc

# THE
# DAR

*B Y*

## Margaret Gibbs

# T H E

*HOLT, RINEHART AND WINSTON*
NEW YORK   CHICAGO   SAN FRANCISCO

# CONTENTS

# THE
# DAR

"WHAT DO THE DAUGHTERS DO?"

"Next time you are asked this question, sincerely reply: The Daughters of the American Revolution work and they work hard, many, long hours to preserve the past, to carry out obligations to the present and to build a firm foundation to safeguard the future."

—*The DAR In Action,*
1963 Edition

"We know full well that the patriotism of common descent is the mere patriotism of the clan—the early patriotism of the tribe— and that, while the possession of a like territory is an advance upon that first conception, both of them are unworthy to be the patriotism of a great cosmopolitan nation . . . To seek our patriotism in some age rather than our own is to accept a code that is totally inadequate to help us through the problems which current life develops."

—Jane Addams, 1911

# I

## "WHAT DO THE DAUGHTERS DO?"

In 1956, Nikita S. Khrushchev announced a new party line which featured the removal of Joseph Stalin as a national idol; six United States Marine recruits were drowned on a forced night march, and their drill instructor, Staff Sergeant Matthew C. McKeon, was demoted to private and sentenced to three months' imprisonment for negligent homicide; the Hungarian revolt was brutally crushed by the Soviet armed forces; President Gamal Abdel Nasser seized the Suez Canal; and Miss Gertrude S. Carraway, President General of the Daughters of the American Revolution called a special press conference to issue an important announcement. When everyone was assembled at the Society's impressive national headquarters at 1776 D Street, N.W., Washington, D.C., Miss Carraway stated that it had been proven that there was a definite link between the members' partiality toward orchid corsages and their first President General, the revered Mrs. Benjamin Harrison.

She reminded the press of the long-standing joke that "if a lady wears one orchid it means she has a genuine admirer; if she wears two orchids, she has a generous husband; if she wears three orchids, she has a boyfriend; if she wears four or more, she's a DAR." Now, she said, she was ready to offer positive proof that the Daughters—for so they like to be called—could wear as many of their favorite flower as they pleased and still remain above ridicule on the dignified plane of an organization dedicated to history, education, and patriotism. The wearing of orchids simply was a way of paying tribute to their original leader.

The discovery was accredited to Mr. Frank E. Klapthor, the new curator of their museum, who was the first man ever employed by the Society in a professional capacity. Fortunately he had a discerning male eye for feminine adornment. While checking the progress of the restoration of a portrait of Mrs. Harrison, he suddenly noticed that she was wearing a lustrous gray silk gown with an unmistakable wild-orchid design woven into the fabric. This intrigued him. If Mrs. Harrison had initiated the love of the flower into the Society, it could become the ladies' traditional badge, rather than a capricious luxury, for nothing is dearer to the hearts of all 186,000 Daughters than tradition.

Mr. Klapthor set out on a pilgrimage to Indianapolis to visit the Harrison museum, where relics of that President's family and administration are housed. To his delight he found that Mrs. Harrison, an able amateur artist, had frequently used orchids as a subject for china painting and watercolors. In 1890, during her term as First Lady, one of her watercolors of a white orchid had actually been lithographed and distributed "in dedication to the mothers, wives and daughters of America." Further research showed that it had been she who introduced the flower into the White House conservatories. It was also discovered that she had often worn them to official meetings of Cabinet wives and at DAR functions, and as Miss Carraway said in her 1956 statement: "The Daughters have been wearing them ever since."

How this information could have remained in obscurity from 1890 to 1956 was never explained; still it was news, not only to the outside world but to many of the members themselves. Certain elderly ones had a vivid recollection of the huge bouquet of roses presented to the exquisite Mrs. Donald McLean upon her retirement as their President General. That was in 1909. Others remembered the stir created in 1913 when the attractive little Mrs. William Cumming Story, another President General, tripped into a luncheon carrying a bunch of daisies given to her as a whimsical tribute to her first name. Then what about violets? Since the annual DAR Continental Congress is always held in the week containing Patriots' Day, April 19, it often coincides with Easter, and until the end of World War I violets were certainly a favorite Easter corsage. Finally, a photograph of the founders, including Mrs. Harrison, shows the ladies in high-neck, long-sleeve, dark dresses without a single adorning flower.

Granville Gude is the only Washington florist authorized to have a booth in the lobby of the DAR auditorium at Constitution Hall. Since he sometimes sells as many as 300 corsages a day—mostly of orchids—during Congress Week, he should be an expert on their history. He recalls that the flower did not become extremely popular with the Daughters until the early 1920s.

In spite of these minor rumblings of dissent, when Miss Carraway gave her official stamp of approval, the orchid took on a sound historical significance. Everyone politely forgot that any other flower might once have had preference.

When the President General of the DAR speaks, it is not considered good form for the rank and file to question her words. This omnipotent power is enjoyed by the entire Board of Management. Furthermore all officers, from the twenty-one vice-presidents down to the Chaplain, are Generals. Among themselves the title is understood only to indicate officers of the "general or national society"; but, intentionally or not, the DAR constitution carries a certain militant flavor. It clearly states: "Daughters of the American Revolution, A National Chapter— independent of state societies, the several chapters standing in the same relation to the Mother Society, as the Posts of the Grand Army of the Republic to the head of the army." Policy is formed by the National Board of Management, and strict adherence to the given policy is expected of all members.

The structure of the DAR is perhaps the unique feature that sets it apart from other women's organizations in which the governing body is responsible to the individual member. For instance, the League of Women Voters requires state and local branches to discuss and vote on all proposals before they are allowed to become part of the agenda at their national convention. DAR delegates, on the other hand, arrive in Washington with only the vaguest overall notion of what they will be asked to approve.

During a Continental Congress, as the DAR convention is called, discussion from the floor—on even the most serious topic —is sternly limited to three minutes for each individual on any one resolution, a span of time hardly conducive to debate. A number of members consider such a limitation an insult to their intelligence, but very few are sufficiently aroused to voice objections.

No one would care if the Board's dogmatic policy were applied merely to orchids and ancestry, but the Daughters make it a habit to concern themselves with issues of national importance. The light tone of Miss Carraway's flower interview is unusual. More typically, again in 1956, when Attorney General Herbert Brownell, Jr., and President Eisenhower were urging a bill to liberalize the McCarran-Walter Immigration Act, the DAR passed a resolution stating that restricted immigration was imperative to our national security. The delegates' passive compliance to the will of the Board is taken so much for granted that almost without discussion, the vote was unanimous. The NSDAR (a term used to designate the official voice of the Society) maintains that attacks upon the McCarran-Walter Act are led by "Communists and other left-wing groups." A 1956 DAR National Defense leaflet states: "These groups have been joined by others who doubtless with good motives have been misled by the barrage of propaganda which has been unleashed against the law."

At the same Congress, again with little or no debate, the Daughters commended the American Legion for demanding the removal of all UNESCO material from our public schools and passed a similar resolution of their own.

The fifty-member Resolutions Committee is even more powerful than the President General. For a week before the opening of each Congress it meets to study the proposals sent from all over the country. These may come from state, chapter, or individual level. The Resolutions Committee has the final and irrevocable say on what will be presented to the delegates for the vote. It works in strictest secrecy, and it is not considered good form to question its judgment.

In 1963, the committee received 288 proposals, covering 121 subjects. In a press interview, the committee's chairman Mrs. Elizabeth M. Cox stated that a certain amount of duplication in the submissions simplified their task. For instance, 16 dealt with patriotic education, 17 with prayers and religious observances in school, 15 with arms control and disarmament, 12 with federal debt and foreign aid, 12 with freedom of the press and news "management," 14 with the Monroe Doctrine, and 12 with the DAR's perennial denunciation of the United Nations. One, demanding the "Preservation of the Bald-headed Eagle," was not considered within the domain of the Society's province. The contents of the remaining 189 were undisclosed.

Out of 288 proposals, only 12 appeared on the agenda. It is unusual for the Daughters to have a mere dozen resolutions to consider. Although only one—which dealt with reverence and respect in the display of the flag—was brought up at their first Congress, in 1891, in later years 50 or 60 questions have been settled at one sitting.

The Resolutions Committee explained that "streamlining" was the reason for a vigorous screening of proposals, but when printed copies were distributed, some delegates felt that "streamlining" had been a master move. Women arriving at the Congress hoping to defend UNESCO or, more particularly in this year, UNICEF were shocked to find that any discussion of separate United Nations agencies was out of order. In past years it had been customary to study a number of the agencies individually, but now they were neatly blanketed under one heading and a general resolution on the UN as a whole had to be accepted or rejected.

A somewhat recent innovation has been the institution of the "standing vote" on certain major issues. In 1957, the parliamentarian, Mrs. Henry M. Robert, Jr. (daughter-in-law of the author of the famous *Rules of Order*), explained that the standing vote allowed greater member participation and lessened fatigue at long sessions.

As a matter of course, the standing vote was used to decide a general resolution condemning the UN as a whole. Pages quickly manned their strategic posts for the counting. (Pages are junior members between the ages of eighteen and thirty who are chosen for their charm and vivacity. Always dressed in white, over 300 of them are a refreshing note during Congress Week. Two of them are the constant attendants of the President General and even escort her to the powder room. The remainder act as "girl Fridays" to the delegates. Vote counting is only one of their many duties.) As soon as the girls in white were ready, Mrs. Robert V. H. Duncan, the incumbent leader, called:

"Those for . . ."

From above, the standing women in their flowered hats looked more like a sleek, well-tended garden than a determined assembly reaffirming its belief in the sovereignty of nationalism. The pages' necks craned, their bodies bobbed, heads darted. For less than a minute they went through the pretense of counting nearly 2,500 women.

"Those opposed . . ."

The few weeds of defiance sprang up, singly or in pairs. Even one quite large group from Glens Falls, New York, looked hopelessly insignificant in a hall that seats 4,000 people. The exact number of the minority was not announced, but they were kept on their feet much longer than the majority. The *Washington Post* estimated that there were about a hundred dissenters. This was somewhat surprising because, in private, many Daughters admit that even if they disagree with a resolution, they do not like to "stand up" in a public vote because they do not want to "stand out." Finally the gavel descended and the resolution was passed to hearty applause and good-natured laughter.

The delegates made short work of the last four resolutions. These dealt with (9) council of state government, (10) Atlantic Charter and Declaration of Paris, (11) personality tests, and (12) domestic peace corps. Opposition was called for and promised to all. The business session ended in time for a good early lunch.

Mrs. Dennis E. Kent, Regent of the chapter in Chappaqua, New York, attended this Seventy-Second Congress and opposed the blanket denunciation of the UN. On May 14, 1963, she told her local chapter that in her opinion the NSDAR was ruled by a small, tight hierarchy. Later she made a formal statement to the press that received countrywide attention. In it she said:

> While the DAR professes no political purpose and claims tax exemption on the strength of it, its policy year after dreary year, monotonously issued from its rubber-stamp

congresses, supports uniformly the position of a certain segment of American political thought. No resolution contrary to positions of the far-right wing is adopted.

It is crystal clear that the DAR has been warped from its original purposes, that the membership at large has no voice of any kind in the formation of DAR policies. It is clear that a tiny band of purposeful people has distorted the patriotic basis of the DAR.

It is also clear that the reason for this deplorable situation is that the membership at large has no chance to express itself effectively. This is perpetuated by the general apathy of the DAR members, the development of a compartmentalized structure to prevent communication between chapters or States except through the national society and by use of subtle devices to insure compliance with national society aims.

Any such organization is subject to easy capture by a purposeful group. The results can be seen in efforts to deny free speech, in suppression of textbooks, in smear campaigns against any who disagree as Communists, and as I have experienced, in naked intimidation.

Later, Mrs. Kent was interviewed on the radio program *Communiqué* by Ron Roby over station WVIP, Mount Kisco, New York. She described being surrounded by angry fellow members during Congress Week whenever a reporter approached her. Since her discontent was already well known within the Society, she said other Daughters refused to let her make a statement to the press and, on the whole, acted as though they were protecting a person of unsound mind from prying news hounds.

Even if some other members secretly share Mrs. Kent's opinions, they rarely express public criticism of the Society. In fact, only a few take exception to the Board's dictates on national and international affairs. To many of these women approval or disapproval of resolutions is not the most important reason for attending Congress. They are there for glamour. Even the trash cans in the cafeteria of their building are sprayed with gold. Delegates often return year after year to see old friends, make new ones, and have a good time in general. The casual remark "This is my twenty-fourth congress" is not unusual.

Still, it must not be supposed that Grant Wood's painting of three elderly women sipping tea is typical of all Daughters. The delegates who come to Washington look very much like any other women at any other large convention. There are tall ones, short ones, pretty ones, plain ones, thin ones, fat ones; of course, there are a certain number of dowdy members but, for the main part, they are exceedingly chic.

Most of them have that extra spring to their walk that is the happy characteristic of a busy, interesting life. The average age seems to run from the mid-forties through the active sixties, and there are numerous very attractive younger women to be seen among the festive throng. By the Society's own count 33 percent of the membership was between eighteen and thirty-five and over 34 percent of the people who joined the organization in 1965 belonged to this age group.

Long ago, wags of a traditionally unsympathetic press dubbed the DAR Congress the "*D*amned *A*wful *R*umpus." Secretly, members take pride in its firebrand reputation; they feel cheated if events run too smoothly. They want a good show and Congress Week tends to be bombastic. For five days they besiege the District. In mock terror the city yields to the onslaught. If it ceased to occur most Washingtonians would miss the sham battle that is as much a sign of spring as the cherry blossoms.

The Daughters are conspicuous even in a convention-jaded town like Washington because of two distinguishing features. One is a bewildering assortment of blue and white ribbons which are proudly draped from right shoulder to left hip. These are called sashes. The officers of the Society are rarely seen without them. Although sashes may not be worn over coats, they may adorn suits if the day is cool. For evening sessions they always embellish formal gowns. (Evening sessions are strictly formal affairs and most members consider it a must to have a different dress for each night of the week.) The President General has the broadest sash of all. Blue with white edging, it measures fully five inches across. All national officers are entitled to similar personal sashes, with width determined by the importance of their post.

All past officials hold honorary lifetime titles. They have their own sashes of distinction—with the blue and white reversed. Past officials make a point of attending Congress whenever possible, so sashes of both past and present vintage dominate the scene.

Another accouterment is even more noticeable. Each active member is entitled to purchase and wear the official insignia, a gold spinning wheel, measuring seven-eighths of an inch in diameter, set on an inch-and-a-half platinum distaff. The rim of the wheel is blue enamel, and the stars surrounding its circumference represent the original thirteen states. The insignia symbolizes the DAR motto of "Home and Country," and must be worn over the left breast. For official occasions, such as the Congress, it is suspended from an inch-wide, blue-centered ribbon which is pinned to the left shoulder by a gold bar engraved with the name of the ancestor through whom the member was admitted to the Society.

A variety of other badges may be attached below the bar. The official DAR jeweler, J. E. Caldwell & Company of Philadelphia, estimates that the firm has at least 200 dies of designs that members can add to the ribbon as they are earned. The badges include twenty-five and fifty-year membership; chapter, state, and national office; and chairmanship of a committee. Then there are supplemental ancestor bars for members tracing more than one Revolutionary hero in their heritage. Some have been successful in proving more than a dozen.

The Society designates that the length of the ribbon must not exceed twelve inches and that only eight pins may be worn on each one. This problem is easily solved by adding another ribbon as soon as the first one is filled up. Of course, no one actually wears all 200 emblems, but many display two or three ribbons full. As a way of conversational emphasis an older member often achieves a magnificent effect by tossing her trophies like the mane of a spirited horse. So adorned, the Daughters are busy every minute they are at the capital.

Congress Week is a precious adventure for most Daughters because, as they put it, it gives them a chance to come *home*. "Home" is the affectionate term they always use when speaking of their Washington headquarters. They are fond of explaining that it is the largest edifice ever conceived, built, owned, and maintained entirely by women. Each Daughter seems to take as much pride in it as if it were her personal property.

Composed of three connecting structures, headquarters runs from 17th to 18th Street, N.W., and from C through to D. It takes eight minutes to walk at a fast pace all the way around it. The entrance to Memorial Continental Hall is on 17th Street. It is a graceful marble building, the original DAR assembly auditorium. When outgrown, it was converted into a genealogical reference library, where 49,000 books and pamphlets and 30,000 manuscripts are housed. The Daughters have good reason to be proud of their library. Only the Library of Congress and the National Archives can compare with this wealth of genealogical material. It is open to the general public, except during April when a number of members spend more time there than attending Congress sessions.

Constitution Hall, their present auditorium, faces 18th Street. Finished in 1929, when the price of marble was prohibitive, it is constructed of limestone which blends harmoniously with the original structure.

The Administration Building, also of limestone, connects the two halls. Here are located forty-four national offices, a chapel, the Americana Room, a repository of historical documents, and the DAR Museum Gallery.

The official opening of the Congress takes place in Constitution Hall on Monday evening of the April week containing Patriots' Day. Quite a few male guests in tails and dinner jackets attend this gala. Every seat is filled in time for the half-hour concert given by the Marine Corps Band—a tradition since the early days of the Society. When the concert is finished, the audience rises and faces the rear of the auditorium to watch the Grand Entrance March of the national officers.

Flanked by pages bearing the Society's banners and the emblems of each state of the Union, the President General leads the long procession. When she reaches the center of the hall, one of the most enormous American flags ever made in this country is suddenly unfurled and extends from the vaulted ceiling almost to the heads of the throng. An ungloved hand flies to the heart of each spectator, in the civilian salute, and there it remains until all the officers are on the stage, towering above the assembly.

After the invocation, the Pledge of Allegiance, the American's Creed, and two stanzas of the "Star-Spangled Banner," everyone is seated and the exercises begin. After the President General reads a message from the President of the United States, she gives a keynote address setting the tone of that year's Congress. She then introduces a number of welcoming dignitaries, including an emissary from the District of Columbia Board of Commissioners and one from the Sons of the American Revolution.

Three daily sessions are held throughout the rest of Congress Week. Between sessions members can inspect the museum or attend open house in one of the twenty-seven period rooms decorated and maintained by individual states. A quick glance at a bulletin board in the Administration Building shows whether the Illinois Drawing Room, the Oklahoma Kitchen, or the New Hampshire Children's Attic is serving refreshments. The lobby of Constitution Hall also offers many attractions. J. E. Caldwell & Company occupies a conspicuous booth, where a Daughter may inspect and perhaps order a new pin or bar to add to her collection. The price of these trinkets range from $3 to $3,000. Then there is Gude the florist, an official photographer, an Ask Mr. Foster Travel Service, Inc., and a bazaar set up by junior members for the benefit of their scholarship fund. A crowd can usually be found around the large booth selling literature published by the Society. Pamphlets issued by the National Defense Committee are popular items.

DAR activities also overflow into every prominent hotel in the city, and taxis shuttle members between Constitution Hall and a series of breakfasts, brunches, luncheons, teas, dinners, and receptions. Daughters have the reputation of being such poor tippers that drivers take care to fill their taxis full, calling out, "Mayflower, Mayflower!" or "Willard!" or "Sheraton Park!"

before starting out for a destination. The Mayflower, the habitual setting of the annual Pages' Ball and the final banquet, has the lion's share of the week's social activities. On Tuesday, April 16, 1963, alone, the hotel's North Room was the site of a breakfast for the Mississippi contingent, while the Program, Public Relations, and Motion Picture Committees were having a joint meal in the State Room. The establishment served luncheon for Delaware in the Jefferson Room, Iowa in the Chinese Room, Kansas in the Pan American Room, Maryland in the State Room, New York in the Ballroom, and South Carolina in the East Room. At 5:30 a buffet supper was given by the Alabama Daughters in the Colonial Room. A little later Colorado had dinner in the North Room, Connecticut in the East Room, and Georgia in the Chinese Room. Because most breakfasts are slated for 7:15 A.M. and evening sessions rarely close before midnight, attending Congress can be a rough experience, but the Daughters thrive on it.

The flurry of social activities serves to keep the Daughters from pondering too much on general policy. A good Daughter, moreover, honestly believes that even if some fault may be found with the existing governing oligarchy, the ideals and aims of the organization itself are beyond reproach. She is convinced that the world does not always understand the motives and procedures of the Society, and she is hypersensitive to outside criticism. She shuts her eyes to unavoidable minor weaknesses. In justification she points to the long list of DAR achievements. These are patiently reiterated by the leaders to the membership at frequent intervals and are proof enough to the loyal Daughter of the Society's virtue. Shortly before Mrs. Dennis E. Kent's outburst in 1963 an official pamphlet called *The DAR In Action* gave an elaborate account of the good works and brought them up to date. It began:

The National Society, Daughters of the American Revolution, was formally organized October 11, 1890, for the purpose of providing and promoting historical, educational and patriotic service. It was incorporated under the laws of the District of Columbia in 1891. A Charter was granted to the Society by the United States Congress and signed by President Grover Cleveland in 1896. This Charter provides that the National Society make an annual report to the Smithsonian Institution, which in turn reports to the United States Congress.

After a short section on membership, it states that "The full DAR Story is primarily one of *service*" and again gives the aims, emphasized this time by capitalization. It then continues:

We are often asked just what are the NSDAR accomplishments. This question is difficult to answer, not because of lack of material, but because the NSDAR, in so many ways, has an outstanding record of contributions. The NSDAR embraces all interests in life: historical, educational, patriotic and cultural.

With a swift change of subjects, the next paragraph gives a lengthy description of the headquarters, which is "worth around $8,000,000 and debt-free." It is emphasized strongly that the money for the construction of the buildings was raised entirely by the Daughters themselves, with no outside assistance.

Then again the reader is reminded that the NSDAR "is a dedicated service organization" and that through the efforts of "23 National Committees" its comprehensive program "appeals to and is designed for the child, the youth, and the adult." The majority of these committees "were established not for the DAR and its members, but to aid and benefit our Country and citizens."

At this point, the article insists that the greatest contribution of the DAR is to "EDUCATION" and it goes on to describe two DAR-owned schools and a number of others that receive partial support from the Society. Furthermore, the American Indian Committee was "established to help American Indians take their rightful place in our American Way of Life." The Indian Committee also aids two schools: St. Mary's for girls in Springfield, South Dakota, and Bacone College in Bacone, Oklahoma.

DAR work among the "foreign-born" is also stressed. This is

taken care of by the Americanism and the DAR Manual for Citizenship Committees. Since 1920, the Society has distributed "nearly 9 million DAR Manuals for Citizenship" and in 1962 alone presented 1,405 prizes to American essay-contest winners, "and $24,248 was spent by the DAR" on this project.

There follows an avalanche of vital statistics, dealing mostly with scholarships, school awards and prizes, on which they expend "around $200,000 annually." The best known perhaps is the Good Citizens Committee's award of a $100 Saving Bond to an outstanding senior girl from each state and the District of Columbia. (Although mentioned here, the national winner of this contest is the Daughters' guest during Congress Week and receives $1,000 scholarship to the college of her choice.)

The account of the National Defense Committee activities is discreetly limited to the information that, in 1962, they also presented "9,288 Good Citizen Medals to boys and girls in the graduating classes of elementary, junior and senior high schools who possessed the four important qualities of *dependability, service, leadership* and *patriotism*. These medals are not to be confused with the GOOD CITIZENS AWARDS which are given to SENIOR HIGH SCHOOL GIRLS *ONLY*."

Since the National Defense Committee receives the major share of the annual appropriations ($30,000 in 1963), it seems curious that so little attention is paid to its other duties. Rather abruptly, the pamphlet goes on to state that also in 1962 "26,000 United States Flags and 40,000 Flag Codes were presented to schools, scout troops and others" and that more than 5,596 History certificates and several thousand medals were given to 5th and 6th grade pupils.

Next, comes a description of the DAR work in architectural restoration, plaques supplied by them for historic sites, and their tireless efforts to locate and mark the graves of Revolutionary soldiers. The functions of the American History Month and Constitution Week Committees are listed. This is followed by a discussion of the Conservation Committee. We find that, aside from feeding "enormous quantities of seed and suet" to birds during the winter and migratory seasons, members have planted "nearly 68 million [67,904,077] trees, shrubs and seedlings."

Finally there is a really impressive account of the National Society's efforts in times of "National emergencies" and the pamphlet concludes with a flourish:

> Pause a moment and attempt to total all of this expenditure of time, energy and money, through the past 72 years, by the Daughters of the American Revolution.
>
> It certainly provides a most impressive answer to the question: "What do the Daughters DO?" Next time you are asked this question, sincerely reply: The Daughters of the American Revolution work and they work hard, many, long hours to preserve the past, to carry out obligations to the present and to build a firm foundation to safeguard the future.

The stated aims of the Daughters of the American Revolution are certainly praiseworthy. A careful reading of this booklet might suggest that the NSDAR had been viciously maligned by Mrs. Kent. In point of fact, *The DAR In Action* shows only one side of the picture, hardly the aspect of the Society which attracts the most public attention.

The pamphlet is misleading because of the vague, innocent way in which the National Defense Committee is mentioned. The power of the National Defense Committee exceeds that suggested by the pamphlet. With the exception of the one devoted to Genealogy, all other committees are subject to either its influence, direction or authority. For example, although the School Committee is allowed to supervise approved DAR institutions, the overall policy of the Society's active, militant educational program is directed by the National Defense group, and Defense is the only committee that issues a monthly pamphlet of its own. Called *The National Defender*, a year's subscription costs $2.50. In the true spirit of public "service," this publication is available not only to the Daughters themselves but to anyone sufficiently interested to subscribe.

The Committee also publishes countless pamphlets, among them the *DAR Textbook Study 1958–1959*, essentially a 20-page blacklist of schoolbooks found in use at the elementary and secondary level. It is still taken as gospel by the members as well as by many other citizens outside the organization who believe that the slightest hint of progressive education is fraught with communist influence. Other pamphlets cover everything from attacks on the National Council of Churches to demands for the prohibition of fluoridation in city water systems. (The Daughters work on the assumption that municipal fluoridation is communist inspired because strong doses of fluoride have been used in the Soviet Union as an aid to "brainwashing.") This literature is available to the general public—mostly for the modest sum of one to ten cents. The committee also distributes the propaganda of other organizations, some of which are so obscure that it is questionable if their output would find an audience unless it were called to notice by the NSDAR.

As a nonprofit, patriotic, educational organization, the DAR enjoys considerable tax immunity. It was Mrs. Kent's contention that the Society has insufficient freedom from political bias and partisanship to justify this fiscal privilege. Even its real estate is tax free (with the exception of Constitution Hall, for which tax rates are determined on the basis of annual rental, rather than on its total property value).

As soon as the hall was completed it became the District's largest and most attractive place for concerts and lectures when not being used for the Daughters' own Congress. Certain Washington businessmen, financially interested in a commercial auditorium, objected to the unfair competition. In 1934, these business men pressured the city government to demand $20,908 from the DAR in back taxes on the building. The city government threatened to sell the building unless these taxes were paid. After a legal battle, a final compromise brought about the present method of taxation. The Daughters now pay about $16,000 a year on rent receipts, but this is certainly a drop in the bucket compared to the actual value of their holdings. A structure covering an entire city block must seem a juicy plum to assessors.

The Society is resourceful when it comes to money matters. The hierarchy encourages every member to participate in one special activity—helping to keep the budget balanced. Each

Daughter is expected to do her share, no matter how small the contribution.

Outside assistance has never been solicited for any of the DAR's projects. The vast sums of money needed for its ambitious building program have been coaxed out of the members without the Board's ever needing the assistance of a professional fund raiser. The campaign is directed by the Treasurer General. Quite often her successful efforts are subsequently rewarded by her election to the office of President General.

The methods used by officers seeking funds are ingenious and original. One of the earliest devices for paying off the mortgage was a "bits and pieces" plan. Each of twenty-seven states "bought" a room in Memorial Continental Hall, which means that they assumed complete responsibility for furnishing and refurbishing it whenever necessary. Variations of the "bits and pieces" plan are called into play whenever cash is needed.

Bronze plaques or markers are a familiar sight throughout the buildings. These indicate that an individual, a chapter, or a state society has "bought" that particular section and given it in dedication to a Regent or in the memory of a deceased relative or friend. The purchase can be of an entire wall as in the case of the tribute to Mrs. Henry B. Joy, venerable leader of the Michigan Daughters, or as modest as a drinking fountain on the first floor inscribed to Mrs. Julius Y. Talmadge and paid for by her Georgia chapter. Every inch of the place, from the outside doors to the rest rooms, is owned by someone. There is good reason to call headquarters "home."

While Constitution Hall was being amortized, Mrs. Russell W. Magna offered space by the cubic foot in the new building. Even the 5,870 feet of the foundation were up for sale. Mrs. Magna, whose nickname was the "Little Gold Digger," explained that in this way it was possible for all to feel the pride of ownership, no matter how small their share. Of course the price of each foot of the foundation was too insignificant to merit a marker. Similarly, markers couldn't be placed on the furniture "sold" by Mrs. Rex Hays Rhoades in 1950. Hard pressed to pay off the debt for the renovation of the Administration Building, she literally ran out of architectural features. She raised an extra $4,000 by convincing the members they should buy the office tables, chairs, desks, lamps, bookcases, and even the books in them.

Although this is the most effective procedure, the Treasurer General will try many things to free the organization of debt. Back in 1913 there was the "penny a day" plan. Each Daughter was supposed to save a penny a day in a piggy bank until $3.65 was accumulated at the end of the year. This amount was intended to be each member's contribution toward decreasing the debt, but the project was soon abandoned as ineffectual. Then there was the "Block plan," named after its originator, the wealthy Mrs. Willard T. Block of Chicago. Caldwell & Company of Philadelphia issued $1 certificates. Of this sum 90 cents was to go toward the mortgage fund and 10 cents to the firm. Neither was this venture very successful. Only $15,000 was raised, and there were 70,000 certificates still on hand. Furthermore, there was some embarrassment when it was discovered that Caldwell had not received a large part of its designated share. Matters were at an impasse until 1917, when the establishment gracefully canceled the debt by earmarking it as its contribution to the Memorial Continental Hall fund. This may be called the only subscription ever accepted by the DAR from anyone outside the membership. Never again have they involved any outsider in one of their drives.

Piggy banks and the "Block plan" probably failed because they lacked color. The Daughters enjoy a little imaginative prodding. In 1949, again during the Administration Building program, delegates wore corsages made of dollar bills rather than orchids. They also enthusiastically pledged the price of their hats to swell the coffers. Nearly $125,000 was collected at that Congress.

The money raisers are never lacking in ideas. In the previous year, at the beginning of the renovation, a huge box elder—dating back to George Washington's time—had to be sacrificed to make room for the new expansion. Instead of being thrown away, it was promptly cut up and converted into bookends and flag stands. These articles were all gone at the end of Convening

Day. In that same year, Mrs. Rhoades made the triumphant report that the Society's fiscal record was so sound that "we are able to borrow $200,000 at 2½ percent interest on our reputation alone." This is the way they have bought and paid for the largest building "ever conceived for women by women."

It should not be assumed that all Daughters are wealthy but it is the rule rather than the exception for members of the Board of Management to be women of considerable means. Only the President General receives a token annual expense account of around $6,000 which does not begin to cover her extensive tours to state conventions and chapter meetings throughout the country. All other officers pay their own way wherever they go and, since they also are expected to make many appearances during their term, it is doubtful if they would run for office unless they could afford to keep up their own end.

When "Grandma" Moses (Mrs. Anna Mary Robertson Moses) was a young girl, her mother told her that she was eligible to become a Daughter but warned her against joining because it was "too expensive." "Grandma" took the advice to heart and did not enter the Hoosac-Walloomsac Chapter, Hoosac Falls, New York, until 1952 after she had gained fame and fortune as an artist. From then on, she was an enthusiastic member and gave one of her paintings, "The Battle of Bennington," to the DAR Museum in 1953. The ever resourceful fund raisers quickly turned the gift to good account by granting Hallmark permission to reproduce the picture. The agreement contract stated that Hallmark would give the DAR 10,000 notecard folders for the privilege of reproduction. These were placed on sale for 10 cents a piece at the Washington Headquarters. The proceeds went to the museum's art fund and were earmarked for the restoration of other canvases.

"Grandma" Moses was by no means the only illustrious Daughter. Over the years many celebrities have swelled the ranks including Lillian and Dorothy Gish and Lavinia Warren Bump who is better known by her professional name of Mrs. Tom Thumb.

# II

It may come as a surprise to some to discover that the DAR is such a relatively young organization. One is apt to think of the Society as old enough to have supplied volunteers for Betsy Ross' sewing bee. Contrary to popular assumption, however, not only the Daughters of the American Revolution but a large number of patriotic societies based on antecedence were originated in the 1890s.

The "nineties" have been called naughty, gay, the Gaslight Era, the Horse and Buggy Days, the Mauve Decade, the Gilded Age. A stiff coat of glamour has been sprayed on Carrie Nation, Salvation Army Nell, the merciless bulls and bears of Wall Street, paupers under Brooklyn Bridge, as well as provincial spooners in fringe-top surreys, the Four Hundred attending a countless round of costume balls, and gaudy ladies accompanying well-heeled politicians down the slippery path of graft. This galaxy is thought to represent the period. Hardly anyone realizes it was also the time when ancestor worshipers began to cultivate a forest of family trees.

Lineage tracing was as much the rage in this decade—and in the early 1900s—as mah-jongg and crossword puzzles in the "roaring twenties." It was not only a favorite indoor sport of dignified elderly gentlemen and lonely spinsters who enjoyed the opportunity for an elaborate research project but heredity digging also titillated a sufficiently large audience for many newspapers to feature a genealogical department. In New York, the Astor Library installed a room for "the large number of searchers after family history" and happily reported that "the attendance there attests the popularity of the fad." By 1896 the *Library Journal* began to offer hints on how to help the public trace their elusive progenitors. Although the east coast was the center of the craze, every city in the country had its fair share of delving buffs.

For some it may have been merely a pleasant pastime, but

most of the researchers were spurred on by an intense desire to become eligible for membership in one of the new and fashionable societies. In 1900, a little journal called the *Patriotic Review* listed seventy patriotic, hereditary and historical associations. Exactly half of them had come into existence during the preceding ten years. The Daughters were part of that day's American Dream.

A current DAR booklet entitled *Is That Lineage Right?* includes an appendix of "Ancestral Requirements for Membership in Various Societies." It lists twenty-two major organizations, all of which have one requirement in common: the participation of an ancestor in the Revolutionary War. Many groups—not the DAR—insist on their members having an ancestor who demonstrated his worth to the country prior to 1776. The list of organizations is illuminating when it is shifted into order of founding dates and, whenever possible, present enrollments are added:

| Organization | Founding Dates | Present Members |
|---|---|---|
| Society of the Cincinnati | May 10, 1783 | 2,150 |
| General Society of the War of 1812 | Sept. 14, 1814 | 1,660 |
| Sons of the Revolution, General Society | Feb. 11, 1876 | 6,570 |
| Holland Society of New York | 1885 | not to exceed 1,000 |
| Sons of the American Revolution | April 30, 1889 | 20,000 |
| Colonial Dames of America (Parent Society) | April, 1890 | 1,863 |
| Daughters of the American Revolution, National Society | Oct. 11, 1890 | 186,000 |
| Colonial Dames of America, National Society | 1891 | 14,000 |
| United States Daughters of 1812, National Society | 1892 | 4,500 |
| Daughters of Colonial Wars | 1892 | 4,000 |
| Daughters of the Cincinnati | 1894 | 360 |
| Children of the American Revolution, National Society | 1895 | 18,000 |
| Order of the Founders and Patriots of America, National Society | 1896 | 900 |

| Organization | Founding Dates | Present Members |
|---|---|---|
| Daughters of the Founders and Patriots of America, National Society | * | * |
| Colonial Daughters of the Seventeenth Century | 1896 | 700 |
| Mayflower Descendants, General Society | 1897 | 11,400 |
| Pennsylvania German Society | 1899 | 1,880 |
| Descendants of the Signers of the Declaration of Independence | 1907 | 750 |
| Colonial Dames of the Seventeenth Century | 1915 | 4,200 |
| Huguenot Society of Washington | 1918 | * |
| Daughters of American Colonists, National Society | 1921 | 10,000 |
| Society of Descendants of Colonial Clergy | 1933 | 379 |

* Not available.

The list brings several pertinent points into focus. Seemingly, this type of organization is more popular with women than with men and the DAR has the greatest numerical strength of all. The list also shows that no major new society of this nature has been created since 1933 and that only two, the Society of the Cincinnati and the General Society of the War of 1812, predate the year 1876.

The Cincinnati is the earliest example of an organization to insist on purity in its member's ancestral lines and was quick to arouse the suspicions of the common man. The name of the society had been inspired by Cincinnatus, the Roman senator who left the plow to defend his country and returned to the land at the end of the conflict. Here, however, democratic principles seemed to come to an end. The stipulations that only officers of the war of 1776 could belong and that they could be succeeded only by their first born sons made many citizens fear that the Cincinnati was an attempt to build up a new aristocracy.

The society was started at Baron Friedrich von Steuben's

headquarters shortly before the disbanding of the Continental Army in 1783. It found instant popularity and within a few months had 2,300 members who were soon wearing an elaborate array of insignia, badges and other regalia.

The insigne itself was called an "Order," which created further distrust in the breast of the staunch republican. Designed by Major Pierre L'Enfant, temperamental city planner of the new capital, it was a gold eagle "suspended from a deep blue ribbon, two inches wide, edged with white, descriptive of the union of America and France." George Washington, original President General of the organization and its leader until his death, received a magnificent replica of the emblem from French officers who served under his command. His medal was encrusted with about 200 precious stones and has become the prized possession of each succeeding President General.

Even though the father of our country was the titular head for 16 years, the Society of the Cincinnati was repeatedly denounced as both unpatriotic and un-American. In the first year of its existence, under the pseudonym of "Cassius," a Supreme Court judge of South Carolina, Aedanus Burke, wrote a bitter pamphlet attacking the organization. Entitled *Considerations on the Society or Order of Cincinnati . . . Proving that it creates a Race of Hereditary Patricians, or Nobility*, the tract was widely read and influenced the public's strong animosity toward the movement.

There was a natural fear that an association of officers—who are almost always better educated and more affluent than the average soldier—might too easily become a powerful influence in national affairs and even take over the government. The possibility raised alarm among a number of our leaders as well as among the common people. Thomas Jefferson, the Adamses and John Jay shared Judge Burke's concern that the Cincinnati could easily become the nucleus of a new ruling class. In 1784, Benjamin Franklin remarked in a letter to his daughter that the founders of the Order had been "too much struck with the ribands and crosses they had seen dangling from the buttonholes of foreign officers." And as late as 1805, Mercy Warren was still accusing Cincinnati members of attempting to build up an American nobility based on heredity that would introduce "stars, garters and diadems, crowns, scepters, and the regalia of kings" into "the simple bosom" of our republic.

However by then, the popularity of the Cincinnati was already on the wane. Normal death rate among the original members was one factor; migration west was another. The charter limited membership units to the thirteen original states; new units could not be set up in newly created states and territories, so interest lagged. By 1832 only six of the thirteen state groups were still active. Although the national body managed to remain intact, it was so ineffectual that it no longer loomed as a threat to those worried about its influence. From then on, and for nearly a century, even the most self-conscious republican was allowed to nurse his plebeian convictions in peace.

The qualifications of the Cincinnati are too rigid to allow for a large membership, yet all the later societies have frankly used this early organization as a model. It is often overlooked, however, that from the beginning the late-nineteenth-century patriotic hereditary groups had two other purposes equally important to the tracing of ancestors. For one, members were dedicated to the preservation of historical traditions and relics; for another —and this is of paramount importance—they felt it their sacred duty to act as guardians of the form of government set up by our founding fathers. The insatiable urge of a certain segment of our population to identify themselves with their lineal ancestors and to believe that this tie of heredity gave them the right to become stewards of the Constitution was a new brand of patriotism which flowered in the late nineteenth century and which still sways opinion in many conservative circles.

Strict adherence to this thought pattern would account for many of the puzzling aspects of the Daughters' policies. To understand the DAR, and all organizations of similar persuasion, it is necessary to examine the age when industrialization was just beginning to bring an unprecedented surge of prosperity to America. Booming industries demanded a flood of immigrants to satisfy their appetite for cheap labor, and many native-born citizens began to see the influx of ignorant, heterogeneous hordes as a serious threat to our institutions.

Between 1819 and 1840 less than a million people came to our shores, but in the next decade the potato famine in their native country forced droves of Irishmen to flee to America. Political unrest on the continent brought numbers of Germans as well. The real tidal wave of immigration, however, did not break until the post-Civil War industrial boom. Within four days in 1865, over 6,000 persons arrived at the port of New York, and in the following year more than 300,000 entered this country. Still, three-quarters of them were British and German subjects with a reasonable degree of literacy, and assimilation was a comparatively simple process. Farmland in the northwest attracted most of the Germans, while the English-speaking Irish stayed in eastern cities, where they easily found immediate employment as laborers and domestic servants until they could accumulate sufficient capital to start a fresh, more independent life in their adopted country.

Southern and eastern Europeans constituted less than 0.5 percent of the foreigners to come to America prior to the Civil War. A sudden shift in the immigrants' country of origin occurred in the early 1880s when burgeoning industries encouraged multitudes to pour in from Italy, Austria-Hungary, Poland and Russia.

It was alarming that only one in thirty could read or write in comparison to the ratio of one in three of the earlier people from Germany and the British Isles. Because of language barriers, the new immigrants clustered in tight ethnic groups and gained little conception of American principles. Admittedly, the "ignorant" newcomers were essential to satisfy the demands for cheap, unskilled labor in industries owned by many "pureblood" Americans, but the original, predominately Anglo-Saxon stock viewed them with growing suspicion and antagonism.

Only a half-hearted attempt was made to mold the new arrivals into real citizens. Charles Francis Adams, Jr., expressed the antipathy of his class for the immigrant when he said that he did not associate with the workmen on his place and added that he doubted if such an association would be "agreeable to either of us." As time went on, Adams charged that the increase of the illiterate vote of the foreign-born was directly responsible for the cancer of the "spoils system" in city government. Many "upstanding" people shared his opinion. They frankly believed in a double standard, one for the Yankee and another for the Mick, the Wop, the Dago, the Sheenie, the Hunkie, the Russky, and the Polack.

Labor tensions accentuated the threat of southeastern Europeans to the American way of life as it had been known. The increasingly violent labor disorders, set off by the Haymarket Riot in 1886, were commonly ascribed to ringleaders with strange, unpronounceable alien names. Cartoons portrayed them as bearded, bomb-throwing, wild-eyed anarchists.

Many of the conservative, affluent members of our population were firmly convinced that native-born Anglo-Saxons must join forces to resist the dangers of inundation from the "foreign element." At the DAR Congress in 1905, it was quite blatantly admitted that one of the reasons the founders had formed the Society was because of the dread that our original stock would be engulfed by the different nationalities entering the country. It seemed imperative to make an effort "to foster patriotism and love of our country and our flag and to make Americans of them."

No matter how altruistic such an aim may have sounded, the formation of patriotic societies as we know them today came in a period when the greatest distinction between the native- and the foreign-born was being made. There is no evidence that these organizations made any serious attempt to break down the social barriers. On the contrary, class consciousness, which had been generally frowned upon in the Republic, was awakened and fostered in this era. A desire for a rigid social order in America was more pronounced from 1870 to World War I than in any other age of our history. Certain of the so-called "pure-blood" Americans began to think of their blood as blue; this seemed to carry an obligation to guard their strain and to prove their superiority.

The game of genealogy was popular in this country even before the 1880s. Its popularity was due to a combination of circumstances: the geographical isolation of our hemisphere, a need for some link with the past, and the restlessness of this nation's shifting population since the early colonies. The endless push to the west had broken down the national continuity of interest and ideas. Lack of communication between the frontier and the east caused a great strain on maintaining family ties. Nevertheless, no matter how many times moves were made, everyone knew more or less who he was and did not think very much about it so long as he remained with his immediate relatives within a tightly knit structure of an agrarian society consisting almost entirely of Protestant Anglo-Saxons. Above all, pioneer settlements were dominated by a strong patriarchal system, which served as a successful substitute for the continuity of ancestral ties.

All this began to change around 1870. Our great pioneering era was coming to a close; a new revolution, the industrial one, was just beginning to gain momentum. Events moved so swiftly that it was impossible for most people to realize what was happening to the simple existence they had been used to. In 1865, General Sherman made the derogatory quip that completion of the Pacific Railroad was so far in the future he would not buy a ticket on it for his youngest grandchild. Yet the golden spike which united the Union-Pacific tracks was driven on May 10, 1869, and the General himself lived to see the day when he could travel in ease from coast to coast over any one of five great systems. The magic of the rails transformed the entire country. Flourishing settlements off the main line became ghost towns; cow pastures mushroomed into cities if they were logical train stops. Mills and factories, meat-packing houses, and oil refineries sprang up everywhere along the line of transit. Accelerated by the Civil War, industry continued to boom and caused a new sort of flux in the population.

After the war, the promise of fortunes to be made in the cities acted as a magnet to the young generation which had been brought up on the farm. The family unit as it had been known became disrupted. The sense of belonging to a familiar community of kith and kin was irretrievably lost to many Americans. And it is the natural obsession of the orphan to want to know who he is.

We suddenly became a nation of "joiners." Fraternal organizations like the Elks, the Odd Fellows, and the Shriners got their start at this time. They thrived because they offered a popular substitute, however superficial, for the warmth of the large home circle. It made transplanted sons of the soil more at ease to call a new acquaintance "brother," "comrade," "sachem"; it gave them a sense of superiority to be able to recognize a fellow Son of Rechab or Soldier of Gideon by a password or a secret handshake. The fraternal ceremony of "meeting in guarded places and wearing spangled dresses" satisfied a craving for excitement and bizarre color in the average drab urban existence. An astonishing tendency among these male organizations was the alacrity with which they recognized the right of women to have similar outlets. By 1875 there was a feminine counterpart affiliated to almost all of them.

It was in this period following the Civil War that veterans' associations also first achieved their real solidarity. Former soldiers had banded together after each of the three previous wars in our history, but because of lack of communication and transportation, they had failed to gain much momentum on a national scale. Now that there were centers of condensed population within easy access of one another, strength through unity became an accomplished fact. It soon became evident that veterans' units not only offered social diversions but could also act as a vital political pressure. Thousands of men felt it advantageous to belong to at least one of them. Here again, women's auxiliaries became a prominent feature.

Neither veterans' groups nor fraternal orders held much appeal for the upper strata of society. The more affluent city dwellers became, the less they cared for the mumbo jumbo of the secret order or the hail-fellow-well-met good cheer of the Grand Army of the Republic encampment. Above all, their wives frowned on such rowdy forms of entertainment. To them, the only acceptable place for a gentleman was "his club," for this was an age of refinement.

George III may have failed to conquer America, but Queen Victoria succeeded. Respectable members of the fairer sex thought of themselves as "ladies," and their ideal was to reign supreme as "queen" of the home supported by a "good provider" with the gumption to build up a huge fortune as quickly as possible.

Such a provider moved his family into grandiose surroundings befitting his recently acquired station in life. Familiar old relationships built up during more modest days were immediately discarded. Often unable to break down existing social barriers in their sumptuous new environment, the parvenus were apt to feel lonely, insecure, and disoriented. A compulsion to appear acceptable to their neighbors, coupled with the popular Victorian anglomania, prodded many of them into a glorification of their antecedence.

An "office of heraldry" was flourishing in New York as early as 1851, but exalted heredity did not become a national status symbol until after the Civil War. Financial ruin made many a southerner pathetically conscious of the past glories of his family tree, and there was in some cases a tendency to graft on elaborate branches not quite true to the original species. However, it was not in the south that the craving for roots threw out the strangest tendrils. It was in the northeast and west, where the postwar boom had brought about meteoric prosperity.

In these sections, successful men were commonly called railroad barons, oil potentates, meat-packing kings, princes of industry, but, as opulence made them and their wives more socially conscious, such titles reeked embarrassingly of vulgarity. The services of professional genealogists were most often enlisted by these tycoons, and the resulting pedigrees sometimes soared to heights of romantic fancy.

In 1867, Charles H. Browning published a book called *Americans of Royal Descent*. The work was taken so seriously that he was able to form a society under the same name, which admitted only men and women "whose lineages are traced to the legitimate issue of kings." With an admission fee of $100 it offered a ribbon of red, white, and blue "suggestive alike of patriotism and royal achievement." By 1894, his book was in the third edition and reached the proportions of a tome, containing 736 pages bristling with thousands of names of persons for whom its author claimed noble origins.

During the last quarter of the nineteenth century in certain circles a family tree, complete with crest, became a must—the more emblazoned the better. Some were satisfied to point to Richard the Lion-Hearted as their original forebear. One genealogist insisted that U. S. Grant, as well as the heirs of thirteen Mayflower passengers, had William the Conqueror as a common ancestor. Research was so profitable and interest so intense that it seemed as if many could not rest until their lines were traced all the way back to Adam and Eve.

In 1904, the Reverend Dr. Charles Wilbur de Lyon Nichols ended his astonishing book, *The Ultra-Fashionable Peerage of America, with a few appended Essays on Ultra-Smartness*, on a discouraging note. "In more than eight out of a dozen instances," he said, "a chasm yawns between the family in the mother country and the first settler in this, which hundreds and sometimes thousands of dollars in genealogical research will not bridge over."

Lineage tracing might have remained the obsession of ambitious Anglophiles except for the unintentional influence of Charles Darwin's *The Origin of the Species* and Sir Francis Galton's *Hereditary Genius, Its Laws and Consequences*.

Numerous popularizers and distorters, on both sides of the Atlantic, quickly brought Galton's genes hypothesis to the attention of the public. Joshia Strong, an evangelical minister, was the most important interpreter of this theory in the United States. His incredible book, *Our Country*, an immediate best-seller in 1885, fitted Galton's theory to Strong's own ends. Consciously emphasizing the Darwinian theme of struggle for existence to apply to struggle for power among nations, Strong expressed excessive confidence in the survival of Anglo-Saxon Americans because of their fitness. He insisted that the United States, a vast reservoir of natural resources, would become the most powerful nation and must indeed dominate the world. If it failed to accept this responsibility, civilization was doomed. He asserted that we were the leaders not only because of our material assets but mostly because of the superiority of American ideals and mores, attributed by him to the predominance of Anglo-Saxon Protestant stock. He urged a militant national campaign to keep the leadership in the hands of this pure strain, imploring them, as God's chosen people, to destroy the rising clouds of Romanism, Mormonism, mammonism, and socialism.

Appearing when an avalanche of southern and eastern Europeans seemed about to crash through the walls of national homogeneity, *Our Country* had a profound effect on the thinking of native-born Americans. Many of them probably discounted the Browning school of heraldry as snobbish nonsense, but Strong's theory of heredity gave fresh, quasi-biological substance to the importance of distinguished ancestors—at least on this side of the Atlantic. (It is another story, but not entirely irrelevant, that the concept of Anglo-Saxon stock, translated into "Aryan" via Nietzsche and Hitler, took hold of the German imagination.)

Strong's clarion call stimulated two instincts in conservative citizens of his day. It satisfied their urge to feel themselves "the best people"; it also gave them support in forming organizations of dignity befitting their stations. What better way than to join together and authenticate their relationship to the founders of the country?

The idea had first crystallized in 1876, America's centennial year. That year might be described as a hive out of which a swarm of hereditary-patriotic societies later emerged. The centennial itself stimulated the birth of the Sons of the Revolution. Subsequent celebrations—in 1883, honoring the evacuation of the British from New York; and in 1889, on the anniversary of George Washington's inauguration—acted as further impetus. In 1890, Henry Hall, a chronicler of such groups, reminisced:

> These observances exerted a remarkable influence on the public mind in every part of the United States. They inspired a pride in Revolutionary ancestry, a shame that the country had come to neglect the annual observance of the Fourth of July and Washington's birthday, and a new respect for the principles of popular government.

In the 1890s, Mrs. Ellen Hardin Walworth, one of the founders of the Daughters of the American Revolution, recalled that her enthusiasm for some unified form of patriotic endeavor was first awakened in 1875, when she read a statewide call in a California newspaper for all men of Revolutionary descent to march in a July 4 parade the following year. According to Mrs. Flora Adams Darling, another DAR organizer, the impressive display of colonial treasures shown at the Philadelphia Centennial Exposition made her begin to dream of a "society" that would provide Revolutionary relics with permanent housing under one roof in the nation's capital.

The Philadelphia Exposition was the climax of a series of nationwide events honoring the end of our first "Century of Progress." It ran from May to November and attracted thousands of visitors. Nothing so elaborate had ever been attempted in this country. The occasion was auspicious enough to merit federal sponsorship, and on July 4 both houses of Congress adjourned from Washington to hold a special session on the fairgrounds. A year before, when U. S. Grant signed the appropriations bill for the exposition, he had used a quill pen fashioned from the wing feather of an American eagle shot expressly for this purpose near Mount Hope, Oregon.

The centennial came in an era when rich and poor alike rolled up their shirt sleeves to get things done. Men bragged about being brought up by their bootstraps on the 3Rs. Too much "book larnin' " was tossed aside as a dilettante's pastime. Fear of God, lip service to our principles, and sharp wits made a man get ahead; the only other thing he needed was Yankee ingenuity. No other period in our entire history to this point had been more painful to those who rejected this self-interest and who placed their faith in "public honor and private happiness." To decent people it seemed time to rejuvenate the original concepts of the Republic.

Two distinct schools of thought arose as to how this could be accomplished. One was made up of intellectuals, sons of well-to-do but not new-rich families, who had attended the best progressive Eastern universities. They believed that social legislation must be passed to deal with the problems of the new industrial revolution.

The second, more conservative school of thought included the Sons of the Revolution, the Daughters, and subsequent patriotic groups based on heredity. These men and women were of the same social stratum as the reformers and on the whole were equally sincere and well educated. As deeply alarmed by the consequences of the industrial revolution, they saw that it was producing a country increasingly diversified in national origin and religion. They blamed this diversity on rising radicalism and labor unrest. They believed as much as the reformers in cleaning up political life, but they did not agree that an urbanized, industrialized system had made many of the standards and bonds of a simpler way of American life obsolete. They felt no need to set up a whole new set of rules and regulations to curb materialism.

With no royal family or national church to create an automatic status quo, conservative native-born Americans became increasingly convinced that nothing but a faith in the founding fathers would save the country from eventual perdition.

In the last quarter of the nineteenth century, patriotism became a secular religion. The flag became a fetish. Impressive monuments were raised as reminders of our past glories; various historical anniversaries began to be observed as sacredly as holy days. Prominent, high-minded citizens considered it their duty to reaffirm publicly a belief in the Constitution and the Bill of Rights. They honestly believed they were setting an example to newcomers to our shores and that these outward manifestations were a more effective way to foster respect for the democratic system than legislation addressed to the abuses of the period.

In that time of stress it is understandable that those who could trace their lines to actual patriots could easily feel that they were the proper people to save our institutions.

Nineteenth-century education had indoctrinated Americans with a lusty respect for all our Revolution's heroes—officers, Minutemen, and bugle boys. Now it seemed only natural to give equal honor to *every* person who had taken part in the struggle. Here was the magic of the Sons of the Revolution. Less exacting than the Cincinnati, it still presented a chance to be singled out from the common throng; above all, it offered a democratic badge of snobbery.

# III

## A D A M ' S    R I B

The original Sons of the Revolution had little desire to organize chapters beyond the boundaries of Manhattan Island. Regarding itself as a sanctuary for such families as the Livingstones, Schuylers, Hamiltons, Pennypackers, Carrolls, and Astors, it was content to let an occasional dignified gathering at Fraunces Tavern demonstrate its outward devotion to the nation —until William O. McDowell became a member in 1884.

McDowell, a resident of Newark, was thirty-six at the time. Born and bred in the country, this true Horatio Alger had left the farm at thirteen to make his fortune. At that time, he took a solemn oath to devote "a part of each day to altruistic work along patriotic lines." By his own lights he never swerved from this early commitment. He had dabbled in mining, railroad securities, and real-estate promotion. Some accounts estimated that he was worth a quarter of a million dollars by the mid-1880s, but financial success was hardly enough to occupy his fertile imagination; as a Son of the Revolution he could soar to new heights to fulfill his early vow.

His affable charm soon found him a place on the Centennial Inaugural Committee. However, co-workers were shocked to see him toss aside staid centennial proposals for a military parade and a costume ball. He insisted: "I felt it was necessary that something should be done to redeem the celebration from being a thing of the day, and to make it an influence world wide, for all time."

Although rather short and physically nondescript, he talked "in a decided way" that carried conviction. But even this quality was insufficient to convert the conservative Sons, who quietly dropped him from the committee. Disgusted by their stuffiness, he threw himself into forming a unit of Sons in New Jersey, where his views were more appreciated. The ruffled New York society not only flatly refused official recognition to the new body; they also publicly denounced McDowell himself, calling his vanity and effrontery unparalleled and declaring that his "insensibility to the usages of polite life is manifest in every movement."

This insult might have clipped the wings of a less dedicated man. But, as early as 1879, the *Newark Daily Journal* had noted that McDowell was "evidentally happiest when running a public meeting." So the harsh rebuke merely precipitated the first "schismatic differentiation."

In this way the Sons of the American Revolution was born in 1889. The zealous McDowell merely kidnaped the original idea of the Sons of the Revolution, seasoned it with his own theories, and launched his own society on a broad national scale. The SAR had instant appeal to men of business and civic eminence. John D. Rockefeller was an early member, as was David Jayne Hill, the traction king. Political leaders like Vice-President Levi P. Morton and Senator Henry Cabot Lodge were quick to join the flock. President Daniel Coit Gilman of Johns Hopkins University declared he was "happy to be one of the cooperators in this excellent work," and the *Chicago Tribune* hailed McDowell as having more spirit of '76 "than could be found in a city full of ordinary business men."

Descendants of old settlers in more modest circumstances also applied in droves. Many of them saw themselves as the genteel survivors of a rural society, forced to exist in polyglot cities that were a direct result of vulgar industry in which they personally had little or no financial stake. It filled them with dismay to be slipping down the social scale into obscurity. The new Sons of the American Revolution offered an excellent opportunity to reassert their position in the community on the basis of antecedence rather than accumulated gains.

Eligible women found the idea particularly inviting, and for a while it looked as though the emancipated SAR might follow the gracious example of fraternal and veterans' organizations in welcoming feminine auxiliaries. Instead, the SAR slammed the door in the faces of the expectant petticoat patriots at its initial Congress, held in Louisville, Kentucky, during April 1890.

Perhaps the ruling was intended more as a rebuff to McDowell than as a discourtesy to feminine aspirants. In one year his popinjay tactics had infuriated his new colleagues. His newest offense was to envision a worldwide movement of groups similar to the SAR. On his own initiative he had sent a circular letter to the presidents of every republic on earth urging them to sponsor bodies composed of the descendants of their respective revolutionaries! In his enthusiasm for the project—which was to include an annual international conclave to exchange views on democracy—McDowell seemed to have forgotten that the majority of the revolutions of his day had occurred in Latin America, many of them so abortive that descendants often found it more convenient to conceal rather than glorify such relationships. Dr. W. Seward Webb, the incumbent President General, called a halt to this flighty scheme by hastily reminding delegates: "The Monroe Doctrine, which is dear to every true American, would seem to limit us to our own country."

This snuffed out McDowell. He never again had any real voice in SAR policy and his extremism was also the undoing of the hopeful ladies. Dr. Webb belonged to an influential clique that felt that woman's place was in the home. Many men who actually favored their inclusion found the global suggestion so preposterous that they joined forces with Webb to defeat McDowell's other resolution, dealing with feminine membership.

The insulted ladies sulked in silence until July 13, 1890, when a letter sharply criticizing the unfair decision of the Sons appeared in the *Washington Post*. It was written by Mrs. Mary Smith Lockwood, a staunch feminist who lived up to her description of "a womanly woman with advanced ideas." Although she appeared to be a tiny, white-haired, cloistered, Victorian widow, she found time and energy to be a tireless club worker as well as to run the Strathmore Arms, a small family hotel located at 810 12th Street, N.W., in Washington. She was the author of numerous magazine and newspaper articles, and her books ranged in subject from ceramics to *Houses in Washington*, in which was included a florid description of her own establishment.

In her *Post* letter, Mrs. Lockwood used the story of an obscure, Elizabethtown, New Jersey, housewife as a stirring example of the important role women had played in the Revolution. She gave a vivid picture of how Hannah Arnett, uninvited, descended upon her husband and a number of other disheartened patriots who were considering capitulation to the British during the hard winter of 1776. Shocked by her "unseemly intrusion," Mr. Arnett whispered: "Hannah! Hannah! This is no place for you. We do not want you here just now." He would have led her from the room, but at the end of her patience, Mrs. Arnett refused to budge before speaking her mind. Mrs. Lockwood's impassioned prose expresses the lady's disdain in such blood-curdling phrases as "you call yourselves men" and "Oh! Shame upon you cowards!" With tears in her eyes, Mrs. Arnett rose to a magnificent crescendo:

> She turned to her husband and gave him a withering look that sent a shock through every fibre of his body. Continuing she said: "Isaac, we have lived together for twenty years, and through all of them I have been to you a true and loving wife; but I am a child of God and my country, and if you do this shameful thing I will never own you again as my husband."

Such a speech, accompanied by the previous epithets, was enough to renew the "strength of strong resolution" of the men before her. Each vowed never to abandon his country no matter what the odds. Mrs. Lockwood ended on a note of dreadful challenge:

> There are names of men who fought for their country and won distinction afterwards, who were in this secret council, but the name of Hannah Arnett figures on no roll of honor.
> Where will the Sons of the American Revolution place Hannah Arnett?

This was precisely the cue needed by the irrepressible McDowell. He promptly seized the banner of the ostracized ladies. On July 21 the *Post* printed an open letter from him. In it he thanked Mrs. Lockwood for recalling his ancestor—it happened that he was a great-great-grandson of Mrs. Arnett—and invited all interested women of Revolutionary heritage to communicate with him. In the best tradition of "schismatic differentiation," he suggested the Daughters of the American Revolution as a name for the new order and offered his assistance in drafting a constitution.

What may appear to be a clever bit of prearranged publicity to arouse interest in the new society was really coincidence. William McDowell and Mary Lockwood had never met. Pursuing the many facets of his patriotic work and reading and writing to leading newspapers had become habitual to McDowell. It was natural for him to pounce upon an item so compatible to his personal aims. By her own statement Mrs. Lockwood considered his offer presumptuous. Somewhat of an organizer herself, she resented male interference, particularly if the man were one of the odious Sons.

Innocent of her disapproval, McDowell forged ahead. He promptly sent a copy of the Lockwood letter to George W. Childs in the hope that his paper, the *Philadelphia Ledger*, might contribute aid to cover the initial expenses of the fledgling society. He distributed other copies to a number of influential people and—with Machiavellian finesse—directed one to Mrs. William K. Vanderbilt, mother-in-law of the antifeminist Dr. Webb.

At least five District of Columbia residents responded to the McDowell plea for action. They were Mary Desha, Eugenia Washington, Mrs. Louise Walcott Knowlton-Brown, Mrs. Mary Morris Hallowell, and Mrs. Hannah McL. Wolff, who was also a descendant of the now illustrious Mrs. Arnett. In reply to the unanimous question of "What can we do?" to get things started, McDowell advised them to call a meeting immediately, elect officers, and prepare for a grand rally on October 11, 1890, the eve of Columbus Day marking the celebration of the centennial of Washington's presidency. Miss Desha, an ardent suffragette, added further radiance to the date by claiming that "it was to a woman's generosity and wisdom that Columbus was indebted for the means to fit out his fleet for his perilous voyage."

Mary Desha had come to the capital from her native Lexington, Kentucky, in 1885 when her brother-in-law was elected to Congress. She soon became a clerk in the Pension Bureau. She has been described as a "forceful and emphatic speaker, of strik-

ing appearance, with the intellectual power and marked personality of her ancestors." Since these ancestors included a famous
Indian fighter, a man who was a Revolutionary soldier at fifteen
and later became governor of Kentucky, along with a female
dispatch rider, she was prepared to take on any number of
projects. She had answered Mrs. Lockwood's appeal even before
McDowell made his. Mrs. Lockwood received a note from Miss
Desha two days after the publication of the Arnett story and,
within the week, the pension clerk had an appointment to call at
the Strathmore Arms.

During that visit the two women made a tentative list of
friends who might be both interested and eligible. Mrs. Lockwood named several women who were among the 818 charter
members, but Miss Desha's suggestion of Miss Eugenia Washington and Mrs. Ellen Hardin Walworth is of particular significance because eventually she and these two friends were to be
designated as the original official founders. Mary explained that
Miss Washington was a direct descendant of Colonel Samuel
Washington and a great-grandniece of the father of our country.
The death of her parents had forced her to earn her own living,
and she was now employed at the Postal Department. Although
somewhat retiring, Miss Washington was a tireless worker and,
quite aside from her distinguished heritage, she would make an
excellent member. Miss Desha described Mrs. Walworth as a
beautiful widow of independent means who divided her time
between the District and her estate in Saratoga Springs. After
raising her family, she had devoted her time to historical and
civic affairs. She was the first woman elected to a local board of
education in New York State and the only feminine trustee of
the Saratoga Monument Association. Such a personage would
certainly be desirable.

The end of the afternoon probably left the new friends satisfied with their progress, but, in Mary Desha's eyes at least,
the results of the little tête-à-tête seem to have paled when
McDowell blazed a new trail with his master plan. His approximately fifteen Washington recruits (Mary foremost among
them) were swift in following his orders, and a meeting was
called for July 27 at Mrs. Knowlton-Brown's.

Mrs. Lockwood failed to attend. Her flimsy excuse of "press-ing duties" was probably a dignified way of calling the whole business a wildcat maneuver. An agreement to wait until "every-one" returned to town in the fall before doing anything really definite seems to have been the main accomplishment of the gathering. Mary Desha was delegated to advise McDowell of the momentous decision. Before retiring that night she wrote him a long, rambling letter covering a variety of subjects. Discussing genealogy, she wondered if legal proof must be furnished and if lineal descent would be necessary. She suggested that she had several friends with "distinguished uncles."

Returning to the meeting of the previous evening, she men-tioned a circular she had sent to McDowell the day before, which described another society, newly organized in Washing-ton, "for the purpose of building a club-house for women." She said the ladies at the July 27 meeting had toyed with the possi-bility of the embryonic DAR taking over one department of the equally embryonic clubhouse to establish an attractive feature of a historical library and picture gallery of presidents' wives.

"What do you think of that?" she asked, then went on to explain that, for so long, women had been limited to activities in hospitals and orphanages that in the dawn of their new freedom they were dreaming of " 'taking to' historical research and the study of parliamentary law, and to the founding of scholar-ships, libraries, art galleries and gymnasiums."

The previous June Miss Desha had thrown herself into organ-izing a club called WIMODAUGHSIS (the WIves, MOthers, DAUGHters, and SISters) whose membership was open to every last woman in the United States of America. Stock at $5 a share was being sold for building a clubhouse in Wash-ington where all members would be welcome.

This was no dream of flighty eccentrics. Anna Howard Shaw, leader of the women's suffrage movement, was president of Wimodaughsis. Among its stockholders were substantial people like Elizabeth Cady Stanton, Susan B. Anthony, Clara Barton, and at least enough of the guests at Mrs. Knowlton-Brown's to make the idea of a merger feasible. Although Wimodaughsis soon faded into limbo, many of its members were eligible as

Daughters and probably brought with them the idea of a club-house. If so, their contribution was enormous, because it is this building program that makes the DAR unique among patriotic societies. McDowell sent an immediate reply to Mary's letter. He was so anxious to harness her abundant energy that he refrained from criticizing the glaring laxity of her genealogical reckoning and was noncommittal about the merging plan. He simply insisted that she must continue with the business of the DAR at once, otherwise nothing would be ready for the October launching.

Dutifully Mary sent out notices that on August 9 a meeting would be held at Mrs. Walworth's. In spite of a severe thunderstorm, she and Eugenia Washington arrived promptly at 8 P.M. After an hour it became apparent that they were the only ones who had inherited sufficient vigor from their forefathers to brave the elements. The meeting was called to order and the trio opened a parcel sent to them by McDowell. It contained full organizational plans, the SAR constitution, and a beautifully bound notebook for the amended and approved DAR constitution, as well as sample application blanks with the word "Sons" neatly scratched out and "Daughters" substituted above. McDowell had inscribed his own name on one of these and enclosed a check for his initiation fee and dues for one year. Thus a man was the initial applicant to the Daughters of the American Revolution.

Mrs. Walworth was careful to stress that she and her companions were innocent of any desire to usurp authority, that they were merely trying to carry out McDowell's instructions. Still, as Mrs. Lockwood pointed out, it later developed that, besides examining the papers at hand, they had also "appointed a number of officers, including themselves."

Mrs. Lockwood was not on the original roster, but a friend of Eugenia's, Mrs. Flora Adams Darling, was. The inclusion of her name made that stormy evening prophetic. For eight months she kept the organization in turmoil, and until her death it was plagued by her tempestuous efforts to prove that she and she alone was responsible for the whole idea.

To protect the "peace and harmony" of the society (a term which has become habitual in the vocabulary of the Board of Management when it wishes to veil unpleasantness) there has been a consistent effort to ignore the history of Mrs. Darling's activities. This policy has been so successful that most present-day Daughters have never heard of her. Among official records only a 1908 history makes mention of Mrs. Darling. Brought out to satisfy persistent inquiries among the membership as to just who was responsible for the birth of the order, this history acknowledges her involvement but minimizes her role in early DAR affairs. It strives to stifle questions by specifying August 9 rather than October 11 as the true founding date and hastens to add that only those who attended the August meeting can be regarded as "true founders." This not only deprives Mrs. Darling of any credit, but neatly disposes of Mrs. Lockwood and McDowell as well. Not until 1929 was Mrs. Lockwood elevated to the roll of honor. Although the title "Literary Founder" sets her a notch below the original charmed circle, her name is immortalized with theirs on the impressive memorial dedicated to the organizers, which stands in a small formal garden on the D Street side of the Washington building.

Just who was Flora Adams Darling? Miss Washington sadly explains that in the beginning of their friendship she had supposed Mrs. Darling to be "a lineal descendant of John Adams, second President of the United States"; she was more than disappointed to find "that Mrs. Darling was proved afterwards to be the descendant of a cousin of John Adams"—and a *fifth cousin* at that, some detractors were delighted to add.

In an effort to refute this accusation, one of Mrs. Darling's books includes her entire genealogy, dating back to Arnulph, Bishop of Metz (d. A.D. 631). Although proof of descent from the illustrious patriot John Adams may have remained inconclusive, the magnificent lineage pattern overshadowed the discrepancy. Her fairly successful novels, with such florid titles as *A Winning*, *Wayward Woman* and *The Bourbon Lily*, or *Romance and Law*, were semiautobiographical, and she had acquired the habit of refurbishing facts to fit fancy.

Born in Lancaster, New Hampshire, the daughter of Harvey

and Nancy Dunster Adams, she married at twenty a southerner twice her age named Edward Irving Darling and went with him to his plantation in Louisiana. When the Civil War broke out, Darling became a Confederate general; he was killed in action in 1863. Left with a two-year-old son, Flora was anxious to return north to her parents. Although she managed to get a federal passport, she was arrested as a spy by Union soldiers before she could leave New Orleans. She was thrown into prison, where she contracted scarlet fever and claimed to have been robbed of a casket of jewels and $25,000 in bonds during her illness. She never received recompense, although her case was kept before Congress for thirty years. She often intimated that President Lincoln had taken a personal interest in her suit and that only his untimely death had prevented him from righting the wrong.

To the end of her days prominent names dropped from her lips as easily as petals from a faded rose. Curiously bipartisan in her relationships, she always insisted that Jefferson Davis' last letter was directed to her. A childhood correspondence with Franklin Pierce while he was president was another favorite topic of conversation. Although her contacts were widespread and influential, many of her stories seemed somewhat improbable.

She had a dynamic personality and an executive ability that should have made her a valuable addition to any board. But, no one recognized the potential danger of her unfortunate flair for taking poetic license with reality.

Her claim of being the only founder of the DAR is one example of this irritating trait. The other contestants were content to date their ambitions from the SAR rejection of women, but she makes the sweeping statement that "The idea of forming an association of women to preserve Revolutionary relics was conceived in my mind during the Centennial Celebration of 1876." Though ordinarily a woman of immediate action, she fails to explain why she did nothing until the summer of 1884, when she let Eugenia Washington in on the secret, or why the two women continued to dream in silence until the spring of 1890, when they finally decided to form a society of women along SAR lines.

Acting as editor of the *Adams' Magazine*, which for a time was the official organ of the society, Mrs. Darling gave a description of her close friendship with Miss Washington:

> It has been our custom for most of the years since then [the war] to spend February 22d together to honor the memory of Washington and Adams, and in forming the Society she has been to me what Hancock was to Adams. She seconded all my motions, and as there were but two engaged in the enterprise last May, we had a majority. We decided to invite a large number of ladies to undertake the work with us.

Eugenia had a reputation for being a person who "would gladly sacrifice life and all that she held most dear for a settled principle." A Desha pamphlet attacking Mrs. Darling quotes Miss Washington in a blunt disavowal of the widow's statement:

> I have never taken dinner with Mrs. Darling on the 22d but three times in my life, and the facts about the first discussion of the "Daughters" are these:
> After the action of the "Sons" at Louisville, excluding women, Mrs. Darling and I were discussing the subject and I said, "Why can't we form a Society of our own?" Mrs. Darling replied, "That is a capital idea, let's do it; you will be President and I Vice-President—Washington and Adams. I will ask General Wright."

General Marcus J. Wright was busily engaged in creating a Washington chapter of Sons. Naturally he too was a "dear" friend of the indomitable Mrs. Darling. Flora told Eugenia that the general had suggested waiting until the following February, when the inclusion of women might be reconsidered. Eugenia's reply showed the true spirit of '76 when she snapped: "We will do it without asking General Wright or the Sons either."

Although Mrs. Darling agreed, she urged her friend to wait until fall, "when Washington society would begin to revive." Whereupon she decamped to Culpeper, Virginia.

Mrs. Darling had no intention of vegetating in the country. Early in June she wrote to Dr. Webb, asking for the credentials of his organization to use as a model for the DAR. At her request, he sent duplicate copies to Miss Washington. Dr. Webb, as accredited leader of the Sons, was certainly the proper channel of approach, and if she had remained steadfast to his faction, refusing all association with the renegade McDowell, Mrs. Darling might have won her claim as true founder—at least on a technicality. Instead she admitted that she had requested and received similar papers from both Washington and New Jersey. The last were undoubtedly sent by McDowell, and from then on he was as deeply involved with her as he was with the ladies in Washington who had answered his call.

For a while Mrs. Darling was his most ardent champion. She insisted that he must be considered "head-centre for at least one year," and she titled him "Pope" to signify his authority. However, with all due respect to his talents, she had no expectation of relinquishing, even to him, her own pivotal position. During the summer, in pure *hauteur*, she suggested that he delay his own arrival until she returned to the District in October. It seemed never to occur to her that he might consider an active Washington spearhead of more value than a lone woman in a small Virginia town. She must have been shocked therefore, suddenly to be informed that she had been appointed to the Desha-Walworth-Washington board and offered a mere vice-presidency. Instead of making a direct frontal attack, she immediately submerged and began to stalk her unsuspecting prey.

On August 30, she graciously accepted a place on the board, but, giving extreme deafness as an excuse, declined the honor of active office. The next time the board heard from Mrs. Darling she was happily ensconced in Mrs. Lockwood's parlor, from which she fired off dictatorial letters into their bewildered forces. According to Mrs. Lockwood the two women had only a slight acquaintance prior to the first week in September, when Mrs. Darling sent a letter offering assistance in an organizational capacity, which Mrs. Lockwood gladly accepted. A rapid correspondence started the splinter movement. Then Flora arrived at the Strathmore Arms. It took only six weeks to complete the destruction of their mutual foes.

The two women struck a crippling blow to the Desha-Walworth-Washington contingent when they gained the tenta-

tive acceptance for titular leadership from the most prestigious
candidate. Both factions knew that a woman of national prominence should become the first president and all eyes were feast-
ing on Mrs. Benjamin Harrison. Dr. John Scott, Mrs. Harrison's
father, had been a frequent guest at Mrs. Lockwood's establishment and this personal contact made it simple for her and Mrs.
Darling to gain an audience at the White House. President Harrison had been an honorary Ohio state leader of the SAR from
the organization's inception, so the First Lady was sympathetic
to the movement. She agreed to accept the post on two conditions, one being that her election must be unanimous, the other
that a competent assistant who met with her approval must be
chosen to take charge of the many pressing duties entailed by
the office.

Probably through Mrs. Darling's influence, Mrs. Lockwood
was reconciled to McDowell; at least she seemed to tolerate his
cooperation as a necessary evil to gain her own ends. The poor
man, still in Newark and unconscious of undercurrent manipula-
tions, became the innocent pawn in the play for power among
the five women. Flora's eloquence was so persuasive that he
sanctioned all her actions, even honoring her choice of a suitable
meeting place for the grand rally. Using McDowell's acquiescence as a damaging weapon, Mrs. Darling demanded sur-
render. She sent a short note to Mary Desha:

> Strathmore Arms, Washington, D.C.
> October 7, 1890

My Dear Miss Desha:

Mr. McDowell will be with me at this hotel to organize
the National Society of the Daughters of the Revolution,
October 11, 2 P.M. It is our joint request that you accept
the office of *President of the Board of Managers* of the
Society. We know of no one better equipped to fill the
position than yourself and trust you will be pleased to
accept.

> Sincerely,
> Flora Adams Darling

The office was extended upon McDowell's suggestion but
there was nothing charitable in Mrs. Darling's compliance to his

wishes. They merely coincided with her strategy. Brief messages were also sent to Miss Washington and Mrs. Walworth. When Mrs. Walworth received her letter she was concluding negotiations with the Arlington Hotel as a suitable place for the first official gathering.

Although Mary Desha replied that she could accept no position until the ladies who had been invited by her "to become members of the board had been provided for," she relinquished the precious constitution and other papers in her possession to Mrs. Darling. The McDowell name had been the real bombshell. Later she explained that she had supposed the switch in authority was by McDowell's order. Although hurt and puzzled, she was still willing to abide by his wishes.

Taking over the helm, Mrs. Darling offered amnesty. Aside from the mystifying claim that she was ignorant of any "temporary" organization, her peace terms could hardly have been more generous. Pleading that she was merely following the direction of their mutual adviser, she begged the "originators" to confer with her on Thursday or Friday so as to eliminate any conflict on the great day. She still refused office because of her hearing and insisted that Miss Desha should be the "true head and must continue as before."

So matters stood on Saturday afternoon, when twenty-four women, supported by an advisory board of sympathetic Sons, arrived at the Strathmore Arms. Mrs. Darling, dressed in her widow's weeds and deaf as a post by her own admission, opened the ceremonies and handed the gavel over to McDowell. The constitution was read and the names of the officers were politely approved by the audience. Mrs. Harrison, discreetly absent, was the unanimous choice for President General. Other posts were filled by the wives of three generals, one admiral, one colonel, and the director of the Smithsonian Institution. Clara Barton became first Surgeon General (an office now extinct). Miss Washington was made Registrar General; Mrs. Walworth, Secretary General; and Mrs. Lockwood, Historian General. As promised, Miss Desha became Chairman of the Executive Board. Mrs. Darling accepted without a murmur of protest when she was named Vice-President-General-at-Large, in charge of organizing chapters. That her affliction would seriously handicap her performance of the duties of this office seemed to have slipped her mind.

On the following Monday morning, a committee called on Mrs. Harrison to make the formal announcement of her unanimous election. They also presented the slate of officers for her approval. Her only objection was to Mary Desha as Chairman of the Executive Board. According to Mrs. Darling, the First Lady felt that anyone holding this key position would be the logical person to represent her "officially at many places and on most occasions" and that it should be held by "a married woman, who had social prominence and a residence of some pretension in Washington."

In self-vindication, Mrs. Darling later wrote:

> I realized instantly that in endeavoring to give Miss Desha a place of such prominence I had committed an error in judgment. I suggested the name of Mrs. William D. Cabell. The suggestion was agreeable to Mrs. Harrison. I wrote to Miss Desha that she must be sacrificed for "the good of the cause."

Miss Desha furiously insisted she had been "decapitated" and held Flora Darling personally responsible for the Harrison ultimatum. During the first stormy months, "decapitation" became a favorite pastime among the leaders. Mary, the first victim, was demoted to one of the seven vice-presidencies, two levels below the original coveted post. Her removal from the chairmanship of the board seems an unnecessary cruelty, because an entirely new office, presiding Vice-President-General, was created for Mrs. Cabell and she was quickly installed.

Mrs. Cabell was a perfect choice. The daughter of a Union soldier from Virginia, she married a Confederate veteran who was himself an active Son. The couple ran a fashionable school for the daughters of leading families in the capital. Not only was she in a position to cultivate new members, but her "residence of some pretension" offered an excellent setting for social functions that brought so much radiance to the organization in the early days.

Mrs. Cabell's conservative outlook became apparent when three months after her appointment, she wrote Mrs. Darling discussing plans for the New York chapter:

> We wish to keep our Sisterhood of Daughters free from entangling alliances with bands of women aiming at any of the "fads" of the day, and to do this we must entrench ourselves within the charmed barriers of Revolutionary descent, *and* social consequence. *Here* we went too fast at first . . .

Couched in these dignified terms is a gentle attempt to conceal another skeleton in the DAR closet: the suffragette leanings of four of the originators. The most obvious offender was Mary Desha, but Mrs. Lockwood also belonged to a Washington branch of the "women's rights" movement. Although unaffiliated with any club, Mrs. Walworth was a warm sympathizer, and even the retiring Miss Washington owned several shares of Wimodaughsis stock.

Among the quintet, Mrs. Darling was the lone disciple of the old school. During early organizational planning she expressed the hope to McDowell that the Daughters "shall be held accountable to the officers of the Sons for our good behavior" and in the same letter confessed her belief in "men for office—women for pleasure."

In her book *D.A.R. and D.R. Societies*, she delights in taking repeated digs at "new" women. At one point, placing Mrs. Cabell and herself in an attractive light as "the weaklings of the order," she states that most of the original board had wanted an "Adamless Eden" and that they continually thwarted efforts to "keep very close to the Sons of both orders." There can be little doubt of her meaning when she says, "Three of the interested ladies stood for 'war to the knife with the Sons' . . .," but unable to resist an additional barb, she continues, "Miss Desha and Miss Washington had no cause for personal prejudice from actual knowledge of 'the total depravity of the man,' but they had no use for mankind . . ."

The majority of the women attracted to the organization were somewhat in accord with Mrs. Darling's point of view. Many prospective members found suffragettes almost as reprehensible as anarchists. "Advanced thinking" was such a handicap that no founder who held suffragette opinions ever attained an office of major importance in the DAR.

A third half-forgotten skeleton is the "mother of a patriot" clause, which declared collateral descendants as eligible as lineal ones. Enemies of the clause pointed out that "a mother might have ten sons, one might be a patriot and nine might be Tories; yet if the clause should be carried it would make the descendants of the nine Tories fully as eligible to the order as the descendants of the patriot . . ."

Today DARs adhere rigidly to lineal descent but in the beginning even some of the officers were not sure their papers were "straight." As late as January 17, 1891, in a confidential letter to Mrs. Darling, Mrs. Cabell complained: "Three of our officers have not yet proved descent. This is very serious, particularly in the case of the Historian-General." Mrs. Lockwood was Historian-General.

The clause was revoked in 1894, but it took a long time for the Daughters to live down the reputation of being notably less stringent on antecedence than other patriotic societies. To these groups, leniency in hereditary matters is the first of the seven cardinal sins.

Miss Desha had been responsible for railroading through the "mother of a patriot" clause at the end of the October 18 meeting. The ladies happily agreed to "dear" Mary's motion. Later it came as a shock to discover that they had opened the gate of their little heaven to the unhaloed.

Mrs. Darling, a vociferous opponent of the clause, snarled that "revenue not patriotism" was the real reason for slackening requirements. Oddly enough, she herself had attended the meeting and at the time had raised no objections, but when Ward McAllister, social arbiter of the day, refused to allow his daughter Louise to become first organizing regent of New York State as long as the odious loophole existed, the clause was suddenly transformed into a valuable weapon to be used against

Miss Desha. Mrs. Darling promptly gave McAllister her personal promise to have it erased in May, when other constitutional errors were to be corrected, and by adroit manipulation created the lasting impression that she had been its foe from the beginning.

Mary Desha, the first martyr to be sacrificed on the altar of "the cause," was soon followed by McDowell, the "Pope and head-centre." Mary complained that his troubles began the minute a certain Mr. Wilson Gill appeared at the October 11 meeting. Although Gill remains a confusing wraith, he is undoubtedly one of the missing links in the "true story." It was Miss Desha's contention that he simply saw a notice of the meeting in the newspapers and asked Mrs. Darling for an invitation, but this could hardly have been true. Because of her connection with the conservative Webb clique, Mrs. Darling certainly knew that Wilson Gill was a New York Son in good standing with considerable organizational experience, but in her high-handed manner she allowed only that he had become interested in "her work."

Mrs. Lockwood gave the real clue to Gill's presence when she credited him, rather than McDowell, with the revision of the DAR's constitution to fit the needs of the Daughters, and indeed the original draft in his own handwriting is still extant. Mrs. Lockwood stated that the "phenomenal success" of the DAR was due to Gill's wise decision to make the organization a national body with completely subservient state societies rather than following the looser SAR pattern of individual state societies that enjoyed some independence from central control.

The revision reverted to the autocratic government of the Sons of the Revolution found so confining by McDowell. The Webb circle, including Gill, hoped to unite the new organization with the parent order. Although this ambition was never realized, the purpose of drawing up a more hidebound structure for the Daughters may have been a delicate hint that the SARs were ready to amend their own charter.

It was gross exaggeration for Mary Desha to pinpoint October 11 as the date of McDowell's "decapitation" and blame Gill for it. Actually McDowell remained in favor for some time to come.

After the initial Strathmore Arms meeting, McDowell had returned to Newark, but he and Mrs. Darling kept up an active correspondence. In one letter he complimented her on her organizational talents. Admitting that before his departure he had feared that "you ladies were at swords' points," he expressed relief that things seemed to be running smoothly. By October 29, however, his tone had changed and he was gently chiding her for her vigorous manner of expression. He suggested that since the organization had become a reality, "you have been elected" might be better phraseology than a blunt "I have appointed you." He felt it hardly diplomatic to write, "I accept with pleasure," when referring to a resignation. "The 'I' naturally grates," he explained toward the end of his masterpiece of understatement.

This marked the real twilight of McDowell's power within the Society. Flora Darling could not abide criticism. In December, when she arrived in New York to organize chapters, McDowell had no place in her plans. Needing an excuse, she suddenly made public a bill of $75, which he had supposedly submitted for his work in the Washington proceedings. (The fledgling Society had a grand total of $33 in the treasury at the end of the first meeting, so this would indeed have been embarrassing.) Although the bill remained unconfirmed, the mere possibility of his sending it placed him in the unfavorable light of a vulgar professional promoter expecting pay for "services rendered." In contrast, she held up Wilson Gill as a radiant example of practical aid and pointed out that he had defrayed all his own expenses. Making McDowell an object of ridicule became an obsession with her. Next she exposed his application for membership. She explained that from the first the form had seemed so ludicrous that she had scrawled this poem across it,

> I want to be a Daughter and with the Daughters stand,
> A crest upon my paper, a check within my hand.
> And there among the Daughters so radiant and so bright
> I'll ring them into glory; the pull I have is right.

She continued that even if she had been willing to consider him "Pope for a year" there was no place for him in the "Sisterhood." McDowell denied both charges in the press, but the damage was done. He had become a public laughingstock. Before the battle was over Mrs. Darling was accusing him of ambitions to become the President of the United States and he was comparing her to the Czars of all the Russias.

For a while, in a vain attempt to dissociate itself from the public brawl, the National Board suffered in silence. Finally, however, matters reached a point where Mrs. Darling had everyone thrashing around in a mire of intraorganizatinal politics. Although she showed a remarkable talent for enlarging the society—sixteen chapters were flourishing by April 1891—her methods soon had the hinterland, as well as Washington, in an uproar. The first rumble came from Chicago, where there was heated disagreement as to the choice of a proper regent, but this squabble was infinitesimal compared with the eventual New York eruption.

Early in 1891, Mrs. Roger A. Pryor, first Regent of Manhattan, refused to accept Brooklyn applicants into her chapter, claiming that Brooklyn was not within city limits. Mrs. Darling preferred to interpret this action as an attempt to blackball Brooklynites because of their lack of social luster. As a retaliation against the Manhattan Regent certain Darling supporters broke from Mrs. Pryor's chapter and formed their own in Harlem. Mrs. Pryor's objection to two separate chapters in one city was just as strong as her insistence to exclude members who lived outside city limits. She immediately placed her case against Mrs. Darling before the National Board. The Board supported Mrs. Pryor and sent a tart letter to Mrs. Darling, condemning her "high-handed method." They particularly admonished her for allowing the new group to call itself the Darling Chapter. Reminding her that names of chapters were supposed to be historical, they acidly implied that as yet she was hardly immortal.

Smarting under this volley of criticism and obsessed by hatred for McDowell, Mrs. Darling blamed him for all her woes. She claimed unreasonably that the Washington group was completely under his control, and in May she informed him that he had been dropped from the DAR advisory committee and that she was preferring charges against him to the New Jersey SAR because of conduct "unbecoming a gentleman." The Daughters' Board promptly denied her the right of such action; furthermore, they dropped her publication, the *Adams' Magazine*, as the Society's official organ and demanded that she cease organizing chapters. In a frenzy she forbade the Board to use her name in any of their dealings and even threatened legal proceedings.

Tired of the whole wrangle, the gadfly McDowell quietly slipped away. Although he remained on friendly terms with the Society, particularly with Miss Desha, he became less closely associated with its intimate, internal workings. He took little or no notice when, on the first of July, the entire Board signed a resolution removing Mrs. Darling from office and expelling her from the order. For mysterious reasons known only to themselves, the Board withheld the news from the press until July 28, 1891, when the *Washington Post* carried a front-page, two-column account of the sensational story. It received headline attention from every leading paper in the country. Charles W. Williams of the Associated Press denied that the item had been carried by his agency. Because he suggested that it may have come through "some special channel," it would appear that even in its infancy the DAR was well prepared to handle its own emergencies.

Mrs. Darling had been vacationing in Canada with her son and his wife. She returned by way of Detroit just in time to be greeted by the glaring streamer MRS. DARLING DEPOSED BY THE NATIONAL BOARD OF THE DAUGHTERS OF THE AMERICAN REVOLUTION NOT ELIGIBLE TO HER OWN SOCIETY. Hastening to New York, she immediately made the statement that it was impossible for her to be deposed since she had resigned on June 18. In retort, Mrs. Cabell thundered, "Mrs. Darling does not see fit to resign. She is removed."

The exquisite pleasure of presenting the Board's formal case against the first DAR dissenter was awarded to Mary Desha. She had prepared a pamphlet that appeared on July 31 and was promptly dispatched to every chapter. The piece ended:

. . . [Mrs. Darling] became bolder and bolder in her false assertions—more and more positive in her assumption of power.

All this was quietly endured, the ladies believing that "peace and harmony" should be preserved at almost any cost—until intoxicated by her own success, and emboldened by their silence, she has falsified history, making the pedigree of the Society of doubtful origin. Believing that under the circumstances it would be highly criminal to remain any longer silent, these ladies now speak, for the truth of history must be preserved.

# IV

Aside from the birth of the DAR, the year 1890 was also remarkable for the publication of *How the Other Half Lives* by Jacob Riis. Many thoughtful Americans were shocked by his frank portrayal of the deplorable conditions in the fetid slums of our cities.

A number of individual Daughters may have responded to the call for compassionate reform, but the Society itself decided to leave such matters to other agencies. It was felt that it was beyond the DAR's province to deal with contemporary social problems. Its purpose was to preserve history, act as custodian for precious relics, and, through education, foster a pride in our heritage. Keeping strictly within these limits, original DAR work among the foreign-born included only a few classes in English for immigrants and a series of stereopticon-view lectures dealing with America, from its discovery through the Reconstruction period.

However, the Daughters were made uneasy by anarchy and labor unrest. The official publication, the *American Monthly*, which had supplanted the *Adams' Magazine*, issued a ladylike plea urging that the Homestead strike should not be allowed to "mar the records of a free country with violence and bloodshed and set an example of lawlessness to the ignorant and the stranger." When Governor John Altgeld questioned the propriety of Grover Cleveland's decision to send national troops into Chicago during the Pullman strike, an Evanston regent branded him "a crying disgrace to every citizen, . . . a man devoid of principles of patriotism, a foreigner and a demagogue of the worst type." Even as early as the first DAR congress, the original Chaplain General questioned the wisdom of trying to absorb "the millions of poor and ignorant" arriving from Europe. In her opening prayer, she wondered if it would be possible to "give them the power to vote, and still keep the purity of our institutions."

On the whole, early Daughters paid scant attention to current events. In those days, most women opened a newspaper merely to turn to the society page, a novel feature just coming into vogue. All social classes found accounts of local activities absorbing, and functions of the national elite—like a Vanderbilt ball or an Astor wedding—merited front-page treatment. DAR leaders realized very early that frequent appearance in the social column was the surest way to capture the public imagination.

Although most patriotic groups based on antecedence preferred to maintain a small and exclusive membership, the Daughters recognized the importance of numerical strength. Perhaps they instinctively took a cue from veterans' associations, with whom eventually they were to share many ideological affinities. Organizational growth was the Daughters' most consuming interest for the first two decades of their history. The Board was shrewd enough to see that a show of social eminence would attract the largest number of desirable members. Mrs. Cabell, acting for Mrs. Harrison, expressed the opinion that "social prestige" was necessary for "anything emanating from the City of Washington." It was decided to give a large and brilliant reception to demonstrate DAR "vitality and enthusiasm based upon American ideals of patriotism."

On February 22, 1891, a profusion of potted palms, flags and yards of bunting transformed Mrs. Cabell's "spacious residence" into a bower of American idealism. A predominant accent of blue and white flowers and decorations represented the Society's colors. A band played patriotic music while the guests filed through a double line of Sons of the American Revolution dressed as Minutemen to be greeted by President and Mrs. Harrison. The press paid minute attention to the ladies' adornment as well as to the decor of the establishment. The splendor of the occasion was enhanced by an entertainment of patriotic speeches, recitations, and a concert, followed by a handsome repast in the supper room. According to Mrs. Lockwood, "The story of this reception in Washington, marked by a spirit of patriotism in speech and song, reached to the farther ends of the country . . ." As a result, "the Nation was awakened with a new light," which became even brighter when the Society was honored by two evening receptions at the White House. The first was on October 11, 1891, and the second on Washington's birthday of the following year. It was the climax of the festivities of the original DAR Continental Congress. On this occasion, President and Mrs. Harrison (in an "elegant pearl white satin gown") received officers and delegates from all over the country. It was one of Mrs. Harrison's final public appearances. Her unfortunate death in October, 1892, was mourned by the Daughters, and although they could ill afford it, they immediately commissioned a life-size portrait of their beloved leader to be presented to the White House.

Both President and Mrs. Harrison had seen great political advantage in the entire movement, and their particular efforts on behalf of the DAR placed the Society in a limelight enjoyed by none of its rivals. Requests for application blanks began to pour in, and between 1891 and 1898 the membership shot from 450 to 23,097. By 1906, there were more Daughters than any force the Continental Army could muster into the field during the Revolution. In 1911, they were proud to announce that they outnumbered the Sons by the substantial margin of 80,000 to 18,000.

A great factor in the popularity of the Society was that it gave middle-class women in small cities the opportunity to bask in the reflected glory of well-known national personages. Although some members complained that their dues were used largely to finance excursions of their officials to Washington, many others derived a vicarious pleasure from the knowledge that a friend and fellow member had lately shaken hands with the President of the United States and had stood in line with Mrs. Potter Palmer or Mrs. Schuyler Hamilton while waiting to do so.

White House receptions became one of the most popular features of the national Congress. After Mrs. Harrison's death, the custom was continued by the President and his daughter, Mrs. James Robert McKee. President and Mrs. Cleveland considered it expedient to receive the delegates, even though Mrs. Cleveland was a life member of the Daughters of the Revolution, the rival organization Flora Darling started after she left the DAR. The McKinleys followed suit and the annual event became a tradition that faded away only when Mrs. Eleanor Roosevelt resigned from the Society.

Local chapters also emphasized the organization's social aspects in their regional activities. New York meetings frequently were held in fashionable restaurants like Sherry's and Delmonico's. In private homes, the ideal hostess was the one who could serve the most delicious refreshments on elegant ancestral china and plate. Minutes of an early meeting in Huntington, Indiana, gave equal space to a speech on the British invasion of New York and to the delicacies of a three-course luncheon.

The National Board used social prestige as a magnet to attract new members. The choice of their chief executives was one of the clues to their initial success. Until 1905, every President General was the wife of a statesman, diplomat, or prominent politician.

For example, after Mrs. Harrison's death, it would have been common courtesy in most organizations to invite Mrs. Cabell, the able Vice-President-General, to step into the top office. Instead, the post remained vacant from October 1892 to February 1893, when Mrs. Adlai Stevenson became the leader. As wife of Grover Cleveland's Vice-President, she was the ideal candidate because of Mrs. Cleveland's close affiliation with the Daughters of the Revolution. Although Mrs. Stevenson had been a DAR for only a week, she was swept into office by a vote almost as overwhelming as that given to Mrs. Harrison. Mrs. Stevenson later explained that the selection of the wife of a high government official "not only elevated the office above the rivalries of personal and sectional interest, but gave the society at once a national basis and was found to be of great importance in keeping out what might eventually end in state and chapter strife."

The *San Francisco Examiner* described her as "a delicate little woman with an oval madonna face and a complexion like the inside of a pink shell." Many members were twice the age of the exquisite Mrs. Stevenson, but she always called them "My Daughters" and they loved her for it. Youthful, able, and popular, she was kept in office from 1893 to 1898 and remains the only President General to serve four one-year terms.

Because of a death in her family, Mrs. Stevenson went into

temporary retirement in 1895. Mrs. John W. Foster, grandmother of John Foster Dulles, assumed leadership until Mrs.
Stevenson resumed her duties after a year of mourning. Mrs.
Foster's husband had been Secretary of State under Benjamin
Harrison and earlier had served as minister to Spain, Russia, and
Mexico. Years in the diplomatic corps had made Mrs. Foster a
fluent linguist and gracious hostess. In the eyes of the Board and
a large number of the delegates she was the logical 1895 candidate but Mrs. Foster was the first member of the Washington
clique to have an opponent.

Mrs. Nathaniel B. Hogg, Pennsylvania state regent, had risen
to prominence in the Society through personal efforts. She had
won fame for championing the strict lineal membership requirement. Mary Desha's "mother of a patriot" clause had become an
increasingly bitter issue, and it was largely due to Mrs. Hogg's
efforts that the clause was finally deleted in 1894. The dictatorial
manner in which the leaders were selected began to irk a number of members, and Mrs. Hogg's supporters felt that the reputation gained in the lineal battle made her position sufficiently
strong to challenge the system. They put on a vigorous campaign, but Mrs. Foster won by a large majority because, no
matter what the accomplishments of others, most Daughters
liked to keep a figure of national importance in the showcase.

The rank and file did not contest either of Mrs. Stevenson's
next two elections, but when she retired in 1898 there was new
evidence of a desire for more rounded representation. Mrs.
Donald McLean, the wife of a prominent New York lawyer,
was determined to break through the charmed circle of the
hierarchy, whose present favorite was Mrs. Daniel Manning. As
regent of a large Manhattan chapter, and adored by the press for
her verve and style, Mrs. McLean had earned the nickname
"Duchess of the D.A.R.-lings." During her regency she had enjoyed more national publicity than any other individual member
in the history of the society.

The rivals were well matched. Both Mrs. McLean and Mrs.
Manning were so beautiful they might have appeared face to
face on the lid of a candy box. They both were descendants of
equally illustrious lines: Mrs. McLean was a Ritchey of Mary-

land, and Mrs. Manning came from New York de Peysters, Livingstons, and Van Cortlandts. Still, Mrs. Manning had one undeniable advantage. Her deceased husband had been a diplomat and Secretary of the Treasury during Cleveland's first administration. This was enough to ensure an easy victory for the favorite of the powerful Washingtonians. At the end of Mrs. Manning's first term, tenure of office was extended from one to two years, and she was reelected without opposition because Mrs. McLean was in mourning for her mother.

By 1901 the "Duchess" was back in the field but, in spite of her strenuous efforts, the post went to Mrs. Charles W. Fairbanks, the pretty, plump young wife of the senator from Indiana who later became Theodore Roosevelt's Vice-President. Mrs. Fairbanks may have had little to offer in competitive glamour, but she kept perpetual open house for visiting Daughters, and her excellent cuisine—as well as her sunny disposition—made her popular. McLean supporters also claimed that her success was due to the personal backing of President McKinley.

Even though Mrs. Fairbanks gained reelection, Mrs. McLean remained optimistic. In the 1905 battle, she decided to carry the fight to the grass roots. This innovation of stumping the country was the weapon that finally brought her victory. Ever since, aspirants have followed her example, and from 1905 on, heated national campaigns have become an exciting part of election year.

Mrs. McLean's victory marked the end of the dynasty of prominent Washingtonians' wives, but its leadership had served an important purpose, laying a firm groundwork for the semiofficial DAR status that is still one of the attractions of the society.

In this early period, most of the lesser offices and places on the National Board were filled with the same care as that of the President General. No wonder events moved smoothly. These women had no need to hound influential men for recognition; they were dealing with their own husbands.

The original DAR charter which ensures the organization perpetual semiofficial standing probably stems from this form of petticoat government. An 1896 act of Congress requires the

DAR to make an annual report to the Smithsonian Institution. The report, a detailed account of their historical and educational activities during the preceding year, is printed at government expense and read into the *Congressional Record* before being delivered to the institution. Only the American Historical Association shares this privilege.

Why should the honor, certainly coveted by every rival patriotic group in the country, have been bestowed upon the DAR? Possibly because at the time of the Society's incorporation, Dr. G. Browne Goode was the director of the Smithsonian. Not only was his wife an active charter member, he had been chairman of the original male advisory board for the Daughters.

The ladies made every effort to cement an imposing national reputation, but they had plenty of energy left to plan an impressive clubhouse. George Washington had expressed the desire for a memorial hall in which to preserve memorabilia of the War for Independence. On various occasions Congress had considered the idea, but nothing concrete was accomplished until the Daughters, when they were exactly one week old, passed a resolution stating their intention to construct a fireproof building that would serve as a museum for Revolutionary relics and as a meeting place for themselves.

In 1891, charter-member fees and life-membership dues were set aside as a nucleus for a building fund. Although these first monies amounted only to $650, the ambitious Daughters envisioned a $700,000 structure to be called Memorial Continental Hall. By 1899, eight years later, the fund still languished at a modest $11,231.88, but the ladies were busily engaged in trying to find a site for their future "home."

During Mrs. Stevenson's term in office, she appointed a committee to petition Congress for a grant of land. True to the DAR pattern, she placed great reliance on her husband's influence, and her confidence seemed justified. Early in 1897, both houses passed a bill that set apart, for the permanent use of the DAR, a plot of land 200 feet square and almost adjacent to the White House! It was soon discovered, however, that the land was part of the Washington Monument grounds and was required by

statute to remain a perpetual reservation. The first grant therefore had to be revoked, but the House promised the DAR a new
site.

The Stevensons lost their power when President McKinley
took office and the new administration proved less sympathetic
to the proposal that the DAR be given federal land. According
to Mrs. Lockwood, "one man defeated the will of Congress by
refusing to recognize the maker of the bill on the floor." The
"one man" was the Speaker of the House, the Honorable David
B. Henderson.

By 1902, reliable sources in high places finally convinced the
DAR leaders that their case was hopeless. They themselves purchased their present location on June 3, 1902, for $50,266.17.
At the time they were called "foolhardy women" for buying such
worthless, undeveloped swampland, but today this site is magnificent. Facing a park known as the White Lot, Memorial Continental Hall and the newer Constitution Hall are flanked by two
distinguished neighbors, the National Red Cross and the Pan
American Union. The White House is only three blocks away,
and in all directions there is no other privately owned real estate.

Ground was broken on October 11, 1902, the twelfth anniversary of the Society. Some 4,000 spectators were present, in spite
of the pouring rain that continued throughout most of the ceremony. A tent was hastily erected over the speakers' platform to
shield the dignitaries, but the incumbent President General, Mrs.
Fairbanks, defied the elements and marched out from under the
shelter. She grasped a spade smelted from Montana copper—the
gift of Montana Daughters. The handle was hewn from a tree
which stood on the trail of the Lewis and Clark expedition. It
was inlaid with pieces of wood from other historic spots in the
state, and adorned with gold and silver from Montana mines, as
well as blue and white Montana sapphires to symbolize the
colors of the society. After "invoking the God of the Nation,"
Mrs. Fairbanks broke the ground and shoveled some of the dirt
into two containers carried by Mrs. Lockwood who stood near
her.

In one pot Mrs. Lockwood planted thirteen Osage orange
seeds to represent the thirteen original states. She told of putting

into the other sufficient earth to supply the remaining thirty-two states with a "Liberty Tree." She failed to indicate how much soil was required for this purpose; nor did she mention the species of the trees thus planted. These plants were officially nurtured in the propagating gardens of the U.S. Agricultural Society. The following year the prospering seedlings were carried home by the various state regents and planted in prominent locations in public parks throughout the nation as perpetual reminders of the memorable dedication day.

A granite slab donated by a patriotic stone dealer marked the spot of the groundbreaking. Later a block of marble was sent from the White House. It was inscribed "From the home of the First President General to the Daughters of the American Revolution." Too precious to be used as a mere marker, the Daughters decided to give it a place of honor inside the finished building, but it was never incorporated because it mysteriously disappeared before the actual construction began.

Although the building fund had soared from a little over $11,000 in 1899 to $82,190.57 in 1902, the land purchase had depleted the treasury. At the groundbreaking exercises the ladies must have carried only change purses, because the total contribution on that ceremonial day was $492. Nevertheless, the NS-DAR was optimistic enough to announce an open competition for architects. Edward Placey won the contest with his graceful design for a "Colonial-Classic" building that had on its south side a portico supported by thirteen columns to represent the original thirteen states. The rules of the contest specified that all materials used in Memorial Continental Hall must be of American origin, so the structure is built of pure white Vermont marble, which is always kept spotless.

The cornerstone was laid on April 19, 1904. In honor of George Washington, who had been a Mason, the service was conducted with full rites by the Masonic Order. Candles were lit at the four corners of the stone, and the trowel was the same one used by the father of our country when he laid the cornerstone for the Capitol in 1793. A variety of objects—everything from Revolutionary relics to a contemporary newspaper—were embedded behind the stone. Then, Mrs. Fairbanks, aided by the three living founders, Mrs. Lockwood, Mrs. Walworth, and Miss Desha, applied the mortar.

A year later, on the same date, dedication services were held inside the DAR "home." Mrs. Fairbanks' second term was drawing to a close. Even though she had increased the building fund to $175,000, construction costs again had depleted it to a paltry $2,000. The hall had only a temporary roof and no interior finish, but a profusion of flowers, wreaths, flags, and elaborate wall medallions softened the severity of the stark white marble. On opening day, a generous pledge of $50,000 by enthusiastic delegates was insufficient to make the place habitable.

When at last Mrs. McLean became President General, a new whisper campaign against her by the Washington clique predicted that if she were elected the building would remain incomplete. As it turned out, it was Mrs. McLean who "evicted the sparrows that made their nests in the temporary roof" because she had the daring to borrow $200,000 from the American Security and Trust Company.

The varied activities of the Daughters received continuous publicity, though not all of it was favorable. At the turn of the century, parades, military band concerts, flag display, commemorative holidays, and erection of monuments to historic heroes were an intrinsic part of the country's life. However, the DAR accent on social events led many outsiders to suspect that members were somewhat a hard-working mutual-admiration society more interested in elaborate dresses and display of jewels than they were in patriotism. The constant emphasis on ancestry opened the DAR and all hereditary groups to criticism. The assumption that antecedence was of paramount importance reawakened the old question about whether this was an attempt to establish an aristocracy.

Public disapproval blanketed the entire movement. Some criticism was serious, but in the 1890s it was more often playful. As a contrast to the stark reality of a new, very real, and often ugly modern social revolution, the petty rivalries of so many hereditary societies with similar names and purposes offered the press convenient comic relief. The miniature war among the organizations was promptly dubbed the "Tournament of Pedigrees," and, to the vast amusement of the uninitiated, reporters played it for all it was worth.

As the feuding over "schismatic differentiation" gradually diminished, most patriotic orders were thankful to retire into a dignified, if ruffled, obscurity. However, in their steadfast determination to keep in the limelight, the Daughters of the American Revolution continued to expose themselves to ridicule. The Society became synonymous with the cartoon image of all ancestor worshipers who consider themselves the rightful watchdogs of the Constitution, the flag, the national anthem, and the proper interpretation of our forefathers' principles.

News value of the DAR was accentuated by the size and strategic location of their annual Congress. Its stormy character soon became—and still remains—excellent copy. The ferment over the "mother of a patriot" clause and the heated electioneering that commenced with Mrs. McLean's original campaign made the internal politics of the Daughters vulnerable to raillery.

Reminiscing about the first Congress in her *Story of the Records*, Mrs. Lockwood excused the ensuing disorder by saying:

> . . . it was easy to see how these inexperienced "delegates" drawn from the most conservative classes, and who were, perhaps, for the first time taking part in any meeting larger than a "Ladies' Aid" in a Church parlour, would inadvertently make themselves objects of criticism for members of the press, who are ever on the alert to seize upon picturesque features accompanying a woman's gathering, considering them as legitimate subject for satire.

It must be remembered that an Advisory Board of Sons presided over the original meeting. Although such a board still exists, with Senator Strom Thurmond as its present chairman, its functions have become merely formal. As soon as the DAR officials became sufficiently acquainted with *Robert's Rules* to become their own parliamentarians, the Society largely discarded masculine supervision over their affairs.

Congresses are now controlled with an iron hand by NSDAR

leaders, but in earlier days members considered it a social insult to wait for recognition from the chair. If a lady had something to say, she got right up and walked down the aisle.

Minutes of the 1896 meeting show that decorum had hardly improved from the time of the first meeting. Various delegates, enraged by stories that had recently appeared in the *Washington Post*, cried, "Shame," "Badman," "Put him out," when the offending reporter came forward to defend his views. It would seem from their own records that there was more truth than exaggeration in the perennial headlines describing "Warring Daughters," "A Gusty Session," and "*D*amned *A*wful *R*umpus."

The press was not always derogatory, however. DAR work during the Spanish-American War won the organization well-deserved and unqualified acclaim. The moment war was declared, the entire Society snapped to attention and offered its services to President McKinley. When they were designated to act as official screening agency for all army nurses, they proved themselves as ready for action as Commodore Dewey's fleet.

The idea originated with Dr. Anita McGee, daughter of the scientist Simon Newcomb. As a physician and the first female assistant surgeon in the U.S. Army, she was hopeful of gaining the recognition for professional women nurses that previously had been withheld by the government. As a loyal DAR and one of the organization's officers, she believed that the Society could manage the task. It is doubtful, however, that the Society would have received the honor if petticoat rule had not again applied pressure. Mrs. George M. Sternberg was a DAR vice-president at the time, and her husband was surgeon-general of the Army. Well known for his strong prejudice against the National Red Cross, he was reluctant to put any authority in the hands of that organization. It was probably a simple matter for Mrs. Sternberg to make him see her sisterhood as the perfect alternative.

Volunteer DAR workers manned their posts from 8 A.M. to 11 P.M. for the duration of the war. They processed 4,600 applications and delivered 1,000 nurses, all of whom had diplomas from certified training schools. Mrs. Lockwood could truthfully say that because of the Daughters the "White Cap and Apron

Brigade had become a permanent adjunct to the Army Medical Corps." It was perhaps due to this constructive and patriotic work that DAR membership increased by nearly 10,000 in 1898 alone.

In gratitude for the Society's splendid effort, McKinley appointed their wartime leader, Mrs. Manning, as official American representative at the Paris Exposition in 1900. On July 3, Mrs. Manning unveiled a statue of George Washington, paid for by the DAR but given to France in the name of all American women. Next day, on the "Glorious Fourth," while the Star-Spangled Banner flew for the first time from the Eiffel Tower she dedicated the plaster model of a statue of Lafayette that, when complete, would be the gift of the American children.

Her public presence was so outstanding that it excited an international admiration for her organization. The Paris edition of *The New York Times* reported that Mrs. Manning "presented a charming picture." She was dressed entirely in white, her hat was a tower of feathers and roses, and old lace trimmed her simple crepe dress. The official decoration of her post, a broad blue sash draped across her bosom, offered a stunning contrast.

The Manhattan faction was bitterly disappointed that Mrs. Manning's rival, Mrs. McLean, who had been largely responsible for raising funds for the Washington statue, had no place in the show. Countess Spottiswood-McKim, French DAR regent, was so much in sympathy with the New York group that she refused to give a reception for Mrs. Manning during the Paris visit. The snub must have left Mrs. Manning quite unperturbed, for she was entertained by the President of France himself and decorated as a chevalier of the Legion of Honor.

Her brilliant performance at the exposition made her the logical choice for president of the Board of Lady Managers at the 1904 St.Louis Fair. For six months Mrs. Manning filled this office with her usual grace. Because of her influence, October 11 was designated DAR Day at the fair, and the grounds became the gala scene of the Society's fourteenth anniversary.

By 1904, the DAR had become quite accustomed to holding a

prominent position at all large national fairs. President Harrison
may have set the original precedent in 1891 by naming Mrs.
Lockwood as delegate-at-large on the board of the Women's
Pavilion for the 1893 Columbian Exposition. The pavilion, the
first of its sort, was to be a feature exhibit, and during the first
DAR congress, the enthusiastic new appointee proposed that the
Society take an active part in the plans. However, minutes of the
meeting show that opinion was violently divided as to how deep
an involvement most Daughters wished to risk. Many women
feared that participation might link their name with suffragettes.
This possibility seemed so distasteful to the majority of members
that Mrs. Lockwood withdrew her resolution rather than have it
suffer the ignominy of defeat. She offered it again the following
year, when the whole country was anticipating the fair with
impatience. This time the atmosphere was more favorable, and
the Lockwood motion sailed through without opposition.

The effervescent Mary Desha was full of ideas. Together
with McDowell, the original DAR mentor, she envisioned a
huge replica of the Liberty Bell as one of the major exhibits.
Individuals and members of all patriotic groups were invited to
contribute ancestral treasures, which would be smelted together
to form the bell. The *Newark Evening News* reported that, due
to the numerous donations, McDowell's attic was rapidly becoming "a curiosity shop." The 1892 Congress found Mary
pleading that "articles of historic interest will be particularly
appreciated—silver, bronze, copper and nickel can be fused." To
make herself absolutely clear she composed this poem, which she
read at the Congress:

> It is not to be builded—this bell we plan
> Of common ore dug from the breast of the land
> But of metal first molded by skill of all arts
> Built of treasures of fond human hearts.

She wanted a complete record of all material sent for smelting.
This information was to be entered into a book that would
accompany the bell wherever it went. Miss Desha continued:
"Things have already been received, historic mementoes of
Washington, Franklin, Jefferson, Hamilton, and others. If your

relic is too valuable to smelt as a whole, send us the smallest filing." As an illustration she added that she had asked the Regents of Mount Vernon for a sliver of the key to the Bastille that had been presented to Washington by Lafayette!

Although this singular memorial was still incomplete at the beginning of the fair, the Daughters themselves were prominently on hand. Mrs. Cabell, acting as their representative, delivered the official opening address at the Women's Pavilion.

Since then, the DAR has played a leading role in at least twenty national expositions. At the end of the seventy-third Congress the President General, Mrs. Robert V. H. Duncan, and 900 Daughters hurried to the 1964 World's Fair in New York, where DAR Day was scheduled for April 25. Mrs. Duncan presented the main ceremonial American flag for the fair to fair officials. Contemporary members are as fond of good food as their predecessors, and the flag exercises were followed by a luncheon at Antoine's in the Louisiana Pavilion.

From the beginning, publicity derived from these public appearances pleased the Daughters, but it was also a constant source of worry, because social aspects often seemed to overshadow the serious educational purpose of the Society. In her day, Mrs. Stevenson complained that the press willfully misinterpreted the real object of the DAR and was largely responsible for the popular doubt "as to the necessity or advisability of founding a national patriotic society on purely sentimental grounds." She went on to say that the main aim of early officers was "to disabuse doubting minds, to overcome prejudice and to start chapters in every state and territory" which would "inaugurate a campaign to emphasize the importance of American history."

The Daughters sponsored a successful series of public lectures by the conservative John Fiske, their favorite historian. Prior to the 1890s American history had been sadly neglected as a college course, and the Society worked hard to rectify the error. However, the ladies were as insistent then as they are now that classroom instruction be handled according to their own special and partisan views of historic interpretation.

These views were largely shaped by men like Fiske and Jonathan Trumbull, president of the Connecticut SAR, who made some extensive lecture tours of DAR chapters. Trumbull was a champion of tradition, right or wrong, so long as it praised the founding fathers. Above all, he was suspicious of an attempt among certain advanced educators at Harvard, Trinity, and Yale to reevaluate and, according to his lights, minimize the motives and deeds of our ancestors. He continually admonished the Daughters to beware of an insidious tendency to tamper with a *McGuffey's Eclectic Readers* type of unquestioning glorification of national heroes. He expressed a paternalistic attitude toward history that was—and still is—characteristic of most patriotic groups.

Although early Daughters focused on higher learning and were content to leave the surveillance of patriotic training in elementary schools to veterans' organizations, they did not neglect young people completely. In 1895, the Children of the American Revolution was organized. The idea was conceived by Mrs. Daniel Lothrop, better known as Margaret Sidney, author of the popular *Five Little Peppers* series. The first meeting of the young people was held at Mrs. Lothrop's home, Wayside, which had once belonged to Nathaniel Hawthorne.

The aim of the new organization was to nourish the proper spirit of '76 in both sexes from the moment of birth to the age of twenty-two. Membership was open not only to the chidren of DAR members but to those of the Sons as well and to all eligible infants whose mothers would enroll them. There was some adverse comment on the advisability of catechizing tiny tots in patriotism, but the movement was so popular that over a hundred units sprang up within two years. The Children raised their small voices for a "safe and sane Fourth" and contributed their pennies to the building of historical monuments. During the Spanish-American War, in a drive sponsored by Mrs. Lothrop, many Children sacrificed the luxuries of candy and sodas to spend their allowances on comforts for our soldiers and sailors.

The educational program of the DAR had one very important aspect. At a time when most citizens were throwing away old things, these women began an incessant campaign to revitalize the past.

From their ranks hundreds of newly awakened amateur historians began roaming the countryside to ferret out the half-forgotten graves of Revolutionary soldiers.They not only supplied appropriate markers for them but also, if necessary, had stones repaired and dutifully tabulated the names of the deceased in DAR archives. Other zealous Daughters spent days in musty back rooms and cellars of town halls, churches, and libraries and often rescued early records from the trash barrel. Members ransacked their own attics and those of their friends in the hope of finding at least one letter or document that might act as a fresh link to our past.

Much of this work was undertaken—and continues—on a chapter level, below the notice of the national press. Occasionally, however, it was brought to public attention by a large project sponsored by the NSDAR. Mrs. Stevenson set an example by raising, among members, the major portion of $11,000 needed to erect a monument in Fredericksburg, Virginia, to the memory of Mary, mother of George Washington. This was accomplished in 1894, when the Daughters had little more than $650 in their own building fund.

By restoring Revolutionary tombstones in an ancient church graveyard, a Hartford chapter shamed the city into tearing down an adjacent tenement district. Another Connecticut chapter made a valuable collection of Revolutionary ballads and songs long before folk singing became fashionable. At 38th Street and Lexington Avenue in New York City, Daughters placed a marker on a mansion where a Quaker lady had diverted the attention of Sir Henry Clinton and his staff with a glass of wine until Washington's army had time to pass a danger point.

In Princeton, New Jersey, Daughters purchased and moved Rockingham, Washington's famous Rocky Hill headquarters, when its collapse was imminent because of constant blasting in a nearby stone quarry. Maine chapters badgered their state legislature until it made its first appropriation for the preservation of historic sites. A Georgia chapter put up a monument to a hero for whom their town was named and who lay in an unmarked grave in Philadelphia. Sibley House, home of the first governor of Minnesota, was opened as a museum by St. Paul members, and the Sarah Bradlee Fulton chapter of Medford renovated General John Stark's headquarters.

Sometimes, however, DAR fervor had curious results. The organization gave the city of Tacoma, Washington, a drinking fountain to commemorate the massacre of Narcissa Whitman. At the following Congress, a Tacoma delegate made the solemn report that an "Indian band of twenty members from the state school for Indians took part in the exercises. They were the descendants of those who perpetrated the massacre. This feature was unique and more than usually impressive."

Names of the chapters are often interesting in themselves. Early Daughters may have been somewhat squeamish about woman's suffrage, but they had their own brand of feminism. Whenever possible, they called the chapters after Revolutionary heroines, most of whom had fallen into even greater obscurity than the men.

One of the most obvious of these heroines was Molly Stark, who served as nurse and doctor when her house became a hospital during the smallpox epidemic that broke out among her husband's troops. There was also Rebecca Mott of South Carolina, who supplied Continental troops with East Indian bows and arrows to set her home on fire while it was occupied by the Redcoats. Emily Geiger, who would have passed unnoticed except for the enterprising Daughters, was also from South Carolina. Acting as courier for General Nathanael Green, she chewed up and swallowed the message she had been carrying when she was taken by the British. After her release, she managed to reach her destination, fifty miles distant, and to deliver the orders from memory. In Brockton, Massachusetts, a chapter is named for Deborah Sampson, a young schoolteacher who actually donned men's clothes and fought for three years in the War for Independence. Her secret identity was discovered when she was wounded, and Washington himself gave her an honorable discharge.

All early members knew and loved to tell the story of Nancy

Hart, a pockmarked, cross-eyed backwoods crack shot from Georgia whose husband ran into the swamp whenever the British made an occasional raid. One day a party of the enemy arrived and ordered a meal. Everything started out quite well. Nancy drank with them while she cooked her last turkey, but at the height of the merriment she grabbed her gun, "Old Bessy," and ordered them to stay where they were. Without blinking an eyelid, she killed two soldiers who didn't take her seriously; she then sent for her husband to come out of hiding because she needed help to string up the remaining captives. A Georgia chapter built a replica of her crude cabin, furnished it, and managed to include a blackened clay pipe that is said to have been Nancy's very own.

The DAR's original work in restoration predates Williamsburg and similar projects by nearly half a century. If it had not been for DAR struggles to rehabilitate the actual sticks and stones and mortar, many of our traditional landmarks would have become mere illustrations in history books. Moreover, their early passion for uncovering and publishing obscure historical data may have acted as a guidepost to magazines like *Heritage* that answer the present popular demand for accurate lively accounts of the nation's past.

In spite of the constructive accomplishments along these lines, the social aspects of the organization reaped the most publicity. The trouble lay in the fact that whether they could belong or not, women all over the country would pounce upon an item describing how every lady wishing to become a Daughter "must be prepared to make affidavit that she had at least six grandfathers." Dry, though more worthy, accounts of historical reclamation bored them. Since the interest of readers increased circulation, editors were pleased to concentrate on what was found enjoyable by the greatest majority.

After elections were given free rein within the DAR, ensuing campaigns always made colorful copy. In the early days it was not unusual for the ladies to throw hats, handkerchiefs, umbrellas, and bouquets into the air as a show of enthusiasm for a favorite. Electioneering among arriving delegates often reached such boisterous heights that it was considered a public nuisance. At one time the stationmaster actually ousted a number of members from Washington's Union Station for disorderly conduct!

In 1905, when Mrs. McLean was finally victorious, her natural flair won the Society a wealth of good-natured notoriety. While her administration was devoted to the solemn task of completing the interior of Memorial Continental Hall and liberalizing the entire viewpoint of the organization, the press doted on her beauty, her wit, and her keen sense of drama. Though the wisdom and merit of her program received scant attention, it soon became common knowledge that she arrived at each Congress carrying a small silk American flag. The originality and taste of her wardrobe quickly gained such a reputation that before each meeting reporters besieged her carriage in order to get a scoop on what she was wearing. She encouraged them by always being dashing and entirely gracious. Mrs. Stevenson described her as "one radiant in the glow of youth, health and enthusiasm." These qualities, coupled with charm and chic, conveyed such a favorable impression to the public that everyone who could wanted to be associated with the order. During her administration, membership grew by leaps and bounds.

In spite of her glamour, Mrs. McLean was not in the least frivolous. Sincerely believing in the real worth of the Society, she tried to enlarge its aims to encompass contemporary problems. If the policies she succeeded in initiating had continued, a 1963 *New York Times* editorial would have had no reason to call the present-day DAR "antediluvians" who are "trying to save the country from progress."

# V

As a loyal supporter of the deposed Washington hierarchy, Mrs. Lockwood complained in the *Story of the Records: D.A.R.* (1906) that, "Mrs. McLean has persistently cherished an ambition to fill this high office, [of President General] and has been encouraged by a large following of those delegates who were inclined to revolt from the constitutional method of selecting candidates from official circles." Of course the "method of selecting candidates" was traditional rather than "constitutional" and it was unfair to imply that Mrs. McLean's motivation was entirely selfish or personal.

Mrs. McLean's majority of 684 to 362 on the second ballot reflected an honest desire to broaden the aims of the organization. The autocratic ladies in Washington had been accustomed to shape policy without interference. Their rigid, conservative aversion to participation in contemporary affairs did not have the unanimous support of the growing national membership.

Mrs. McLean and many others within the ranks believed that the DAR should join other leading women's clubs in a vigorous crusade for national civic improvement. Under the dynamic leadership of Theodore Roosevelt, the progressive reform movement was making headway with antitrust laws, and serious consideration was beginning to be given to labor legislation.

The philosophy of Mark Hanna and "rugged individualism" appeared to be outdated. Tycoons who had employed ruthless means to amass huge fortunes now were engaged in vast philanthropic programs. The richest man in the world, Andrew Carnegie, took the lead in establishing a policy called "wealth in motion." It prescribed that in order to ensure a healthy, democratic society every responsible person of means must use some of his gains for humanitarian purposes. The theory soon found popularity among the powerful rich, and John D. Rockefeller, an energetic SAR, was one of its most ardent exponents.

Mrs. McLean lost little time in fulfilling her promise to lead the Society into an active role in the reform movement. Like her predecessors, she devoted much of her attention to the organization's debt and to other problems of the building program. Yet by the end of her first term, she had established the Committee on Legislation Pending in the United States Congress, which advised the DAR to concentrate on—and lend support to—a few worthy bills each year. Restrictive child-labor laws and conservation of natural resources were suggested as the most pressing issues.

To ensure effective and intelligent action, the Child Labor Committee, which had a Washington information bureau, was set up in 1907. It kept regents abreast with the latest developments in the field, and an intensive program was carried on throughout the year at the chapter level. In 1908, the Conservation Committee undertook similar duties. Members in the hinterlands accepted the new activity with enthusiasm. They kept up a constant barrage of letters to senators and congressmen, and often attempted to sway the viewpoint of local politicians. Petticoat influence had been well understood by the National Board in Washington. Now all members were offered an opportunity to exhibit their dexterity at the game.

The *American Monthly* reported that on April 19, 1909, the opening day of the eighteenth DAR Congress, "The sun shone bright. Washington had put on her most beautiful robes of green adorned by flowers of every hue." The sun also shone on the group's progressive policy. The keynote speaker was Gifford Pinchot, champion of conservation in public domain. Complimenting the ladies for their aid in his battle against private-interest "land grabbers," he gave them his personal recommendations for future effective action.

The chairman of the Child Labor Committee made a twenty-three-page detailed report covering the astonishing progress of each state in the fight for the enactment of humane laws. Although it was the longest paper read, delegates gave it close attention.

Every Daughter was then urged to join the National Child Labor Committee, whose chief aim was to establish a children's bureau as an official branch of the Department of Commerce. It was stressed that unified DAR support would be an effective method of securing federal legislation to control abuses.

Mrs. McLean's final year in office was 1909, and she was anxious to leave the Society in the hands of a vigorous liberal. She made an excellent choice in backing Mrs. Matthew T. Scott. Mrs. Scott was a sister of the admired Mrs. Stevenson and also was a progressive woman of unquestioned ability. As a widow, she had managed her own considerable interests for years. These included a 20,000-acre model farm in Illinois where living and working conditions were ideal and where, at her expense, employees attended agricultural school to learn modern methods. Under her guidance, the DAR was bound to keep on the path Mrs. McLean had initiated.

Mrs. Scott's opponent was Mrs. William Cumming Story. As New York State Regent, she had a large following, and her reputation for being among the organization's best-dressed women prejudiced many delegates to favor her rather than the plain Mrs. Scott. Mrs. Scott, appearing in a succession of dowdy Queen Victoria bonnets, sat quietly on the sidelines while her sponsor, Mrs. McLean, waged a battle of *haute mode* with the ambitious Mrs. Story.

Disregarding serious issues, newspaper accounts emphasized that the outcome of the election hinged on the result of a duel of fashion between the two beauties. The *Washington Post* declared that, before the opening of the 1909 Congress, Mrs. Story already had worn a whole trunkful of ensembles and still held plenty of fresh ones in reserve to woo the votes of clothes-conscious members. But Mrs. McLean's wardrobe seemed to be winning.

At one evening session, Mrs. Story appeared in a yellow satin gown and a black plumed hat. With her arms full of flowers sent by admirers, she floated down the aisle to give a belated regent's report. She advanced toward the beautiful Mrs. McLean, who stood on the platform in a white crepe de Chine dress that billowed into a flowing train. Mrs. McLean also wore a black picture hat, quivering with blue ostrich feathers. An emerald dog collar with matching bracelets completed the most stunning outfit ever displayed at a Congress. As Mrs. Story approached the podium, Mrs. McLean brusquely dismissed her for having failed to give her report earlier in the day when she had been called upon to do so.

Partisanship for the rival fashion plates became so spirited that before the delegates went to the ballot box, Mrs. McLean felt called upon to issue a warning. "We are a body of American gentlewomen," she said, "and we are going to behave as such all this day of election."

Mrs. Scott slid into office on a margin of only eight votes. No matter how slim the plurality, it ensured the continuance of a liberal policy, and even her most bitter opponents were somewhat mollified when she induced President William Howard Taft to address the 1910 opening session, the first to take place in the fully completed Memorial Continental Hall.

Following this precedent many chiefs of state made personal appearances. The custom continued, almost without interruption, until Franklin Delano Roosevelt prefaced his remarks to the DAR with the salutation of "Fellow immigrants . . ." Although the personal visit has been discontinued, the Daughters still receive an annual letter from the president. Of late these messages have often contained veiled criticism rather than praise of policy, but when President Taft sat on the platform in 1910 the organization was one of the most progressive of the day.

In her induction speech, Mrs. Scott pointed with pride to past DAR accomplishments. Stressing the importance of lending their unified strength to "divers good causes," she placed particular emphasis on their drive to abolish the abuses of child labor. Obligations to public education and public morality covered a variety of areas, including the responsibility of trying to improve hygienic conditions among "the least fortunate dwellers in our cities and centers of industry, where American wealth is being produced on a scale unprecedented in the world's history."

She praised the Society for having become a potential national influence for righteousness in so short a time and went on to suggest a further extension of activities. She urged the Daughters to join the great international peace movement to which so many responsible citizens were devoting their energies. In an eloquent appeal she explained: "It is particularly fitting for the Daughters, representatives of a victorious citizen-soldiery, to dedicate themselves as such,—to the great modern crusade for arbitration of international disputes—to the new-born war against war."

As early as the 1890s, a faction of both SAR and DAR members had shown sympathy to an international court of arbitration. Walter S. Logan, an influential Son, had expressed a hope for "a Congress of Nations with a jurisdiction which shall enable it to provide for the settlement of all international disputes and make possible the disbanding of all armies and navies." However, Mrs. Scott's proposal, which became a resolution, represented the only official affirmative stand on the question ever taken by either organization.

Pacifism must have appealed to the bulk of the 1910 membership because in the following year Mrs. Scott was reelected by a substantial majority, even though the popular Mrs. Story was again her opponent. Early in her second term, she set up the Committee on International Peace Arbitration which remained active until America entered World War I. During Mrs. Scott's entire administration the Society's only seeming concession to reactionary prejudice was a unanimous protest issued to the Secretary of the Navy, objecting to the acceptance of a silver service from the State of Utah to the battleship *Utah* "unless the figure of Brigham Young is erased from the pieces."

In this period there was a surge of public feeling that our country should take the initiative in promoting peace among the nations of the world.

In 1905, Andrew Carnegie had made his first great public antiwar gesture by assuming complete financial responsibility for the construction of the Palace of Peace at the Hague where international disputes would be settled by arbitration. Progress made here had been so encouraging that many thought the battlefield was almost a thing of the past. In 1910, the American imagination was caught by the enormous potentialities of a $10 million fund given by Andrew Carnegie to found the Carnegie Endowment for International Peace.

Carnegie himself was optimistic enough to feel justified in

qualifying his 1910 "endowment" with the provision that when the threat of war became nonexistent the money should be used for the abolishment of "the next most degrading evil whose banishment . . . would most advance the progress and happiness of man." Popular interest was so great that even a foremost humorous periodical abandoned its joking tone long enough to devote an entire issue to a peace symposium. Liberal educators and reformers, led by Dr. David Starr Jordan (president of Stanford University) and Jane Addams, called the first Emergency Peace Council in New York City to discuss practical means to give reality to the dream.

Peace hopes did not fire the imagination of progressives alone. President Taft gladly accepted the post of honorary president of the Carnegie Endowment. Elihu Root became its active head. Not one of the conservative members of the board of trustees could possibly have been mistaken for a "flighty idealist." Faith in the peace movement remained so firm that for a long time a large block of substantial patriotic citizens believed it was America's duty to stay out of World War I in order to act as arbitrator between hostile nations.

It was in this atmosphere that Mrs. Scott led the Daughters into the peace crusade. In 1912, President Taft again beamed down on the members and spoke of the "pleasant annual duty that falls to the President of the United States of welcoming the beauties of spring and the beauties of the Daughters . . . I hope that your deliberations this year may be as useful as those which you have had in the past."

He had every right to praise their record. Making good their pledge to work for peace, the organization had developed an intensive program of antiwar education aimed at the elementary-school level. Conservationist Pinchot also found them hard workers who had used their considerable influence to help pass the Alaskan coal bill, La Follette's legislation to regulate grazing, and the Appalachian bill. This year Pinchot advised them to get behind laws to ensure public interest in water power.

The year 1912 was triumphant for the DAR mainly because they had the satisfaction of seeing the Children's Bureau become a permanent branch of the Department of Commerce. Julia

Lathrop, the first woman to serve the federal government in an official capacity, was named director, and the Daughters of the American Revolution were among her most ardent champions. Although her appointment was a real triumph for the suffragettes, the Board of Management of the National Society had so far outgrown its original antipathy to the women's rights movement that Mrs. Scott could exclaim in this moment of victory: "No amount of eloquent verbal appreciation of heroic ancestors will absolve this generation of its difficult task of working out ethical and humane solutions for all the pressing economic and social problems of our times."

Mrs. Scott also took this opportunity to remind her constituents that although women still lacked the vote, three important avenues of public service were open to them. Since teaching was the one profession in which they had long held an accepted place, women should try to extend their influence in the educational field, whenever possible, by gaining admittance to school boards. Next, pointing to the fine example of Miss Lathrop, she outlined the vast possibilities of social-service work as a career. Last, she proposed that even if members remained housewives, they should regard home economics as a science rather than a drudgery. Contemptuous of "bargain hunters," she begged everyone to join the Consumer's League in its war on unfair labor practices, emphasizing that this was a way in which women could exert an unrealized potential power over business and industry. She ended her speech by saying:

It may seem in these lines of work—somewhat unique —and heretofore undefined as patriotic, that I am departing from the usual address on patriotism. But I ask your careful consideration of this subconscious knowledge in every woman's breast that at least every issue . . . has its foundation in life and action—the surest meaning of noble and holy patriotism applied in the broadest and deepest sense.

Mrs. Scott's administration ended in 1913. With the Children's Bureau an accomplished fact, one of her last acts in office was to expand the duties of the Child Labor Committee to include the welfare of women as well. As late as 1916, the DAR agenda bristled with a series of liberal recommendations favoring regulation of women's work hours, universal marriage and divorce laws, a ban on new tenements lacking proper facilities, the improvement of sanitary conditions in stores and factories, tuberculosis control, compulsory education, work-hour limitation and work permits for anyone under sixteen, federal control of child labor, juvenile courts, and the prohibition of the sale of cigarettes, drugs, and liquor to minors.

However these liberal resolutions reflected merely a formal, somewhat apathetic reaffirmation of past policy rather than a burning desire to support progressive measures. The period of active DAR participation in social reform was drawing to a close.

World War I had come along and diverted their attention. Chapters were now too deeply involved in war relief work and pushing the preparedness effort to devote much time to domestic improvement. The switch in emphasis had been a gradual one.

On November 5, 1914, in immediate response to President Woodrow Wilson's plea for the country to remain an "island of sanity" refusing to enter the conflict, the Board of Management passed a unanimous resolution pledging the organization to neutrality.

As devoted disciples of George Washington, they were bitterly opposed to all foreign entanglements and, with Wilson, wanted no part in the struggle. However, protection of our own shores was also a fundamental principle of Washington's philosophy, and a firm belief in this doctrine prompted the DAR to support such staunch militarists as General Leonard Wood and Theodore Roosevelt who were issuing loud warnings that the strength of our armed forces was insufficient even to defend our neutrality. These men claimed that the growing strength of the pacifist movement had weakened our army and navy, and, as a result, America's ability to protect herself in case of emergency was in jeopardy.

Wilson was decidedly cool to any form of preparedness, and a number of Daughters began to lose their original ardor for his program as a result of his message to Congress on December 6, 1914 in which he said: "We shall not alter our attitude toward the question of national defense because some of us are nervous and excited." Although he mentioned no names, obviously the slur was intended for Wood and Roosevelt.

In prosperous, conservative financial and professional circles, these distinguished men were highly respected as practical realists. To hear their opinions dismissed as "nervous and excited" enraged their champions, and before the year was out, many influential Americans steered away from Wilson's "island of sanity" to support General Wood, who had bluntly declared that the United States inevitably would be drawn into the conflict on the side of the Allies and that we must be prepared for the crisis. Wood's disciples formed the National Security League. Its admitted purpose was to alert fellow citizens to the imminence of danger and to bring about action by public demand in spite of President Wilson, whom they considered the dupe of pacifists.

The League launched an aggressive, efficient campaign to keep its views before the public. It recruited numerous members from the same strata of society that were attracted to the patriotic-heredity movement, but its real strength lay in the heavy backing of powerful financiers like H. H. Rogers, the Guggenheims, the Du Ponts, John D. Rockefeller, and J. P. Morgan. Mrs. Finley J. Shepherd (who had been Helen Gould before her marriage) was one of the most generous contributors. She was also a prominent DAR and easily may have swayed opinion among sister members.

In 1915, the League's efforts were supplemented by the American Defense Society, another powerful preparedness association, which was formed as a direct result of the sinking of the *Lusitania*. Theodore Roosevelt became the Defense Society's patron saint. In addition to lobbying and pamphleteering, this younger organization kept in the limelight by sponsoring a rapid succession of patriotic exercises in schools and auditoriums, where over 100,000 huge photographs of the beaming "Teddy" were unveiled by members and adoring "friends" who always made appropriate remarks to whip up enthusiasm for American intervention.

Unlike the National Security League, the Defense Society made little effort to attract dollar members. Instead, it relied largely on the generous support of two wealthy angels, Franklin Remington, of the Remington Arms Company, and Mrs. George E. Owen, whose sincerely militant convictions were in sharp contrast to the stubborn pacifism of her father, William Cullen Bryant.

Mrs. Owen, along with Mrs. Shepard, was a loyal and influential Daughter of the American Revolution. Although she was unable to convert her own father to her viewpoint, it would seem that as the war intensified she gained many pro-Allied sympathizers within the sisterhood.

Certainly Mrs. Shepard and Mrs. Owen had a willing confederate in Mrs. William Cumming Story, who finally had been victorious in the 1913 race for President General. Mrs. Story was an entirely new type of DAR leader and her views were in marked contrast to those of her liberal predecessors. She may have appeared to be merely a frivolous butterfly to many of her most ardent supporters, but on closer examination it is obvious that enlightened women like Mrs. McLean and Mrs. Scott had good reason to suspect the motives behind her consuming ambition to become head of the Society.

Daisy Story was a superpatriot. At the time of her election, the DAR magazine noted with some pride that she also was vice-president of the National Society of Patriotic Women. This organization had no ancestral requirements and lacked the Daughters' preoccupation with preserving our historical past. Its major functions included maintaining flag ritual, upholding the Constitution, and increasing the power of the United States. Its firm stand on strengthening our military forces was at direct odds with the peace policy favored by the Society when Mrs. Story took office.

The *National Cyclopedia of American Biography* states that Mrs. Story was an Episcopalian, an expert golfer, and a painter of sufficient talent to exhibit at the National Academy of Design and the American Art Association. However, above all, the account stresses her outspoken antagonism to pacifism and radicalism and her untiring efforts to further the cause of universal military training and strong national defense in peace as well as in wartime. However, neither Mrs. Story nor any other member of the higher echelon was solely responsible for the Daughters' change of attitude. In fact, little headway was made in weaning the Society away from its progressive policy until Mrs. Story's second term.

By this time, there was a different climate in America under which continued neutrality was beginning to appear a cowardly position. The bulk of the DAR membership belonged to the segment of our population that was quick to resent any slur on our national honor. As the proud guardians of "Old Glory" and all it stands for, the Daughters felt they had no choice but to repudiate pacifism and adopt the spirit of militant patriotism, which since that time has remained uppermost as a determining factor in every action of the organization.

Soon after the beginning of hostilities in Europe, the Daughters of the American Revolution received their first rebuff from official circles. On September 9, 1914, Mrs. Story gained a personal interview with President Wilson in order to suggest that the Daughters be put in charge of a refugee relief program. Her prompt action was entirely in keeping with the DAR's splendid record in the Spanish-American War. Wilson told Mrs. Story that, in his estimation, the Red Cross seemed a more efficient agency to handle the task. Even though he hastened to add a courteous request for the DAR to give its closest cooperation, it must have been a blow to the DAR to relinquish the honor to their old rival.

Nevertheless on the very day of Wilson's reply Mrs. Story ordered every regent to follow the President's directive. The Daughters seem to have accepted the subordinate role in good grace and worked "hard, many, long hours" within the framework of the American Red Cross. However, they insisted on certain nice points that enabled them to retain DAR identity. Woven name tapes soon appeared with the words "American Red Cross, DAR Navy Auxiliary." These were inserted into all DAR gifts sent through that agency, while others marked "Daughters of the American Revolution" were attached to articles coming directly from the Society. To make the distinction even more pointed, a 1918 resolution ordered all DAR members to wear their pins and insignia when working under Red Cross auspices.

In spite of this small display of wounded pride, DARs had every reason to be proud of their record of cooperation. They also contributed time and money to Belgian Relief, the French Red Cross, and the American Society for the relief of French War Orphans. In its zest to aid ravaged Europe, the National Society adopted the French village of Tilliloy as its own, and provided generous funds for extensive rehabilitation.

At the time of the unanimous November 1914 resolution that pledged NSDAR support to Wilson's neutrality policy, Mrs. Story had showed no signs of disagreement. However, less than a month after the Board issued its public declaration favoring nonintervention, she sent a letter to the War Department asking in what ways the DAR might help the armed services. The department suggested that gifts of books would be welcomed by troops at home and abroad. Although this could hardly be considered a militant assignment, it is significant as Mrs. Story's earliest attempt to alter the Society's stand on pacifism. For the duration of the war, a similar communication to the War Office became an annual DAR custom. It was not long before the military recognized the potential value of the cooperation of a powerful women's patriotic organization, and DAR assignments became much more significant than the distribution of reading matter. Not only Mrs. Story but most Daughters were pleased to be promoted to the pivotal position of acting as goodwill ambassadors in furthering American preparedness.

At the spring Congress in 1915, Mrs. Story's reelection was threatened by stiff competition from Mrs. George Thatcher Guernsey who took as her main campaign issue the fact that the Story administration had been unsuccessful in reducing the $60,000 mortgage on Memorial Continental Hall. Mrs. Guernsey promised to liquidate the entire debt through current receipts over a three-year period.

Long-suffering delegates, accustomed to being pressed for generous contributions to amortize the debt, probably found the proposal tempting, but a serious handicap stood in the way of Mrs. Guernsey's victory. She lacked glamour. Wearing her straight hair parted in the middle with a severe knot at the nape of her neck, she favored cap-sleeve evening dresses and took pride in the title "the plain woman from Kansas." Although admittedly less of a businesswoman, Daisy Story won an easy triumph; the vote once more confirmed the DAR preference for a beauty in the showcase, particularly since the year 1915 marked the twenty-fifth birthday of the DAR and the President General was scheduled to make a number of important public appearances.

The climax of the Silver Jubilee festivities came on the natal day, October 11, when over a thousand Daughters flocked to their "home" to attend an anniversary party. The largest cake ever baked in Washington was served at an evening banquet. It was 36 inches in diameter and 3 tiers high and weighed 120 pounds. One glowing description of the gastronomic masterpiece ended: "Twenty-five silver candles were held erect by twenty-five silver roses and on the icing were the initials 'D.A.R.' and the two dates, Oct. 11, 1890–Oct. 11, 1915."

Many Daughters may have been unaware of the fact, but the day was memorable for a far more serious reason than the innocent celebration of a birthday party. This was the day on which Mrs. Story committed the society to a new policy of militant patriotism from which it has never once deviated.

At the afternoon session, previous to the banquet, President Wilson appeared before the assembly. At the end of his address, Mrs. Story made a fervent plea for every DAR to take an active part in a new crusade that was encouraging American women to demand adequate national defense.

There was little in the contents of President Wilson's magnificent speech to warrant her strong demand for preparedness. To be sure, he said: "Neutrality is a negative word. It is a word that doesn't express what America ought to feel . . . ," but he clearly qualified that statement with his next words:

> America has a heart and that heart throbs with all sorts of intense sympathies, but America has schooled its heart to love the things that America believes in and it ought to devote itself only to the things that America believes in; and believing that America stands apart in its ideals, it ought not to allow itself to be drawn, so far as its heart is concerned, into anybody's quarrel.

Mrs. Story's reference to a crusade for preparedness had little to do with the President's actual utterance. It may be that by this time she and many other Daughters were more attentive to Teddy Roosevelt's battle cry for a show of "100 percent Americans" ready to go into action than they were to any plea for tolerance and reason. President Wilson's October 11 address to the DAR came after the sinking of the *Lusitania* and the August scare created by German sabotage of industry in this country. Pro-Allied feeling was running so high that anyone daring to oppose intervention—even a perfectly loyal native-born pacifist —was suspected of being a German sympathizer.

Wilson's procrastination was making him unpopular with staunch defenders of the country's honor like the DAR and indeed with most conservative Americans. At the time of the *Lusitania* disaster, an infuriated Teddy Roosevelt roared that "we owe it not only to humanity but to our national self-respect" to declare war on Germany. As the war intensified, Roosevelt was applauded when he proclaimed that, while loyalty to the nation was indispensable, it was questionable whether loyalty need be extended to a "namby-pamby" leader who was trying to dissuade the United States from its clear duty to join the Allied cause.

The Daughters soon were in the vanguard of the intervention crusade being staged by the National Security League and the American Defense Society. Only a few months after Mrs. Story's call for preparedness, the National Security League made a daring, major move to win over the Daughters completely.

The League's headquarters was normally in New York. To win political friends for intervention, it staged a three-day Washington conference in January, 1916. To wind up the conference the DAR "home" was the scene of a major rally. The Daughters offered a perfect mouthpiece to voice criticism of the pacifism that was still being supported by most of the national women's clubs.

After an introduction by Mrs. Story, the meeting was turned over to Major John P. Mitchel, the Mayor of New York City, who also held a reserve commission in General Wood's pet "civilian army." On this occasion, he described the benefits of Plattsburg, the new "businessman's camp," where he had spent five weeks during the previous summer.

Plattsburg was one of a series of reserve corps units set up by General Wood in an attempt to bolster the strength of the regular army in case of emergency. It received wide publicity because many of the 1,200 recruits represented the cream of New-

port, Bar Harbor, and Wall Street. Volunteers included such
notables as Richard Harding Davis, then fifty-one, and Sergeant
Robert Bacon, an executive of US Steel and formerly Secretary
of State, who dutifully snapped to attention before his own son,
a first lieutenant. Although it was an incongruous group of all
ages and the short training period was admittedly insufficient to
fit soldiers for modern combat, General Wood's businessman's
camp succeeded in dramatizing the growing demand for some
form of military conscription. It may be assumed that Major
Mitchel's persuasive arguments at the League's January meeting
in Memorial Continental Hall were partially responsible for
arousing enthusiasm among the Daughters who were in the
audience.

The American Defense Society soon made a determined effort
to woo the entire DAR. During one session of the 1916 Congress,
President General Story urged sister members to cooperate
closely with that organization. Then, after announcing the Defense Society's New York address, Mrs. Story urged the ladies
to contact a Mr. Sterling P. Story for further information. Mr.
Story was her youngest son.

In the years to come, both these preparedness groups provided
glamorous officers as speakers to captivate DAR ladies at the
most modest chapter meeting, held in some provincial parlor, as
well as to grace the platform of the DAR Washington headquarters. Largely due to this influence, the DAR remains a steadfast
champion of a system of compulsory military duty that their
revolutionary forebears detested.

By 1916 pro-Ally feeling had gained such momentum that in
order to gain reelection, Wilson was forced to make concessions.
However, he still clung to neutrality and refused to admit the
inevitability of our entrance into the war until Germany, on
February 1, 1917, announced that henceforth the American
merchant marine would be the target of unrestricted submarine
attack. The ultimatum left Wilson no choice. He severed relations with Germany on February 3.

Connecticut State Regent, Mrs. Elizabeth Barney Buel,
promptly dispatched a strong letter of DAR support to the
Commander in Chief. Undoubtedly all patriotic groups shared

her expressed feelings of relief that at last our nation had awakened to its duty and was about to plunge "into the fight to save liberty and democracy."

On Washington's birthday, the SR, the SAR, and the DAR staged a huge joint rally that packed Memorial Continental Hall. President Wilson and his entire family sat on the platform; so did most of the Cabinet, Supreme Court Justices, and the majority of the Allied foreign diplomats. After the Marine Corps Band had played "The World Turned Upside Down," the handsome Senator Atlee Pomerance gave a rousing keynote address. The DAR magazine reported that he had been chosen because he could make aggressive statements on the subject of intervention inappropriate at the moment for the President and that "the audience, to the last person in it, sat up and 'took notice' as if galvanized by an electric battery."

The National Board of Management issued application blanks to all DAR members with orders to classify their individual talents for active service in the "Women's Civilian Army." The response was so quick that the Daughters were ready to "do their bit" as soon as war was declared on April 6, 1917.

A few days after that declaration—and almost a month before the draft became a law—the ladies at twenty-seventh DAR Congress jumped to their feet to pass a resolution favoring a permanent and democratic system of defense based on universal military service and training. Enthusiasm for the motion was aroused by the stirring speech of Lieutenant General S.B.M. Young, president of the National Association for Universal Military Training. He complimented the Daughters on being the "first great Women's Society to raise its voice in support of this fundamental principle of the Nation's military policy" and declared: "We will never have a Nation in the highest sense of the word until all of our citizens render equal National Service." Delegates applauded these remarks without considering that many of their own ancestors would have been the first to question the general's assumption that conscription was a "fundamental principle of the Nation's military policy."

A rousing ovation was given to the Georgia state regent when she made the motion for all members and visitors to wear a small

American flag during Congress Week. The DAR magazine described how Mrs. Guernsey was finally swept into office at this time by a band of "purposeful women" who were "waving flags" and listening to "inspiring patriotic music and eloquent addresses." In fact, Mrs. Guernsey's victory was quite unrelated to war but, rather, was based on her renewed promise to liquidate the debt on the DAR "home" through current receipts.

Two other planks of her platform, which also received enthusiastic endorsement, had a lasting effect on future DAR policy. The first was innocuous enough: it merely proposed to extend the term of the President General from two to three years, a custom that still prevails. The second, proposed that an individual be allowed to speak at the Congress, no more than five minutes on any given subject. Many delegates welcomed the idea of limiting debate because endless quibbling and filibustering had disrupted previous Congresses. They did not foresee that strict adherence to the new time limit (shortened to three minutes a little later) was a potential weapon with which the National Board might silence opposition to its decisions.

Preoccupation with internal reform did not keep Mrs. Guernsey from fanning the superpatriotic flame that had burst out among the Daughters. Even the peace-loving Mrs. Scott was sufficiently excited to accept the chairmanship of the new National Committee on War Relief Service. It was she who brought the eventful twenty-seventh Congress to a close with a "fervent appeal to patriotism" and instruction to members that it was their duty "to stop petitioning and go home and plant potatoes."

The Daughters took to war work with the same zest they had exhibited for all their projects. They purchased $130,000,000 worth of Liberty Bonds and offered vacant land behind their hall rent-free to Herbert Hoover as a site for temporary headquarters for his Food Administration. When the land was refused as too small an area, they promptly gave it to the National Council of Defense, who became gratis tenants of the Daughters for the duration.

Hoover's slogan "Food Will Win the War!" was one that

both pacifists and militarists could agree on. Many DAR chapters cut down on refreshments; twenty-three abstained entirely and nineteen served only tea and wafers at meetings. A column of recipes, utilizing substitute foods, became a monthly feature of their magazine, and the Daughters were urged to try them no matter how unsavory they might seem.

Some members sold tinfoil, some collected peach stones. Others listed as their contributions the number of hours their limousines and chauffeurs had been active in patriotic service. "Busy fingers," in the Mary Isham Keith Chapter of Fort Worth, Texas, "wrought seventeen full sets of knitted garments." An Illinois chapter made "two barrels of jelly." In spite of the sugar shortage, jelly was a popular item as a national project. Some 93,752 jars were recorded in all. The society set a cash value of 20 cents on each jar, and the overall contribution made to the cause from this commodity alone came to $18,750.40. In fact, most DAR gifts were assessed at cash value and amounted to $3,730,385. A total of 1,711,322 gifts remained unpriced.

One chapter had to its credit the purchase of vestments for 2 chaplains, 2 ukuleles, 53 pounds of candy, and 2,048 picture puzzles. The same chapter also entertained 3 sailors as weekend guests for 3 months. Hospitality was a favorite war work: the national headquarters was open for the convenience of the armed forces, and throughout the country the Daughters played hostess to 42,398 servicemen as house guests, 98,329 as table guests, and 50,109 at public restaurants.

The Children of the American Revolution were also on the front line of action. While on duty, the little girls wore a red veil with a white band displaying the blue seal of the CAR; boy workers had red, white, and blue armbands. Mrs. Lothrop donated a complete twelve-volume set of her *Five Little Peppers* to various groups, and the books were read aloud during the work periods. As of March 16, 1918, a Washington children's contingent had turned out 213 needle cases, 344 pinballs made from milk-bottle tops, 703 cards of darning thread for "comfort bags," and one eye bandage.

Attending to the needs of the "doughboys" was, however, only part of the job. Wartime hysteria had focused on the serious threat of subversion at home. Strict espionage and sedition laws were passed June 15, 1917, and strengthened on May 16, 1918. These laws included penalties against any person—alien or native-born—who was accused of expressing contempt for the President, the government, the Constitution, the flag, or the uniform. Even saying or doing something likely to obstruct the sale of war bonds was considered a crime. Although dangerous suspects often were proven to be innocent victims of the overfertile imagination of some patriotic amateur detective, the "civilian army" was given official encouragement to ferret out the slightest infringement of the laws.

The Daughters were quick to participate in this exciting new hunt. No misdemeanor was too small to attract their attention. Early in the summer of 1917, the "Vigilante" column became a feature of the DAR magazine. The July issue expressed anxiety over the proper ritual of the flag.

One of the contributors to this issue, Gelett Burgess, wrote a vivid description of the shameful desecration of the Star-Spangled Banner by many businesses and department stores. The crime was punishable by a fine not to exceed $100 or thirty days in jail or both. Nevertheless, stores continued to display the flag on neckties, paper napkins, and "party crackers," which, when pulled at both ends, forced merry makers to tear it to shreds. It was also being used on party rattles, so that at each sound a hammer hit "Old Glory." Whenever Burgess found a guilty shopkeeper, he considered it his patriotic duty to haul him into court and demand the full penalty of the law. He cited the case of one emporium that was featuring a 75-cent silk handkerchief with the flag printed on it. The owner objected to Burgess' protest, wanting to know who would blow his nose on a 75-cent handkerchief. His flippancy proved useless—the culprit promptly followed the path of the other offenders. Burgess said that his tireless work was discouraging "dollar patriotism" in New York City, and he urged the Daughters all over the country to join in his crusade.

The DAR local flag committees already had their hands full.

Mrs. Lyra Brown Olin, committee chairman in Joliet, Illinois, faithfully attended every naturalization session at the county court and presented a flag to each new citizen. She appeared on all army registration days to distribute flags and even made a trip to the women's state prison, telling the women the story of *The Man Without a Country* and again giving out flags.

On the whole, amateur sleuthing had many more serious aspects than finding "Old Glory" delinquents. Now that America's intervention was accomplished, the National Security League and the American Defense Society turned their attention toward "suspicious characters." They compiled an impressive dossier on anyone who in their estimation might retard the war effort. Under this heading they blanketed all people who threatened the powerful military machine (and profits therefrom), which the leaders of preparedness associations were anxious to continue into peacetime.

Their lists included not only Germans and possible sympathizers, but hundreds of anarchists and syndicalists, who had always been dreaded by big business. Special attention was paid to the Socialist Party, to labor leaders, and to political and civilian reformers. An increasing number of highly respected clergymen and educators began to appear on the lists. In order to discredit the entire pacifist movement as despicable and unpatriotic an enormous amount of adverse publicity was given to the "slacker's oath" taken by conscientious objectors.

The sedition laws opened a door through which the findings of the Defense Society and the Security League could enter and be dutifully filed away in the Justice Department for future reference. Streamlined propaganda from these two organizations continued to bombard the startled ears of the Daughters and other patriotic and civic groups, who accepted the findings as solid fact. Mrs. Guernsey's message to the 1918 Congress shows to what an extent she was influenced by the constant warnings of subversion:

> In the name of "free speech" and "personal liberty" we have unwisely refrained from closing mouths that have too long and too loudly proclaimed treason. . . . We stand ready as Daughters of the American Revolution to back up

the government in a procedure for more stringent censoring of *speech* as well as press . . .

That year, the agenda bristled with resolutions demanding the prohibition of German-language courses in public schools and the suppression of foreign newspapers. One motion offered violent objection to the funeral of two German soldiers who, having died in Fort McPherson prison, had been buried under their native flag, with military salute, in the National Cemetery at Marietta, Georgia.

Peace came in November. To most of the nation it seemed abrupt and unreal. People were just beginning to be geared to the prosperity of wartime economy as well as to the antagonistic emotions that war engenders. It is impossible to revive a feeling of brotherly love for all mankind simply by declaring an armistice. As Wilson said in 1917 to Frank Cobb, editor of the New York *World*:

> Once lead this people into war, and they'll forget there was ever such a thing as tolerance; to fight you must be brutal and ruthless, and the spirit of ruthless brutality will enter into the very fibre of our national life, infecting Congress, the courts, the policeman, the man in the street.

Opinion was sharply divided on the wisdom of Wilson's policies of "peace without victory" and the League of Nations. He did not receive his Democratic majority at the mid-term election. Reflecting the feeling of many people in this country one DAR spokesman snorted: "The Armistice was viewed with disappointment and foreboding by many who had hoped to see our boys march into Berlin through a humiliated Germany."

Yet, the Society at its 1919 Congress gave its support to Wilson's League of Nations. The Daughters may have been pleased and flattered by a novel form of entertainment offered during a DAR victory banquet at the Willard Hotel on April 15. A model of an "aerial mail carrier" sailed through the ballroom, and when the machine reached Mrs. Guernsey, a carrier pigeon was released. It bore a personal message to the DAR from Colonel E. M. House, who at the time was with President Wilson in Paris. Mrs. Guernsey read the message aloud to the delighted members: "Daughters of the American Revolution, we need you!" Next day, at the business session, a unanimous resolution was passed in favor of the League of Nations.

# VII

After the first flush of victory, the average American began to wonder if winning the war had really made the world "safe for democracy." President Wilson may have sailed across the sea to discuss peace terms and promote his League of Nations, but the communists were winning the revolution in Russia, and the danger of the Boche paled before the new peril of the Bolshevik. The "Red plot" was admittedly an international attempt to force the ideology of state ownership onto every capitalist country. Nothing could be more frightening to Americans, who were dedicated to the institutions of free enterprise and individual property rights.

Many alarmed conservatives sincerely believed that our government was in danger of being overthrown by "sinister and subversive agitators." Internal safety seemed far more crucial than international idealism. The Espionage Act remained intact, and investigations of radicals were speeded up by popular demand.

A. Mitchell Palmer, who became Attorney General in 1919, was uncompromising in his enforcement of the Espionage Act. At the time he entered office there was some real cause for alarm. Freed of wartime controls, labor was in ferment. The Industrial Workers of the World (IWW), whose leaders were predominantly foreign-born syndicalists, was gaining ground. There was a wave of violent strikes, with occasional demands for key industries to remain nationalized rather than be returned to private ownership. Bomb scares in May and June seemed to justify Palmer's harsh, indiscriminate persecution of "radical alien agitators." Proud of his nickname, "The Fighting Quaker," Palmer used methods that were undemocratic and, in many cases, unconstitutional. However, because he raised the battle cry of restoring America to Americans with good old-fashioned American ideals, his strong-arm tactics met with general applause.

Although the 1919 DAR Congress had supported the League of Nations, the majority of its resolutions reflected the hysteria that Palmer was engendering. Mrs. Guernsey's farewell address showed the contemporary distrust of foreign-born minority groups when she asked how an "American soul" could be grown in a New York tenement or an "American conscience" developed in a Dakota Mennonite community. She said that if she had her way, she would transfer thousands of Minnesota Scandinavians into the south, Wisconsin Germans into New England, and New York Jews into the far west. Even British-aping Americans did not escape criticism. Mrs. Guernsey asked point blank what could be hoped "from the Americanism of a man who insists on employing a London tailor?"

She offered some solutions to existing problems: In her opinion, membership in any organization retaining allegiance to a nation other than America should be prohibited; "All foreigners should be compelled to cease telling how they used to do it in their native country," and, above all, foreign youths must be taught to understand that conditions here are superior to those of their original homeland. She issued a prophetic postwar DAR directive by calling for an acceleration of the Americanization Committee. She declared: "Our Society in this crisis will continue to teach proper reverence for the heroism and noble deeds of our forefathers because our Society is particularly adapted to carry on an educational program."

Far away in Europe, President Wilson seemed unconscious of the domestic turmoil. Returning in early summer, he was too ill and still too preoccupied with the fate of the League of Nations to strip his Attorney General of the extraordinary power he had usurped. Palmer's reign of terror was allowed to extend through most of 1920.

Many patriotic societies joined in the initial postwar witch hunt, but the Daughters remained somewhat aloof from the turmoil. To be sure, they were adamant in their stand for a powerful army and navy. They passed an annual resolution to keep armed force strength at the 1920 quota. In 1922, along with the Sons, the DAR pledged to expel objectionable history books and other unpatriotic material from public schools, but on the whole, these years were comparatively placid ones for the Society. The organization again had become involved in financing a building program. Mrs. George Maynard Minor succeeded Mrs. Guernsey as leader in 1920, and a much-needed Administration Building was started at the rear of Memorial Continental Hall. When it was completed in 1923, 1776 D Street, N.W., became the DAR's official address.

The public image of the Society was greatly enhanced in 1921 when Memorial Continental Hall became the meeting place of the Conference on the Limitation of Armament. The *Washington Post* wrote that the entire United States owed the DAR a vote of thanks for playing hostess to this international assembly and for agreeing to extensive temporary renovations of their auditorium to fit the needs of the meeting. With such favorable publicity, DAR membership increased at the rate of 1,000 a month.

The year 1921 was memorable for the DAR for another reason. Although the Society joined the SAR and other patriotic groups in firm support of every law restricting immigration, it also determined to do something constructive about the hordes of confused aliens pouring into the country as a result of the war. The National Society began to levy an annual assessment of 25 cents per member in order to publish a *DAR Citizens' Manual*, which offered immigrants practical aid in their own language.

The idea was not an entirely new one. Back in the days of Mrs. Scott, Connecticut Daughters had discovered a book called *Guide to the United States*, written in Italian by John Foster Carr. It was so helpful to immigrants that the state society spent $5,000 of their own funds to distribute it. The project was so successful that Connecticut Daughters persuaded the Society to put the program on a national basis and translate the book into the language of every nationality coming to America. The manual came to be known within the DAR by the affectionate nickname of "the little green book," and by 1915 editions were appearing in Polish, Yiddish, and English as well as Italian.

In 1921, Mrs. Elizabeth Barney Buel revised the guide and included the latest useful advice on legal, medical, and economic problems of daily life. The *Manual* has remained an absorbing interest of the Daughters. At one time, it appeared in as many as eighteen languages, and over 9 million free copies have been distributed to date.

During this period the DAR's program among the foreign-born was so constructive that, with the official sanction of the federal government and at their own expense, the Society set up an occupational-therapy center at Ellis Island. The center eased the strain among immigrants during the anxious period of detention and, at a later date, the government requested a similar installation at Angel Island in California.

It was not until 1923 that the Society focused its full attention on the grim visions of subversion which had been haunting the dreams of other patriotic societies since World War I. That year, President General Minor issued a "clarion call" to the DAR Congress. She demanded that every member do her duty by stamping out the "debauchery of youthful minds" by radical societies masquerading as "peace and freedom organizations." Reminding the Daughters that *"large families* gathered about the hearth" were a natural heritage from the original patriots and that the destruction of the family unit was the intention of communism, she warned:

It is not *birth control* that America needs today, for this control will not be practiced by the foreigner and the poor whom it professes to benefit. *It aims straight at the heart of the American home and the most sacred relations of life.* Make no mistake about that.

On the subject of education she was equally certain. She said:

Better the man or woman who teaches truth and integrity, orderliness and obedience, loyalty and love of country, than the most brilliant mind you can hire for the money ... it is well known that there is an organized movement of *many years standing among radicals to insinuate their doctrines into schools and colleges* . . . there are *over eight*

*thousand teachers* in our schools who are not loyal to the
government and the Constitution of these United States
and who are using their opportunities to teach disloyal
doctrines and to throw discredit upon the ideals and principles of our National Government.

Calling this a fertile field for "watchful care," she prescribed a
number of ways to curb the trend—including dismissal of suspected teachers:

*We want no teachers who say there are two sides of every
question including even our system of government; who
care more for their academic freedom of speech and opinion (so-called) than for their country.*

By the time Mrs. Minor issued her warning, the general public
was embarrassed about the hysteria of the last few years. Most
Americans were trying to forget the whole nightmare of alien
radicals, but a new menace was looming before a large audience
of conservatives. They were shocked to be told that conniving
foreigners were only one of the dangers and that many native-
born and prominent educators, pacifists, clergymen, reformers
and labor leaders also were taking orders from Moscow.

After the war, the drive to stamp out pacifism and to check
"federal paternalism" intensified rather than diminished. The
National Security League and the American Defense Society
continued to function and, during the early 1920s, when it became evident that keeping conservatives "informed" on the subversive activities of American liberals could be turned into a
profitable business, a number of new "red-baiting" organizations
quickly formed. The new groups often were organizations in
name only. They consisted of nothing more than a high sounding title, some impressive stationery and an executive secretary,
or director, who in his own day was commonly called a "patrioteer." For a fat fee, he was willing to supply "inside" information on radicalism through newsletters. For a greater consideration, he would make platform appearances.

In his book *Only Yesterday* Frederick Lewis Allen described
the prevailing atmosphere:

Elderly ladies in gilt chairs in ornate drawing rooms heard from executive secretaries that the agents of the government had unearthed new radical conspiracies too fiendish to be divulged before the proper time. Their husbands were told at luncheon clubs that the colleges were honeycombed with Bolshevism. A cloud of suspicion hung in the air, and intolerance became an American virtue.

"Facts" sustaining the "patrioteer's" charges were often based on the 1920 Lusk Report, four fat volumes of largely inconclusive testimony of the Lusk Commission which had investigated seditious activities in New York State. This report had been repudiated as untrustworthy by every reliable agency. Other "facts" were taken from a series of articles written by Calvin Coolidge when he first became Vice-President and published in the *Delineator* in 1921. The underlying theme of the Coolidge articles was that a firm stand must be taken to guard our youth against the communist menace. In his summation, Coolidge insisted that in order to counteract these diabolical forces "the influence of religion must be brought into play, the influence of patriotic and fraternal societies which are through and through American." Above all, he emphasized, "This is essentially a job for women." Women's colleges were the chief target of his criticism and his disclosures lent great weight to an attack on all feminine liberals, many of whom were active pacifists and advocates of progressive education.

Perhaps the Daughters were particularly responsive to Coolidge's views because, soon after his election, he proudly announced that his mother had been a Daughter and that he himself had won an SAR essay prize contest in 1896. (His wife was also a Daughter, and the President's aunt Mrs. Sarah Pollard of Proctorsville, Vermont, and her daughter-in-law Mrs. Fred Pollard both attended the 1924 DAR Congress as delegates.)

Mrs. Anthony Wayne Cook of Cookstown, Pennsylvania, succeeded Mrs. Minor as President General in 1923. In DAR annals Mrs. Cook is remembered as a somewhat ineffectual leader whose main desire was to convert the Society to the support of the doomed Volstead Act. However, a careful study of her years in office—1923–1926—shows that it was she who diverted the Daughters' anxiety over the communist menace in the areas of general education and focused their full attention on a drive to combat pacifists who were offering determined resistance to the militarists' efforts to preserve our standing army at its 1920 quota, which was the largest in our entire history.

A powerful military machine in peace time was decidedly unpalatable to many civilians and the pacifist movement had a great popular upsurge in the post-war period. In 1921, a Congregational minister, Frederick J. Libby, succeeded in uniting 35 associations in the National Council for the Prevention of War. It included not only peace societies but also numerous sympathetic organizations with broader aims such as the YMCA and the YWCA, the National Education Association and the National League of Women Voters. With a membership of around 10 million, Libby's Council became a substantial voting bloc to oppose the mounting military budget.

The new threat of communism was used as a bogeyman to confirm militarists' arguments for continued strength and anyone even remotely connected with the peace movement became suspect. Certain members of the War Department were guilty of employing unethical methods to sway public opinion toward increased appropriations. General John J. Pershing, with the consent of the army, made a nationwide lecture tour under the auspices of the American Defense Society while that organization was at the height of its Red baiting. Pershing preached the necessity of a big army and navy as the only way to ward off a surprise attack from Russia. He did not fail to point out that "at home our situation is seriously complicated by the teachings of numerous pacifist organizations . . ."

The Daughters were among the first to lend a sympathetic ear. "Blackjack" Pershing was one of their favorites. He made it a habit to drop in on their Congress unexpectedly and often vaulted out of his box onto the stage to say a few impromptu words. If unable to come himself, he made sure to send a representative.

Many other high-ranking officers tried to curry civilian favor, and a certain clique stationed in Washington belonged to a curious civilian organization called the National Patriotic Council. The president of this group, Mrs. Noble Newbold Potts, was a Daughter whose fine singing voice gave her fame in the Society. Year after year they had enjoyed her solo. She had welcomed Mrs. Scott as the new president general by singing "Illinois" accompanied by the Marine Corps Band.

Although the membership of Mrs. Potts' council was supposedly open to any American promising to uphold the Constitution and to fight radicalism, the council never numbered more than 200. There was no paid staff, and all business was conducted from Mrs. Potts' palatial residence. Her board included Major General Eli A. Helmick, Inspector General of the U.S. Army; Rear Admiral William A. Moffett, Chief of Aeronautics; and Major General Amos A. Fries, Chief of the Chemical Warfare Service. Prominent pacifists accused each of them of overstepping the privilege of his commission by distributing anti-pacifist propaganda, either by personal utterance or by literature. At least two of them were husbands of prominent Daughters: Mrs. Helmick became Registrar General and Mrs. Fries served two terms as publicity chairman.

In 1922, The American Defense Society had opened a Washington branch with R. M. Whitney as executive secretary. It proved to be an excellent channel through which to push military opinions.

Under Whitney's guidance the Defense Society's branch in the capital became a collection center for information on subversives. He made constant use of the confidential files of both the Justice and the War Departments, which were inaccessible to the press and even to those innocent organizations and individuals under attack.

One of Whitney's most successful literary efforts was *Peace at Any Old Price*, a pamphlet in which he purported to expose the "secret" conference of the Women's Third International. In reality he was reporting on the first American meeting of the Women's International League for Peace and Freedom. Jane Addams, its president for years, became one of the most viciously maligned of the peace advocates. Because of its international nature, the WIL was particularly adaptable to the purposes of patrioteers. Representatives from 21 countries were expected to attend its conference held in Washington, March 13–16, 1923.

The meeting was viewed with such suspicion in superpatriotic circles that before the opening of the conference Republican Congressman Clarence McLeod urged the Justice Department to look into the charges that the WIL was maintained by Soviet funds. Mr. Whitney was not the only man to cover the conference. The War Department sent officers in mufti to "attend" each session. Then, realizing that this ludicrous spying made "an officer and a gentleman" appear unchivalrous, top officials hit on the solution of enlisting the aid of women's patriotic organizations to combat the growing popularity of pacifism. Shortly after the WIL conference, the DAR Mrs. Nobel Newbold Potts, of the National Patriotic Council, called together a group of interested women and the powerful Woman's Patriotic Conference was the outgrowth of this gathering.

Although not officially involved in the Woman's Patriotic Conference at first, the NSDAR showed its intention of accelerating its activities to combat subversion. Almost immediately after the WIL meeting, the National Board of Management voted unanimously in an Executive session that "our Society would not be true to its lofty ideals of patriotic service if it did not take more active measures than it has yet taken in opposing the disloyal individuals and organizations that are striving to pervert our national ideals."

Whitney's pamphlet "exposing" the WIL made such an impression on the Daughters that "Peace at Any Old Price" became, and still is, their slogan to express contempt for the peace movement. Elated by success, Whitney wrote *Reds in America*, a book that gave him the undisputed reputation of the greatest living authority on communism and led to a rash of quasi-exposés of subversives by other authors. All of them became gospel to the DAR and other patriotic societies. *Reds in America* so alarmed President General Cook that she promptly dispatched a copy to every State Regent and national officer of the Society. The Daughters were particularly shocked by the section dealing with women's clubs.

Whitney had leaned heavily on the "Spider-Web Chart," a photostatic copy of an ink drawing measuring one by two feet. Three columns appeared under the heading "The Socialist-Pacifist Movement in America Is an Absolutely Fundamental and Integral Part of International Socialism." The first column listed women's organizations—even the Needlework Guild of America was not above suspicion. The next two gave names of specific leaders active both in women's clubs and in the peace movement. A web of lines connecting the offending organizations and individual culprits earned the document its nickname of the "Spider-Web Chart."

The page was designed to show that there existed in the women's clubs of America a vast Moscow-controlled "interlocking directorate." Anyone remotely connected with the National Council for the Prevention of War, the Women's International League for Peace and Freedom, or the Women's Joint Congressional Committee was part of a "conspiracy" to undermine the government.

The chart had been made by Mrs. Lucia R. Maxwell, a loyal Daughter, who was librarian at General Fries' Chemical Warfare Service. A poem of her own creation embellished the bottom of the page. With a little coaxing it can be fitted to the tune of Yankee Doodle. It read:

> Miss Bolsheviki has come to town
> With a Russian cap and a German gown
> In women's clubs she's sure to be found
> For she's come to disarm AMERICA.
> She sits in judgment on Capitol Hill
> And watches the appropriation bill
> And without her OK it passes—NIL
> For she's come to disarm AMERICA.
> She uses the movies and lyceum too
> And alters books to suit her view
> She prates propaganda from pulpit and pew
> FOR SHE'S BOUND TO DISARM AMERICA.

The chart was inscribed to Mary G. Kilbreth "with appreciation for her work" and was printed in Miss Kilbreth's paper, the

*Woman's Patriot*, a Washington antisuffrage biweekly dedicated to "defense of the family and state and against feminism and socialism." The *Woman's Patriot* was popular with the DAR all over the country.

Mrs. Maxwell's chart was also distributed to every branch of the armed services, including the ROTC. Some copies were accompanied by a letter of endorsement written on War Department stationery.

The chart was full of minor inaccuracies, half-truths, and downright falsehoods. When Mrs. Maude Wood Park, chairman of the Women's Joint Congressional Committee, brought complaint, War Secretary John W. Weeks made a courteous apology. Regretting that "charts containing the errors pointed out by your committee were circulated by any branch of the War Department," he promised to have them recalled and destroyed or, at the very least, publicly repudiated. He also issued a reprimand to General Fries but did not remove him from his post. Moreover, Mrs. Maxwell was allowed to remain tucked away in the chemical-warfare library, where she continued to spin webs around a gigantic card index of victims who were cataloged as all the way from dangerous "Red" to "Only Pink." Along with the Lusk Report and the Coolidge articles, Mrs. Maxwell's work became a classic in the patrioteers' library.

The year 1924 was a time of mounting tensions between preparedness and peace advocates. Popularity of the Reserve Training Corps had suffered a gradual decline since World War I; interest in the college ROTC program was also weakening. General Pershing hit upon a novel plan, which he hoped would dramatize civilian training. He announced that on September 12 the whole country would take part in an experiment to see how rapidly maximum fighting forces could be mobilized. It would be declared a national holiday called Preparedness Day. One wag suggested that its purpose was to "break the tedium between the Glorious Fourth and Hallowe'en." The title of the day seemed so absurd to most citizens that it was suddenly changed to Defense Test Day. Elaborate arrangements for its celebration proceeded at top speed.

According to DAR records, Mrs. Cook, the President General, had the honor of serving as "Chairman of the National Committee composed of nearly one hundred Veteran and Patriotic Societies which rallied to the Government's appeal for cooperation in helping to carry out its Defense Test Day Program." In the four months preceding the great day itself, the DAR turned over a room in their new Administration Building for the exclusive use of this committee.

Young cynics tried to laugh the event into oblivion, but older, more sober pacifists decided to fight back. The Women's Peace Party staged a "No More War Day" on July 26, urging members and sympathizers everywhere to march in protest of the mock mobilization. Almost simultaneously Frederick J. Libby's National Council for the Prevention of War announced that ministers throughout the country would deliver a sermon the next day, Sunday, July 27, on world cooperation.

In spite of opposition, Defense Test Day went off on schedule, although it may have lacked some of the verve and sparkle anticipated by those who had worked so hard to make it a success. The organized animosity of the pacifists was not forgotten. On the opening night of the 1925 DAR congress, Mrs. Cook warned sister members: "The spread of pacifism and the undermining of our ideals of national service by foreign agencies and by our native-born emotional theorists, who have been swept loose from the staple mooring by skillful propagandists, has reached a dangerous stage."

The new Speaker of the House, Nicholas Longworth, gave a rousing speech later in the program that was described in the DAR magazine as "one of the hits of the evening." In it, he cried, "To my mind there is little danger now from enemies without; what we have to fear are the enemies within."

The Coolidges, faithful followers of DAR proceedings, sat in the presidential box during Mrs. Cook's and Longworth's pronouncements. The following morning, in appreciation of the society's hospitality, Mrs. Coolidge sent a huge basket of flowers to the hall from the White House conservatory.

All week long, speakers kept the Daughters in constant ferment over the dangers confronting the nation, and finally, at the business session, delegates passed one of the most important resolutions ever to be introduced before the organization:

> *Resolved*: That the National Society recommend a definite, intensive campaign to be organized in every state to combat "Red" internationalists and that State Regents be asked to appoint a chairman to direct the campaign of "Cooperation on National Defense."

The defense program got off to a good start, particularly below the Mason-Dixon Line. At the 1926 North Carolina convention, the state Regent, Mrs. Edwin Clark Gregory, sounded the alert that plans were afoot "for a *Red Russian invasion* of the South" and that their state would be the first target. Brigadier General Albert J. Bowley, stationed in North Carolina since 1924, was largely responsible for Mrs. Gregory's apprehensions. The General was a forceful speaker who warned of the imminence of a communist-inspired Negro revolution. His favorite metaphor for pacifists was "whelps and cats," and he cautioned that every college, chautauqua, or forum that sanctioned the appearance of peace advocates was a breeding ground for skullduggery. It was quite natural for a good Daughter like Mrs. Gregory to have implicit faith in the alarming disclosures of such an important officer. She was determined to keep her state free of contamination.

Goaded on by the impetus of the DAR's new defense policy, North Carolina Daughters lost no time in joining with the American Legion in a demand that all teachers be compelled to take a loyalty oath to the government and to the principles of private ownership. In addition, the North Carolina DAR concentrated on the Greensboro Open Forum, exerting pressure to ban dangerous speakers.

Georgia Daughters were also in the fray. Early in the fall of 1925 their State Regent, Mrs. Julius Y. Talmadge, had started a heated correspondence to bar Mrs. Lucia Ames Mead from a scheduled tour of southern colleges in November and December. She carried her campaign beyond state boundaries, and in a letter to Dr. Hamilton Holt, president of Florida's Rollins College, Mrs. Talmadge disclosed that "through the assistance of the Military Order of the World War and other patriotic organizations" the DAR had succeeded in gathering authentic data on Mrs. Mead, which offered definite proof not only that she was the vice-chairman of the National Council for the Prevention of War (a group that promoted "socialist and radical ideas") but that she had had a long career as a leader in many similar un-American movements. She should not be allowed to sully the innocence of southern youth.

Dr. Holt was himself a pacifist and had organized the League to Enforce Peace in 1915. He sent a strong reply to the Georgia Regent, in which he stated that Mrs. Mead was a personal friend and that for twenty years they had appeared at the same conferences and conventions.

In a gallant defense of his friend's integrity, Dr. Holt declared, "Mrs. Mead is not a Communist, although you doubtless remember that the early Christians were," and insisted that no woman was "rendering abler, wiser and more devoted service" to America. He reminded Mrs. Talmadge that peace and goodwill among men should be the goal of every patriotic citizen and ended the letter by suggesting that this was peculiarly the duty of the Sons and Daughters of the American Revolution, "who surely can never forget that the great founders of the Republic were the preeminent peace statesmen of their time."

Mrs. Gregory and Mrs. Talmadge were not the only Daughters to wage war on communism. By the end of Mrs. Cook's administration, and largely due to DAR efforts, speakers on pacifism and industrial reform had been silenced in Windsor, Connecticut; Boonton, New Jersey; Morgantown, West Virginia; and many other places.

When the new slate of national officers took over the defense program, they extended the original plan of "cooperation." Grace Brosseau, the new President General, was the wife of Alfred J. Brosseau, president of Mack Trucks. She had become a Daughter while living in Michigan and when her husband's interests increased to include subsidiary companies, the couple moved to New York. There, Mrs. Brosseau started an active career in National Society affairs. She made a name for herself as the first chairman of the Ellis Island Committee. Wealthy, domineering, and aggressive, she quickly rose to the innermost circle of the oligarchy and attained the post of Treasurer General in 1923.

By then, DAR membership had become so large that there was barely sufficient room to seat the delegates in Memorial Continental Hall. As a temporary solution the Daughters rented a public auditorium for the 1925 Congress, but plans were already under way to build the vast Constitution Hall. No Treasurer General was ever more energetic in prodding money out of members than Mrs. Brosseau, and she was rewarded by being elected the next President General.

Mrs. Brosseau was not the fashion-conscious kind of leader earlier Daughters had chosen. The only indulgence she shared with most former Presidents General was a fondness for jewelry. Over the years, her husband had given her a magnificent collection of rubies, which she wore on all formal occasions. Other than her love of jewels, the cloche hat was Mrs. Brosseau's only concession to fashion. Although knee-length skirts were the rage, she stuck to a ten-inch hemline and she always wore sensible shoes and a pince-nez.

But times had changed, and the Daughters' interest was centered on less frivolous matters than high fashion. Mrs. Brosseau was known for her intense preoccupation with adequate preparedness and with war to the death on radicalism.

During her term as Treasurer General, she found a sympathetic ally in her co-officer Mrs. William Sherman Walker, who was Organizing Secretary General, and a warm friendship sprang up between them that lasted until Mrs. Brosseau's death. Unlike most DAR officers, Mrs. Walker was a lady of modest means who had risen in the NSDAR through the sheer force of her dynamic personality. Sleek, well groomed in tailored suits, she had been assigned to accompany President General Cook on extensive field trips to numerous state conventions. Years later she admitted that the Brosseau-Walker team might have influenced Mrs. Cook.

Mrs. Brosseau's first message to the Daughters had a decidedly militant flavor. In the June issue of the Society's magazine she referred to herself as the "new general" and to her officers as the "new captains and lieutenants." She commanded members to regard themselves as "shouldering arms."

A glance at her slate shows that the wives of two of the directors on Mrs. Potts' National Patriotic Council were included: Mrs. Fries remained the publicity chairman, and Mrs. Eli A. Helmick became Registrar General. Perhaps as a reward for her untiring correspondence, Mrs. Talmadge was made a Vice President General. Mrs. Lowell Fletcher Hobart, who had founded the American Legion Auxiliary, filled the key post of Organizing Secretary General. Most important of all, Mrs. Brosseau's close friend Mrs. Walker took over the duties of "Cooperation on National Defense."

"General" Brosseau's 1927 New Year's "Message" had an ominous ring to it. In it she laid down eleven "Resolves" to be accepted by all good Daughters. Among them:

> TENTH: that I will pledge my unswerving loyalty throughout this year to my leaders—Chapter, State, and National. I will offer only constructive criticism and will not willfully obstruct any move that is sponsored by an intelligent majority, even if I do not happen to approve of it. In other words, I will try my best to consider at all times what is the greatest good for the greatest number.

Mrs. Brosseau was soon to test the sincerity of the pledge to the tenth resolve. On February 9, 10, and 11, 1927, the Woman's Patriotic Conference on National Defense (which had been started by Mrs. Potts) convened at Memorial Continental Hall. Since there is no record of a delegate vote approving the meeting, it may be assumed that Mrs. Brosseau and the National Board represented "an intelligent majority" and assumed full responsibility for the action.

In April, at the thirty-sixth Congress, Mrs. Brosseau reported that she and Mrs. Adaline W. Macauley, president of the American Legion Auxiliary, had issued a joint call for the conference. The Daughters had contributed the "gratuitous" use of their auditorium while the Auxiliary had assumed all other expenses. Whether DAR members approved or not will never be known.

However, the announcements did not take them by surprise because the event had been given extensive coverage in the March issue of the *Daughters of the American Revolution Magazine.*

Featuring a photograph of the spare President Coolidge standing between the mountainous Mrs. Brosseau and Mrs. Macauley at a White House reception for the delegates, the article stated that the conference had been well attended by ten or more representatives from thirty organizations. Naturally the list included such superpatriotic groups as Mrs. Potts' National Patriotic Council, Women Builders of America started by Mrs. Story in the Post-war period, and the Government Club, Inc., which was the present pet project of Mrs. Ruth Owen (the DAR who had lent such heavy support to the American Defense Society during World War I). Most veterans' groups sent representatives to the conference, as did, astonishingly enough, almost an equal proportion of such pillars of quiet respectability as the Daughters of the Cincinnati and the Order of the First Families of Virginia.

One of the most interesting aspects of the conference was the unprecedented unity of purpose between ordinary veterans' organizations and the more elite societies based on antecedence. During their previous history, members of the latter group had held themselves aloof from such mingling. Now an emergency had arisen and, in spite of their differences, all were determined to present a united front against the common enemy.

The Daughters of the American Revolution and the American Legion Auxiliary seemed to have the strongest bond. Mrs. Brosseau presided over the first two sessions of the conference, then handed over the gavel to Mrs. Macauley, who, incidentally, was also a DAR. In her opening remarks Mrs. Macauley said that her organization was proud to unite with the DAR "to take up the gauntlet women pacifists have thrown down."

Not one of the delegates to the 1927 DAR Congress questioned Mrs. Brosseau's high-handed methods in arranging the February conference and they dutifully rubber-stamped the majority of the resolutions passed at that meeting. The Brosseau-Walker team was in supreme command, and their Red-baiting, promilitary, antipacifist policy became the new DAR line.

Mrs. Walker's National Defense Committee report to the delegates was published in full in the July magazine for those members who hadn't attended the Congress.

It began: "Sunrise! Dawn! The glow of morning! The new day of Co-operation on National Defense . . . is just beginning." It went on to describe in detail Mrs. Walker's indefatigable work "on a limited budget"—letters, digests, files on subversives, research, book reviews, exhibits, interviews with hundreds of callers, "supplying information to press, platform and pulpit," and, of course, speech making all over the country. At the end she pleaded for financial donations, no matter how small, and for volunteer workers to aid in the great cause.

A later report told of another addition to the list of Mrs. Walker's heavy responsibilities. In June, the Daughters had broken into radio with a regular weekly half-hour broadcast from Chicago's WBBM, then the most powerful station in America. Because theirs was an educational program, the Daughters were allotted free air time. Suitable material was chosen by the Radio Committee, which consisted of Mrs. Walker as chairman, Mrs. Fries, and Mrs. William J. Sweeney, the Illinois state Regent. The program was such a success that by 1931 seventy-seven stations were giving the Society free time.

Although Mrs. Walker was fond of reminding fellow members that she was only one woman doing the work of more than three, no one ever heard a word of complaint from her. Her cheerful perseverance soon earned her the affectionate nickname "Pooh-Bah," which in DAR language means a willingness to tackle many different jobs at once. She was so efficient in completing every task that at the 1928 Congress she was rewarded by being elected a Vice President General. She was happy to fill this post in addition to her ever-increasing defense duties.

# VIII

In July 1927, a liberal periodical, *The Woman Citizen,* printed "An Open Letter to the D.A.R." by Carrie Chapman Catt. Until that time, the Daughters had retained their halo of respectability, and most Americans were a little in awe of them. Mrs. Catt's exposé came as a shock to the general public.

In her article, Mrs. Catt bluntly accused the Society of being "active distributors of literature that slanders other women as well educated, honest and loyally American as are you—" She also charged:

> The Chairman of your Defense Committee sent out on February 25 an appeal to members to subscribe for four papers and she asked that the information concerning these papers be passed on to your chapters. These are the chief hysteria-stimulating, slander-spreading sheets in the country.

Mrs. Catt denounced the "campaign, directed and financed by parties unknown, that your leaders are assisting" because it had failed to unearth any conclusive proof of a Red plot to overthrow the government. "Instead," she said, "it has made slanderous, mendacious and brutal attacks upon thousands of Americans who never saw a Bolshevik in their lives."

She gave a number of pertinent examples of the increasingly irresponsible behavior of the Society, among them that delegates had voted to print and distribute a speech delivered by Captain George L. Darte to the 1927 Congress. (The captain was Adjutant-General of the Military Order of the World War, an inflammatory veterans' organization pledged to civilian as well as military usefulness. Both he and his order had been helpful to the Daughters on numerous occasions. They had supplied much of the information used by DAR to ban Mrs. Mead and other pacifist lecturers.) In his 1927 speech Darte had branded Rose Schneiderman as "the Red Rose of Anarchy" although, as Mrs. Catt pointed out, it was common knowledge that Miss Schneiderman, president of the Women's Trade Union League of New York, long had been in the vanguard of opposition to communism in the ranks of labor.

The main body of Mrs. Catt's "letter" concentrated on two pamphlets known to be circulating within the DAR. One, *The Common Enemy*, unmistakably had been printed for or by the Society and passed out by members at chapter meetings. The other was a thirty-six-page reprint of the July 3, 1926, *Congressional Record*. At that time Senator Thomas A. Bayard had read from the floor a document issued by the Woman Patriot Publishing Company and signed by its officers:

President: Mary G. Kilbreth, Southampton, N.Y.
Vice-President: Mrs. B. L. Robinson, Cambridge, Mass.
Secretary
    Treasurer: Mrs. Randolph Frothingham, Boston, Mass.
Directors: Mrs. John Balch, Milton, Mass.
          Mrs. Rufus M. Gibbs, Baltimore, Md.
          Mary G. Kilbreth
          Mrs. B. L. Robinson.

Late in 1920 Miss Kilbreth, formerly president of the National Association Opposed to Women's Suffrage, had announced that she and her associates would use the vote thrust upon them to block all progressive measures upheld by the victorious suffragettes. She carried out her threat as editor of the *Woman Patriot*, the Washington bi-weekly in which Mrs. Maxwell's Spider Web chart had appeared. Her paper had enormous influence on DAR readers. The Bayard reprint purported to oppose the Sheppard-Towner Maternity Act (which had established national Children's Bureau Clinics in 1922 and would expire in 1927) but, according to Mrs. Catt, in reality it was a "wholesale attack upon the patriotism and honor of individual women and women's organizations." It was supposed to be used as a key for *The Common Enemy*.

Mrs. Catt disclosed that the title page of *The Common Enemy* acknowledged the use of material supplied by the Key Men of America, whose director was Fred K. Marvin, an all-powerful patrioteer. He had been generous enough to supply *The Com-*

*mon Enemy* with a list of over 200 subversive organizations. The DAR pamphlet named no names but placed "some" of the offending organizations under three headings. The first gave "The best-known Communist organizations." The other two categories listed "dupes" of the world revolutionary movement. They were headed "The best known of the open Socialist organizations" and "The most prominent 'liberal' and Pacifist organizations." Ths list included fourteen associations. Foremost among them, of course, was the Women's International League for Peace and Freedom.

Referring to the Bayard reprint, Mrs. Catt discovered that here, through innuendoes and indirect processes, WIL's president, Jane Addams, was damned as a Bolshevik. So were Florence Kelley, for 28 years general secretary of the Consumers' League; Lillian D. Wald, promoter of the National Child Labor Committee; Julia Lathrop, original director of the Children's Bureau, and her successor Grace Abbott. All of them were women the Daughters had been proud to support in President General Scott's day and Mrs. Catt intimated that the Society had become captives of reactionary forces.

Mrs. Catt took up the "gauntlet" thrown down by the NSDAR Defense Committee and declared: "You say we, on this side of the fence, are either Bolsheviks or dupes. Just now the folks over here are beginning to take notice. The voices are rising and they are saying 'The Daughters! Why, those Daughters are dupes themselves!' " She finished the article on a humorous note, pointing out that red was the antisuffrage color as well as that of the revolutionary flag and that on June 19 it betokened Fathers' Day. "Under these confusions even a patriot should be able to wear a red rose without fear of arrest."

Mrs. Brosseau treated the "Letter" with disdain. She said that Mrs. Catt did not impress any sense of guilt upon the DAR and that she was misinformed, or unobservant, if she did not see evidence of communism in America. Too many leaders, including Kellogg and Coolidge, believed in the claim, as the DAR did, to dismiss it. She ended with a quote from the 1905 president-general: "When there is some reason to be in want of an American Eagle, Congress and the White House may send for the D.A.R. We have a nest full."

In spite of Mrs. Brosseau's dismissal of it, Mrs. Catt's article shattered the public illusion that the Daughters of the American Revolution was a completely praiseworthy, if somewhat conservative, organization that concerned itself chiefly with ancestor worship and restoration.

The "Letter" appeared at a time when Boston was a particularly fertile field upon which to carry the blacklist fight to its conclusion. The date for the execution of Sacco and Vanzetti finally had been set for August 27, 1927, and because of the frantic last-minute attempts to save their lives, tensions were running high in the city which was divided into two irreconcilable camps. Conservatives believed that American institutions would be endangered if clemency were shown to the Italians. Liberals were equally convinced that the men were the innocent victims of hysterical racial prejudice, class hatred, and intolerance of socialism.

Because of the unusual concentration of universities around greater Boston, the battle between modern trends and old-fashioned mores reached a greater intensity there than anywhere else in America. Unified by the pressure of the Sacco-Vanzetti issue, intellectuals felt strong enough to defy the flood of censorship that seemed about to engulf the freedom of speech and action in the whole country.

Conservatives, among them the DAR, issued attack after attack on what they considered dangerous radicalism. Their material was often supplied by two flourishing local propaganda mills. One was the Massachusetts Public Interests League run by Mrs. B. L. Robinson, prominent on the board of the Woman Patriot Publishing Company. The other was E. H. Hunter's Industrial Defense Association. He supplied two lists, "Doubtful Men Speakers" and "Doubtful Women Speakers" that were given wide circulation by the DAR in an effort to control "subversives."

Boston was rocked by the controversy and it was a Boston

Unitarian minister, Vivian T. Pomeroy, who coined the phrase "the blue menace" which soon became the battle cry of the liberal opposition all over the country. Early in January 1928, in an address before the Unitarian Club, Reverend Pomeroy admitted that evidence of real radicalism should not be ignored but pointed out that some Americans were taking the "Red menace" too seriously. Appealing to the inherent native American sense of humor in his audience, he said:

> Since color is being splashed about so freely in these days, I call it the blue menace . . . a small but pestiferous bug with the general disposition and technique resembling those of the mosquito. Unlike the mosquito, its favorite haunts are not solitary and swampy places, but the clubs and parlors of small towns and even big cities. It can be found buzzing and stinging in some churches. It is quite an interdenominational insect. Of late it has been swarming in Boston.

Boston liberals resisted being silenced by the censorshp of the city's conservatives, but the heated battle might have remained on a local level except for a DAR descendent of Anne Adams Tufts, a decorated Revolutionary heroine who had nursed the wounded under fire at the Battle of Bunker Hill. On April 1, 1928, Mrs. Helen Tufts Bailie exhibited the true courage of her Tufts ancestry when she rose before the Boston Ethical Society and calmly declared that the Daughters of the American Revolution were being used as a cat's-paw in "a tremendous conspiracy to crush free thought, free speech and even liberty itself." She said she had absolute proof that Massachusetts DAR officials were not only distributing screeds listing such prominent local personages as Dean Roscoe Pound of Harvard Law School and Rabbi Harry Levi of Boston's Temple Israel as "doubtful speakers" and "communists" but, even worse, reaching out to include such national figures of impeccable character as former President Taft; Senator Thomas J. Walsh of Montana, instigator of the Teapot Dome investigations; President William Alan Neilson of Smith College; and Mary E. Woolley, who had been president of Mount Holyoke for twenty-seven years and who was an honorary member of a DAR chapter in Pawtucket,

Rhode Island. Mrs. Bailie pointed out that she was naming only a few of the maligned citizens and that there were a "host of others against whom the charge that they were unsafe to address a group of women like the DAR is preposterous."

The minute the DAR was brought into the scandal, the impropriety of the Boston lists became a national issue. If such lists were appearing in Boston under DAR auspices, they also must be circulating in every major city in the Union. The entire press immediately took up the hue and cry, and for months Mrs. Bailie's course of action remained front-page news.

Newspapers reported that a series of events had led up to the April exposures. Mrs. Bailie was described as ordinarily a somewhat inactive Daughter with pacifist sympathies. However, since March 15, 1927, she had paid close attention to an alarming new trend in the Society's policy. At that time Mrs. Stephan P. Hurd, state chairman of the National Defense Committee, had made the following announcement during the annual Massachusetts conference: "A list of names of individuals and organizations which seek to embody Communist principles in the management of our government has been forwarded to the regents of every chapter in the country as part of the work in overcoming these influences."

Later in the month, Mrs. Bailie discovered that the program chairman of her own chapter had been surprised, when lining up speakers for the fall season, to hear that most of her suggestions had been ruled out by the Regent as "unacceptable." The Regent substituted a number of "acceptable" names, all of them notorious Red baiters.

Further investigation showed the procedure to be the rule rather than the exception. The "packing" system was highly effective. On December 8, 1927, Boston papers heralded a meeting of the Bunker Hill Chapter under the banner of: D.A.R. WARNED OF RED MENACE. The gathering was treated to a double-feature program of Mrs. Robinson and Melvin M. Johnson, a Boston lawyer who had been lambasting Iowa's Senator Brookhart ever since 1925, claiming repeatedly that Brookhart had said, "Lenin is a greater man than Washington or Lincoln; he established a government destined to rule the world."

Mrs. Bailie was so outraged by Johnson's irresponsible charge that on December 17 she wrote to the senator, calling his attention to the accusation. Brookhart replied:

> Several years ago I made a trip to Europe and visited 15 countries while abroad, one of these countries being Russia. I was escorted through Russia by Gen. Haskell of the American Relief Commission, under instructions from Secretary of Commerce Hoover. On my return from Russia I was asked by various people to give my impression of the country, and also what the people of Russia thought of Lenin. I told the parties who interviewed me that the people of Russia at that time looked upon Lenin with the same reverence that we in the United States looked upon Washington and Lincoln; but some of my bitterest enemies changed my statement and circulated false reports that I had claimed that Lenin was greater than Washington and Lincoln which is absolutely untrue in every particular.

This evidence of bald misrepresentation strengthened Mrs. Bailie's determination to take action. With great difficulty she managed to procure one of the blacklists circulating among the Regents, and found there the name of the husband of a friend and fellow DAR member Mrs. E. Talmadge Root. The Reverend Root was the executive secretary of the Massachusetts Federation of Churches.

On January 4, 1928, Mrs. Bailie and Mrs. Root called, by appointment, on Mrs. Charles Peabody, State Regent, and Mrs. Hurd, chairman of Massachusetts Defense Committee, at DAR state headquarters. The visit was far from satisfactory. When Mrs. Root asked why her husband had been blacklisted, Mrs. Peabody said she would look into the matter. When Mrs. Bailie asked who made up the lists, Mrs. Hurd refused to answer. Both officers agreed that any speaker must be "acceptable" to the state officials and must talk along lines approved by the National Board of the DAR.

Mrs. Bailie then wrote a private, personal protest to Mrs. Brosseau. Her first letter, of February 2, 1928, was ignored, so she wrote another, to which Mrs. Brosseau made this reply:

"The petition you addressed to me personally I shall take great pleasure in presenting to the National Board of Management, for I assure you that it does not share your point of view."

There matters rested until March 12, when the Reverend Root brought the issue into the open by discussing his experience of being on the DAR blacklist at a meeting of the Congregational Ministers of Greater Boston. He explained that he had accepted the post of adviser to the Fellowship of Youth for Peace but had acted in that capacity only once in several years. Even this slight connection with an organization that had had its meeting broken up in Concord in 1926 by the American Legion, at the incitement of E. H. Hunter was enough to make him suspect. Root told his colleagues:

> The ladies of the DAR do not realize the seriousness of the Black List they are abetting. A good name is rather to be chosen than great riches. It is the chief asset of a clergyman. Is a man who is unfit to address the DAR, fit to represent the churches? The unthinking may assume that a certain military coloring justifies and authorizes such black lists. To my mind the very connection constitutes a danger compared with which the danger from the "Red Menace" is negligible. If once we admit that our army and navy and those formerly connected therewith are by that fact constituted censors of public opinion, their power will insensibly grow and the liberties of America will be lost.

The speech received a rousing ovation and was reprinted in full in the March 13 *Springfield Republican*, which began to run a series of explosive articles exposing the tactics of patrioteers. Root had held his fire with a definite purpose in mind. He spoke on the eve of the 1928 Massachusetts DAR state conference.

If they attended the conference, Mrs. Bailie and Mrs. Root remained silent, but Mrs. William F. Anderson, wife of the Methodist Episcopal bishop of Massachusetts, rose to protest because her husband's name was also included in the odious lists. She was rebuffed by Mrs. Peabody, who immediately shut off discussion by referring the matter to a committee. "It needs no action here," Mrs. Peabody explained. (That year Massachusetts' only recorded gift to the museum at the DAR "home" in Washington was a "handmade mousetrap, used in the family of Samuel Brown of Concord, who served in the American Revolution." It was presented by his descendant, Miss Sarah Marion Chase, Paul Revere Chapter.)

After the affront to Mrs. Anderson, Mrs. Bailie refused to remain silent. Not only did she make the address at the Boston Ethical Society but a few days later she made a statement to the press and gave reporters copies of the lists. *The Christian Science Monitor* quoted her as saying that there was "a whole system of espionage, innuendoes and aspirations, which has been flourishing in more than seventy patriotic societies. Boston harbors two groups of blacklisters screened under high sounding names. In California, Illinois and other states, there are similar blacklist factories."

In a blaze of publicity, Mrs. Bailie's next move was to form the Committee of Protest, which included fifteen other dissenting Daughters. In a pamphlet entitled *Our Threatened Heritage* they stated their case against the Board of Management. They charged that the officers of the National Society had led the complete membership into the Women's Patriotic Conference on National Defense with no previous action or consent by delegates.

They also objected to Mrs. Walker's appearance before the House Naval Affairs Committee on February 17, 1928, when she alleged that the DAR gave unanimous support to the "big-navy bill." The pamphlet explained that although a resolution favoring the bill had been passed at the 1927 Congress, it was part of a rubber-stamp acceptance of the complete platform of the Women's Patriotic Conference. Because of the complicated nature of the wording, none of the resolutions sponsored by the conference had been read in full. (In order to make Mrs. Walker's action constitutional, Mrs. Brosseau had been forced to send a telegram to every state requesting endorsement. Due to the imminence of the hearing, the endorsement was given in each case, except one, by the top state officials without being referred to chapters for discussion or action.)

The gravest charge was that Mrs. Brosseau and Mrs. Walker were directly responsible for the distribution of the blacklists to state officials, that they were "hypnotized" by a certain professional Red hunter, and that his was "a domination which our officers are unable or unwilling to repudiate."

They were referring to Mrs. Brosseau's well-known friendship with Fred K. Marvin, whom she had praised publicly on numerous occasions. "I am perfectly in sympathy with Fred Marvin and his ideas, as well as his particular brand of patriotism . . .," she said on one occasion, and Mrs. Walker had written to him: "I feel that the work of the National Defense Committee would be half accomplished if our members were receiving and reading your Daily Data Sheets." These sheets were issued to all members of the Key Men at $6 per annum and were to be saved for future reference. They constituted a "bible" for believers.

Although any specific documentary evidence was lacking to support such a theory, the public was beginning to feel that Marvin was the real father of the DAR blacklists. It did little good for Mrs. Brosseau to deny the charge by announcing that *"No man or woman* during the two years of my administration has dominated me." The *Springfield Republican* quickly countered with the disclosure of a letter that the paper had received from Marvin the previous summer. It suggested a subscription to his *Daily Data Sheet* on the grounds that "we furnish newspapers special reports on radical or subversive movements, agencies, individuals, etc., either for confidential or public use." It was typed on Key Men stationery, and on the reverse side of the first sheet was printed a list of the organization's advisory council. Among others appeared these names: Mrs. Alfred J. Brosseau, Captain George L. Darte, General Amos Fries, Mrs. Lucia Ramsey Maxwell, Mrs. Margaret C. Robinson, H. A. Jung of the National Clay Products and at least two prominent Boston DARs. The public seemed amused by Mrs. Brosseau's "domination" statement, and even further delighted when the press, asking for a comment on the Committee of Protest, quoted her as saying, "Not one of the women of this 'committee' is known to me personally. Therefore, their combined judgment could hardly be said to be reliable . . ."

Mrs. Bailie's committee was not alone in voicing a protest. The Pawtucket Chapter refused to recognize any list upon which Mary Woolley's name appeared. The Lewis and Clark Chapter of Eugene, Oregon, wrote a long letter to Mrs. Brosseau stating:

> When we are informed by our State Chairman of National Defense that we are untrue to our duties as citizens and members of the D.A.R. when we allowed Kirby Page and Judge (Ben) Lindsey to speak in Eugene, we resent the implication, for we believe in the free and open discussion of all social and political issues, and are opposed to this type of censorship.

A vigorous one-woman battle was started in New Jersey by Mrs. Mary P. MacFarland. As well as being a DAR, she was state president of the American Association of University Women, and her husband, Dr. Charles S. MacFarland, was active in the Federal Council of Churches. Both organizations figured heavily in blacklists, and Mrs. MacFarland reached the end of her patience after being subjected to a scurrilous Marvin speech at a chapter meeting. She opened a stormy correspondence with Mrs. Brosseau. When this proved to be of no avail, Mrs. MacFarland also began to circularize members and give public exposure to the lists.

Mrs. MacFarland had other grounds for indignation. She had attended a chapter meeting at which the Regent called for a "rising testimonial" to the resolutions passed at the 1928 Congress. Mrs. MacFarland had remained seated, explaining that she could not endorse *en bloc* the action of the Congress. She then received a public reprimand for "refusing to renew her allegiance to the society."

Mrs. Brosseau tried, without success, to confuse the issue by blaming the exposé on a "few pacifists within our organization who oppose our support of the Navy bill." She continually stressed that the dissidents "who have undertaken to vilify this society are not even what we classify as active working members. One of them has never held an office in her chapter while the other has not attended a chapter meeting in two years."

It was not so easy to dismiss another insurgent, Mrs. Eleanor Patterson St. Omer Roy, a delegate from Kansas and the author of a resolution to go before the 1928 Congress which proposed the following reform measures: (1) all questions of national importance should be referred to chapters for discussion and action before the annual Congress *or* the National Board *or* any officers committed the Society as a whole to any given policy; (2) all sides of a question should be discussed at chapter meetings; (3) chapters should use their own discretion in choosing speakers; and (4) an outline of the policies of the National Defense Committee should be submitted to chapters for approval or disapproval before being put into practice.

Mrs. Henry B. Joy, resolutions chairman, presented the motion without recommendation. Mrs. Roy spoke for its adoption and was seconded by Mrs. Eleanor Dutcher Key of Maryland. Then, according to the *Daughters of the American Revolution Magazine*, Mrs. Frank Greenawalt of the District wondered why the committee should bother with a measure "which if adopted would be so paralyzing and destructive to our patriotic work." The same source tells that discussion arose and Mrs. Roy asked for tabling of her motion. The motion was voted down and Mrs. Joy reread the resolution.

Now President General Brosseau stepped forward. "Those in favor rise," she said. About eight women "in scattered parts of the auditorium" stood up. Next came the call for "nays," and "two thousand women sprang up with alacrity and the place resounded with cheers and applause."

When quiet was restored, the President General said she wished to make an announcement. It was in part:

> Now in regard to the alleged blacklist, I want to say once and for all that the National Society of the Daughters of the American Revolution issues no such list.
> An editor in Kansas made the statement in his paper that the President General of the Daughters of the American Revolution compiled a list without the authority of her Board of Management. I did not take the time or the trouble to answer that in public, but I fling the challenge here and now to everybody in the world that I am not responsible for any such list . . .
> I have seen no less than twenty-five different lists issued by

twenty-five different organizations. If other organizations
reserve the right to advise their members, we certainly
have the same privilege . . .

Mrs. Brosseau's speech ended on the same defensive note:

This is my final statement in regard to the lists. There is no
such word in our vocabulary as blacklist, but so long as the
leaders of the States wish they may advise for or against
speakers to appear before the organization.

At the conclusion of her remarks, "the Congress rose spontaneously to its feet and gave its President General a prolonged
ovation." As far as the delegates were concerned, that was the
end of Mrs. Roy and her reform measures.

On the previous evening, "Navy Night," Mrs. Walker had
referred to the Committee of Protest by name and had spurned
their objection to her recent visit to the House by saying:

I hold there is nothing mysterious or contradictory to the
policies of the D.A.R. about an American woman appearing before a Congressional Committee to state the stand
taken by a well-known American society, declaring in
favor of an American navy to protect the life and treasure
of America.

Her statement was greeted by thunderous applause. No direct
reference was made to Mrs. Bailie or Mrs. MacFarland during
Congress Week. Everyone knew that their judgment would be
meted out at a later date.

Mrs. Brosseau's defense of her own position and that of her
subordinates brought down an avalanche of criticism outside the
organization. William Allen White, the Kansas editor to whom
she made reference in her denial of blacklists, took the lead. At
one time he said that the DAR had been "lured into the Red
Baiting mania by the tea gladiators of Washington"; at another,
"It shows what happens when the brass buttons of retired Army
officers in Washington hypnotize the nice old girls of the
DAR." White had previously laughed the KKK out of the
state of Kansas. Now he declared, "The DAR has yanked the
Klan out of the cow pasture and set it down in the breakfast

room of respectability, removing its hood and putting on a transformation."

The historian Samuel E. Morison, whose grandmother had been one of the original incorporators of the Society, dubbed the Daughters "Grandmothers of Reaction." Oswald Garrison Villard imagined that Jefferson would sink in Mrs. Brosseau's estimation "were she to learn that as President he hauled our effective warships up on the beach" or that it was the "heretic Ben Franklin who said even after the Revolution that 'there never was a good war or a bad peace.'" Mercer G. Johnson, director of the Baltimore Open Forum, suggested, "What the DAR needs is a good stiff drink of the simon pure brand of the spirit of '76."

The *Literary Digest* featured the blacklist and ran nationwide comment on it. *The New York Times* reminded the Daughters that it was fortunate for the organization that DAR ancestors "were not afraid to have issues threshed out in public" and it continued, "Fancy Sam Adams of Boston proscribed because his utterances might be radical." The *New York Graphic* wondered what George Washington would think if he knew that the DAR was trying to eliminate liberals from speakers' lists. The *St. Paul Pioneer Press* made the comment that the organization "might have displayed some sympathy for Russian revolutionists, since they came from revolutionary ancestry."

*The Nation* proclaimed that the DAR blacklist was "an honor roll of American life" and on May 9 gave a party at the Level Club in New York City for all individuals fortunate enough to be included on it. The program was made up of stunts and speeches by Heywood Broun, Groucho Marx, Arthur Garfield Hayes, Norman Thomas, Art Young, James Weldon Johnson, "and others whose talents sprang spontaneously from the rich soil of 'sedition.'" Two of the most honored guests of the evening were Mrs. Helen Tufts Bailie and Mrs. Joseph Whitney, who had led a number of New Haven DAR into protest resignation.

Testimonial letters from a host of blacklisted personages unable to attend the party were read. Clarence Darrow wrote that since he was a poor boy he had never been able to get a college degree so "this is the first degree I have ever had and I am proud of it." The Liberal Club of Harvard expressed delight "to see our name on the D.A.R. Honor Roll." A letter from Victor L. Berger, the persecuted New York Socialist Senator, said that he had always considered Judge Landis' jail sentence as his "croix de guerre and any blacklisting can simply add a ribbon or another decoration."

*The Nation* had been courteous enough to send Mrs. Brosseau a special invitation to their party as well, but she was unable to attend because on May 10 she was being "presented to the British King and Queen at Buckingham Palace!" *The New York Times*, which gave the event extensive coverage, explained that on May 9 Mrs. Brosseau was practicing the "low, sweeping curtsy which she would perform before King George." The *Times* had interviewed Mrs. Brosseau after the presentation and the report continued:

> "It was all a very delightful experience for an American, very delightful," beamed Mrs. Brosseau, after she had curtsied low before King George and Queen Mary tonight . . . "I went in early," said Mrs. Brosseau, with a slight touch of triumph, "and I was in the Throne Room from the beginning of the ceremony. . . . All I can say in describing it is that it was very ceremonious, in fact, I would call it dignified and wonderful."
> The D.A.R. head wore a blue brocade gown with soft irridescent flower figures of pale gold and pale rose embroidered with pearls [This presentation gown became her favorite for state conferences during the coming season].

Refreshed by her British social triumph, Mrs. Brosseau returned to the serious business at hand, the formal expulsion of Mrs. Helen Tufts Bailie. This took place on June 21, 1928. Mrs. Walker reported the proceedings in her monthly national-defense article in the July magazine: "Mrs. Helen Tufts Bailie, of Cambridge, Massachusetts, the self-confessed author of 'Our Threatened Heritage,' has been expelled from the National Society, Daughters of the American Revolution, by the unanimous vote of the National Board of Management." She was found guilty on five counts of "conduct calculated to injure the good name and disturb the harmony of the Society..."

Mrs. Walker hastened to add that there was "no rushing nor railroading nor steam-roller process about this hearing." At 11 A.M. on the fatal day, Mrs. Bailie appeared, represented by George W. Alger of New York and Lawrence G. Brooks of Boston. Apparently Mrs. Bailie had a number of witnesses, but Mrs. Walker saw fit to name only one, Mrs. Roy, whose resolution had been ignored at the April congress, and who was described as an "office secretary" for the Women's International League for Peace and Freedom as well as a DAR member. Mrs. Walker also made a point of implying that Mrs. Bailie had received financial aid from the WIL to conduct her defense.

Mrs. Walker emphasized "the President General's unfailing courtesy" throughout the hearing, which lasted seven hours and covered 216 pages of testimony. The triumph of the trial came when, under cross examination by the DAR counsel, H. Ralph Burton, Mrs. Bailie had been forced to admit that "she had never seen a copy of such a list as she had described outside the State of Massachusetts and that she had never known of any National officer of the D.A.R. possessing any such list." On the strength of this statement, Mrs. Walker claimed the exoneration of the National Board from all responsibility for the blacklisting charge.

Meanwhile Mrs. MacFarland was busily engaged in collecting a set of affidavits from Kansas to prove that the lists distributed in the Sunflower State were almost identical with those making the rounds in New Jersey. In November, the Board made short work of this nonsense. Mrs. MacFarland also was rewarded with expulsion. When asked if she planned to try to be reinstated, Mrs. MacFarland shrugged. "The Continental Congress can learn the facts and do justice if it so desires," she said. "If it doesn't desire, nothing I could say would move it."

Mrs. Bailie was more stubborn and finally was granted an appeal to have her case reviewed by the 1929 Congress. This was again an election year, and the nearly completed Constitution Hall also was to be dedicated. Under parliamentary rules the Bailie case came under the heading of new business and would not be brought up until Saturday. However, on Tuesday morning, probably by prearrangement, a delegate rose to move consideration of her appeal. Mrs. Brosseau approved, saying that it was unfair to wait for the end of Congress since many delegates would have left by then. The motion was carried and Mrs. Brosseau ordered the meeting into executive session. Addressing reporters and guests, the President General explained: "I will have to ask you to leave for a moment—maybe for a few hours." As they filed out a wave of laughter went through the group remaining in the auditorium.

Because of the element of surprise, neither Mrs. Bailie nor her attorney, George Alger, was in the hall at the time. As it turned out, this mattered very little, for the action was cut and dried. Making it quite clear to the delegates that they must fully understand that they were not trying Mrs. Bailie, merely considering her appeal, Mrs. Brosseau stated that nineteen members had filed charges against the accused and that the National Board had acted upon these charges. An Iowa Daughter immediately rose to sustain the expulsion. It was promptly seconded and the entire auditorium rocked with the burst of "Ayes," reaffirming the members' faith in their President General.

The DAR magazine reported that "A solitary voice was raised in protest when the Congress voted to sustain the action of the Board." To whom this voice belonged was not recorded and the lone dissenter remains anonymous to this day. In all it took ten minutes for the supreme legislative authority of the DAR—its Congress—to render the final verdict against Mrs. Bailie.

A triumphant Mrs. Brosseau announced to the *Washington Daily News*: "The 38th Congress has spoken. You can figure from this what the DAR thinks of Mrs. Helen Tufts Bailie." When interviewed, Mrs. Bailie said she was glad she was "through." She added: "I'm glad it's over. I had to keep on fighting—I couldn't stop without an appeal. But I don't want to belong to such an organization."

# I X

While the memory of the blacklist controversy was still fresh, the DAR was dragged into another ugly scandal. It broke only a few months later in September 1929, when William Baldwin Shearer took the stand at a Senate investigation probing shipbuilding interests.

Shearer was a suave, mustachioed cavalier who had been somewhat of a mystery man ever since the 1927 Geneva Disarmament Conference. Unreservedly in favor of a strong American navy, he had arrived in Geneva flourishing letters of recommendation from the DAR and a number of other patriotic societies. Shearer implied that he was representing these groups.

In spite of his seemingly innocent credentials, it soon became apparent that Shearer had remarkable access to highly confidential information and he became the most influential individual at the meeting. From the first he was courted by delegates from this country as well as from England and Japan. Shearer was a lavish entertainer, and his hospitality made him extremely popular with American reporters. He issued them a daily "progress" analysis sheet. Since the nautical technicalities of the conference were beyond the comprehension of the average layman, the reporters were grateful for his sheet and used it almost verbatim for home consumption. These releases were written so as to make acceptance of the limitation of Naval arms proposals unpopular in America, and public opinion exerted enough pressure on our delegation to cause a breakdown in the proceedings.

When negotiations collapsed, a leading Geneva newspaper accused Shearer of being "The Man Who Wrecked the Conference." At the time, Wythe Williams, *New York Times* correspondent, suggested that Shearer's backing was more extensive than he had acknowledged, but nothing could be proven about his real connections until the summer of 1929, when he filed a joint claim for $250,000 against the New York Shipbuilding

Company, the Newport News Shipbuilding and Drydock Company, and Bethlehem Steel. He revealed that these firms had promised him a stipend of $25,000 a year over a period of ten years if he would represent their interests at the conference without appearing to do so. He was bringing suit because they had failed to live up to their agreement.

The disclosure was sensational. President Hoover demanded a Senate investigation of the accused firms. Shearer was not subpoenaed, but he appeared voluntarily and was a valuable witness. He revealed that his portfolio at the Geneva conference had contained not only letters of endorsement from patriotic societies, the DAR among them, but also confidential U.S. Navy statistics, under official frank, and the expert briefing of his shipbuilding backers.

He testified that as soon as he had "wrecked" the conference, he had returned to America to compose a series of violently anti-British propaganda papers, which were widely circulated by the Republican National Committee and which helped sway the Irish vote to Hoover.

After Hoover's election, he had showed himself unsympathetic to the fifteen-cruiser bill that the DAR's Mrs. Walker had endorsed in February 1928. The shipbuilders then sent Shearer to Washington to wage a campaign in favor of the legislation. He admitted that, at the same time, he also was being paid $2,000 a month by William Randolph Hearst to attack the League of Nations and the World Court. Combining his dual interests, Shearer wrote a new series of pamphlets, including *The Cloak of Benedict Arnold*, which threw discredit on all individuals and groups favoring the League, the World Court, and armaments limitation. The DAR were the most zealous distributors of these pamphlets.

At the hearing, Shearer took full personal responsibility for his actions and minimized his connection with patriotic societies. Describing himself as a "Protestant and a nationalist," he insisted that the organizations in question had only supported him in his own ideals. The investigators tossed aside this explanation. They wanted to prove that the societies had allowed themselves to be used as a shield of respectability for selfish interests.

Republican Senator Samuel M. Shortbridge of California kept hammering away at this point. He asked the big-navy agent if he had not said "in so many words" that he was the representative of certain patriotic associations. Shearer replied: "I will not say 'representative,' I said 'endorsed.' If you wish to interpret that as representative I will acknowledge it." Senator Shortbridge refused to be put off by the evasion and wanted to know if he had not mentioned the DAR specifically by name. Shearer was forced to admit he had. While he was on the stand, the Society's name was mentioned so frequently that it became irrevocably linked with the tawdry proceedings. Ironically enough, at one point Shearer admitted that his original interest in naval affairs had been aroused at the Memorial Continental Hall conference in 1921.

The Reverend William L. Stedger of Boston's Copley Methodist Church was still smarting from vicious DAR attacks on leading clergymen. It must have given him great satisfaction to tell his congregation that the Senate should investigate the DAR and the rest of the organizations that had allowed themselves to become the tools of the big-navy agent. Emphasizing the particular guilt of the Daughters, Stedger accused them of being "a lot of old ladies who sit at home basking in the unearned increment of dead ancestors, satisfying their feeling of self-importance by sending forth the stupid propaganda of war and allowing Mr. Shearer to use their organization as a cat's paw to rake his hot coals out of the fire . . ." The indignant minister continued that the DAR again had been Shearer's willing dupe by flooding the country with his hate literature about President Hoover in which the President's delay to build cruisers was called unwarranted, unsafe and unconstitutional.

The DAR attorney, H. Ralph Burton, threatened to sue Reverend Stedger and all others who allegedly had made disparaging remarks about the order, but no suits materialized. Public reaction was one of disgust. Never again would the high-sounding phrases of the Daughters go unchallenged as pronouncements of disinterested patriotism.

Except for Burton's unfortunate outburst, the Daughters rode out the storm in silence. However, among themselves, a general distaste for the scandalous proceedings was strong enough for the DAR magazine to devote a great deal of space to the reprints of all national press comments that upheld the organization's position. This was the first time in DAR history that the Board of Management made an effort to vindicate its actions to members. Still the pressure of internal criticism was insufficient to bring about a change in policy. If anything, demands for strong defense, isolationism and stricter immigration laws were intensified. The Daughters also continued to aid their old friend Fred K. Marvin in his purge of subversives.

Because of its bad odor, the Key Men had faded into oblivion, but in the spring of 1929, Marvin turned up with a brand-new organization called the American Coalition of Patriotic Societies. The Coalition was launched at a banquet in New York City, where fifty-six people, claiming to represent sixty-three leading patriotic societies, vowed to continue the campaign to "clean up" America. One of Mrs. Brosseau's final acts as President General was to attend the banquet and, again with no formal consent, pledge DAR support. Many Daughters may have been ignorant of the new affiliation since the National Board maintained a tactful silence about Mrs. Brosseau's farewell commitment.

The Coalition consisted of a network of national "Study Clubs." They received a series of Marvin's lectures in pamphlet form, which before circulation were delivered in person on two separate occasions: first to a group of women at the New York Army and Navy Club, then to men belonging to the Manhattan Chapter of the National Sojourners. Mrs. Finley J. Shepard, the DAR who had contributed so heavily to the National Security League, sponsored the women's group.

A quick glance at the Coalition's roster shows the usual pattern of interlocking officers. Mrs. Shepard was chairman of the "Educational Board." The vice-chairman, the Honorable Josiah A. Van Orsdel, was listed as associate judge of the District Court of Appeals, Washington, D.C. (He was also incumbent President General of the SAR, and his wife was acting DAR Registrar General.) Two other members of the board were Major General Amos A. Fries, now described as "Past National President, National Sojourners; President R.O.T.C. Association," and Mrs. William Sherman Walker. In Marvin's initial lecture, he crowned Mrs. Walker with laurels for possessing the most comprehensive library on subversion in the United States of America.

Mrs. Lowell Fletcher Hobart, who succeeded Mrs. Brosseau as President General in 1929, was as militant as her predecessor, but she did make one concession to adverse criticism. She appointed a new publicity chairman, Mrs. William Louis Dunne. Mrs. Dunne was a former newspaper woman with a good sense of public relations. She was deeply concerned by the unsavory image the society was creating and did her best to erase it.

Mrs. Hobart retained Mrs. Walker as Defense Chairman and the work of her committee was subsidized by an annual assessment of 15 cents per capita. Mrs. Hobart had an intense, personal interest in American Legion affairs. Proud of being the founder of the women's Auxiliary of the veterans' organization, she took every opportunity to cement the bonds between Legionnaires and the DAR. During her administration her efforts were aided by at least two Auxiliary presidents who were also Daughters: Mrs. Donald Macrae (1930) was a member of long standing, and her successor, Mrs. Robert L. Hoyal (1931), became a Daughter soon after her election.

All three women certainly shared Mrs. Brosseau's original enthusiasm for the Women's Patriotic Conference. When the Daughters moved into Constitution Hall in 1930, the conference went right along with them. In fact, its fifth meeting, January 29, 30, 31, predated the DAR initiation of their own auditorium and was hailed by the *Daughters of the American Revolution Magazine* as the first important function to be held on the premises. As usual, in April, the DAR Congress rubber-stamped most of the resolutions passed at the conference. One of them was to cause the Society considerable embarrassment.

On the opening night of the first Congress in their new "home," President Hoover made a major policy address. The 1930 London naval conference had succeeded in creating a naval holiday among the three rival nations—the United States, Great Britain, and Japan—which was to last until 1936. Hoover spoke of his part in these negotiations, then made an eloquent plea for Americans to consider entering the World Court. The speech was received with warm applause, and on Tuesday morning a letter of appreciation for his appearance was sent to the President. On Wednesday, however, the press reported that the Society had passed a strong resolution condemning the court.

Public reaction was immediate, indignant, and derisive. Probably upon Mrs. Dunne's advice, Mrs. Hobart tried to dismiss the unfortunate situation as a misunderstanding. She insisted that reporters had failed to differentiate between resolutions passed, those endorsed, and committee reports that were read and filed without action.

Technically, Mrs. Hobart's explanation was correct. The Society itself had not *passed* a resolution repudiating our entrance into the World Court. Nevertheless, it had *endorsed* a resolution passed at the Women's Patriotic Conference that opposed "the commitment of our Country to entangling alliances which could operate to limit full liberty of decision in international affairs . . . "

A droll rumor was soon circulating in Washington that the President's sister-in-law, Mrs. Theodore Jesse Hoover of California, was defeated in a race for DAR Vice-President General because the Daughters had disapproved of the World Court speech. Mrs. Hobart dismissed the gossip as "too silly for words," and Mrs. Brosseau snorted, "Absurd." Nevertheless, the fact remained that seven out of nine candidates were elected and Mrs. Hoover was not among them, but defense-minded Mrs. Charles Peabody of Massachusetts was.

Although the President continued the custom of the White House reception and the First Lady attended at least one session of each annual Congress, Hoover never again addressed the Daughters of the American Revolution. His wife, herself an Iowa Daughter of long standing, always expressed regrets for his absence, but he did not send the personal letter that became the customary method of communication of most presidents following Hoover. The President General's explanation seemed to satisfy most members, but in some instances the World Court resolution caused even more discontent in the organization than the blacklist controversy. With the thirty-ninth Congress still in session, Mrs. William Thayer Brown of West Orange, New Jersey, sent in her resignation. She had been a generous member and felt entitled to write Mrs. Hobart a personal note expressing her displeasure. Blacklists, disarmament, and the World Court were her principal grievances. Mrs. Carroll Miller of Pittsburgh resigned at about the same time and for the same reasons. Mrs. Miller had seconded Al Smith's presidential nomination at the 1928 Democratic convention. Both women were prominent enough for their views to create a stir. Mrs. Hobart tried to counteract the impact of the two withdrawals by calling them "another attempt to use the DAR for peace propaganda."

In the week after Congress two more well-known members left the Society. They were Mrs. Lois Kimball Mathews Rosenberry, wife of the chief justice of Wisconsin's Supreme Court, and Margaretta Fort, another West Orange member, the daughter of a former New Jersey governor and sister of Democratic Representative Franklin Fort.

On May 16, 1930, nearly half of California's Stanford University Chapter left the organization in a body. The group, including the wives of Dr. John Cooper Brannon and Dr. David Starr Jordan (both former presidents of Stanford), issued a public, formal protest against the "political activities and reactionary policies of the National Board of Management in regard to peace, disarmament and the World Court." They also objected to the methods of administration that gave chapters no effective voice in determining the national organizational stand.

Although the Board was forced to concede a loss of 1,905 members in 1930, Mrs. Hobart pointed with pride to the gain of 9,450 new ones in the same period. The shower of resignations was attributed to the depression, but disapproval of the oligarchy was certainly a factor. (By 1934, the membership of Daughters was reduced to 150,980, and it continued to dwindle until it stood at 141,882 in 1941. The Society then revived and through vigorous membership drives managed to climb to the present 186,000. The gain, however, was never at the fast pace of earlier days.)

In spite of handicaps, Mrs. Dunne, the new publicity chairman, made the most of any favorable news for the Society. One bright moment was the 1931 Congress, when Will Rogers arrived as the guest of Vice-President Charles E. Curtis, whose sister, Mrs. Dolly Gann, was an ardent DAR. Donning a sash of the Society and holding a huge bouquet, Rogers made an impromptu speech. In it he admitted that he had no right to the sash, since he was not a DAR or even a DAR's husband; he suggested the ladies might think of him as sort of a "mother superior" because he also believed in a strong navy and army, which he wanted to keep at home rather than "messing around" in foreign countries. He called the Daughters "you old sisters" and had the audacity to admit that he had no service record because, during the war, he had been busy saving follies girls from doughboys, but the audience loved it. At the conclusion of his remarks, he was swamped with autograph seekers.

Mrs. Dunne was always ready to play up a touch of humor even if it happened to be at the Society's own expense. One evening in 1932, the last year of Mrs. Hobart's administration, the statuesque President General appeared in a gown entirely fashioned out of florists' ribbons saved from bouquets received while in office. Her costume was described in the DAR magazine as follows: "Its close-fitting bodice was of golden bands in basket weave on diagonal lines, and its billowy skirt was of rainbow-tinted ruffles. She carried an old-fashioned bouquet of artificial flowers made of gay bits of ribbon."

Moments of frivolity such as these were rare during the Hobart term. Not only were the Daughters pulled along in the wake of the policy of the Women's Patriotic Conference but they were constantly subjected to Mrs. Hobart's denunciation of the evil forces of communism. She blamed communists for all the "disagreeable events" of the depression such as riots, walkouts, sitdowns, street demonstrations, and protest marches.

Even so, her statements were mild in comparison to Mrs. Walker's extravagant claims. At the 1931 Congress, the Defense Chairman divulged that runs on banks were being started by communist whisper campaigns and insisted that investigation of these activities had "become a question worthy of the best intelligence." Her monthly feature articles in the DAR magazine were full of tales of Bolsheviks. They were lurking in the long, miserable soup-kitchen lines. Shanty towns were nothing more than training camps for the pending bloody revolution. Hoover may have seen prosperity "just around the corner," but Mrs. Walker could see nothing but subversive infiltration into shops, factories, mines, mills, railroads, and steamship lines. All strikes were dress rehearsals for the "takeover." Reds were enlisting by the droves in the armed services to undermine efficiency. She claimed to have evidence of their cunning, organized opposition to the CMTC, the ROTC, and all forms of cadet work in high schools. They were even out to smash the Boy Scouts and the Campfire Girls. References to the *Daily Worker* peppered Mrs. Walker's articles. From its pages she learned that industrial intraorganizational sports events were fraught with danger since the Trade Union Unity League was largely responsible for the arrangement of athletic contests. Also in the *Daily Worker* she discovered that a songbook was published by the Communist Party that included such tunes as "Capitalism Is Falling Down," "We'll Confiscate the Bank on the Corner," and, worst of all, "Onward Christian Soldiers" revamped into communist language "too vile and blasphemous for reprinting in a legitimate publication."

By 1932, the Daughters' reactionary policy seemed to be so firmly entrenched that no outside observer could have believed that many members might be thinking in terms of "time for a change." However, several months before Franklin Roosevelt coined that catchy phrase as a campaign slogan, an attempt was made to modify the Society's outlook.

In 1932, when Mrs. Russell William Magna won a unanimous election as the unopposed candidate, *The New York Times* predicted that she would lead the organization down more moderate paths. The *Times* based its prophecy on the facts that (1) Mrs. Dunne would stay on as publicity director and that (2) Mrs. Walker had not been invited to continue as chairman of the National Defense Committee. (Mrs. William A. Becker of New Jersey had been appointed in her stead.) The paper admitted that the ladies would remain staunch supporters of military preparedness and a large reserve corps but suggested that there were indications of a growing feeling within the ranks that the communist menace was absorbing a disproportionate amount of the Society's energy. To outsiders, Mrs. Magna was known mainly for her imaginative, untiring efforts to amortize the mortgage on Constitution Hall, but among members she had a sound reputation for moderate views. The *Times* pointed out that her good sense accounted more for her popularity than her fund raising ability and made the hopeful forecast that she and Mrs. Dunne would calm down the Daughters' emotions.

Beyond dropping Mrs. Walker, Mrs. Magna took no other decisive step until January 19, 1933. Then, practically on the eve of the Women's Patriotic Conference, she quietly announced the withdrawal of the DAR from the alliance. Making no charges against the conference or former DAR policies, she simply said that "at the time of the depression" members were unable to sponsor the meeting in conjunction with the American Legion Auxiliary. Nevertheless, the significance of her understatement was fully apparent, especially when she emphasized that any Daughters wishing to attend the gathering were at liberty to do so only as individuals, not as representatives of the Society.

The resolute Mrs. Brosseau appeared at the Women's Patriotic Conference as usual and it looked as if she would lead a determined minority who wished to reinstate the DAR in the conference. However, much to everyone's surprise, Mrs. Brosseau abided by Mrs. Magna's decision. At the 1933 Congress she reminded malcontents that "the President General is willing for any member to cooperate personally with other societies," and threw her weight with the majority of delegates who voted to uphold Mrs. Magna's January ruling. In the following year, a resolution was passed that made it illegal for the Daughters of the American Revolution to ally themselves with any outside organization. For better or worse, from that time on their policy has been the result of independent thinking. Lacking DAR support, the Women's Patriotic Conference died a few years later. After the blow-up, most Daughters saw little of the former defense chairman Mrs. Walker, although backstage she kept her hand in DAR affairs and was vice-chairman of the all-powerful

Resolutions Committee from 1950 to 1957. (Most of Mrs. Walker's time was devoted to the American Coalition of Patriotic Societies, of which she became executive secretary upon Marvin's death in 1939.)

The vote of confidence on her decision to sever relations with the Women's Patriotic Conference was only one of Mrs. Magna's personal triumphs at the 1933 Congress. Through her efforts, the liberal Eleanor Roosevelt became a life member of the Society only a day or so after Mrs. Brosseau had crushed the insurrectionists. The Daughters were so eager to have this particular First Lady on their roll that they paid the necessary $100 initiation fee for her themselves and at the White House reception gave her an embossed certificate inscribed with the names of her six Revolutionary ancestors.

"Avoid adverse criticism" became and remained the watchword of the Magna regime. At her final Congress in 1935 she reminded the Daughters that the Society's strength lay in its nonpolitical, nonpartisan nature. She said she had tried to keep the organization from being the prey of propaganda and exploitation and begged future leaders to keep away from extremism. However, in spite of her good intentions, Mrs. Magna had failed to change the DAR public image.

On April 4, a few days before her last message, a rally was held at Madison Square Garden under the joint auspices of the American Civil Liberties Union and the American League Against War and Fascism. Approximately 17,000 people answered the call to protest stricter alien and sedition bills pending in the House. The DAR, Hearst, the American Legion, and the Chamber of Commerce were denounced as the chief proponents of this legislation. Gigantic cardboard effigies of all four had a prominent place on the speakers' platform, and after the meeting they were auctioned off for several hundred dollars.

If Mrs. Magna was sincere in her aim to moderate the Society's stand on controversial matters, why was she willing that the DAR give its solid support to these bills and to other reactionary measures? After one timid flirtation with the New Deal, when they supported the National Recovery Administration, the Daughters had renounced Roosevelt's government experts for trying to destroy the Republic through a communist-inspired planned economy. To them, and to many other conservatives, it was frightening for the government to usurp the role of benevolent private charities. They were sure that taxes and labor unions would bring an end to the free-enterprise system. To them perhaps the gravest heresy of all was the nonchalant way in which "brain trusters" twisted the interpretation of the revered Constitution to make it pliable enough to fit the complicated new needs of the people. After the first stunned silence, the Daughters soon found their voice and became an integral part of the old guard that tried to balk liberal legislation.

In the 1920s, the Daughters had earned the animosity of youth, which was managing to break down the moral code of the late 1800s. That contest won, enlightened young men and women of the 1930s committed themselves to politics and social reform. This was a grim, impatient generation, which often exhibited flashes of bitter satire when called upon to defend its principles. The young people had no tolerance for any person or group who clung to the type of thinking that they held responsible for the country's economic crisis. They gave no quarter to the Daughters, whom they saw as a symbol of the dwindling yet vicious minority that was using a nineteenth-century yardstick to measure the ills of the depression.

Though Mrs. Magna's administration was wise enough to muffle the new defense chairman, still, with men such as Martin Dies and Lamar Jeffers as their favored speakers and representative contributors to their magazine, many Americans continued to dismiss the DAR program as undemocratic and rabble-rousing.

Although perhaps less flamboyant, Mrs. Becker was as zealous in the execution of her duties as Mrs. Walker had been. A Becker article in a 1935 DAR magazine announced that over 225,000 pieces of defense literature had been distributed to "members and teachers and to many others in public and private life." She also stated that, upon the request of its chairman, she had given a documented report to the senate committee investigating un-American activities. She emphasized that her findings dealt with the torrent of Red propaganda being disseminated among American youth and showed evidence of its dangerous infiltration into the armed services.

Mrs. Magna's desire to "avoid adverse criticism" was hardly possible if she remained so out of step with the nation's current attitudes. Nevertheless, something constructive might have resulted from her desire for moderation if, in 1935, Dr. Flora Myers Gillentine rather than Mrs. William Becker had succeeded to the presidency.

Mrs. Gillentine had been a university professor for twenty years and now was head of the psychology and education department at the State Teachers' College in Arkansas. Although the DAR Congress did not convene until the fifteenth of the month, both she and Mrs. Becker had set up campaign headquarters by April 8. The battle was a bitter one.

Dr. Gillentine distributed a broadside advocating that the Board of Management survey the four committees supported by per capita levies. In it, she made it clear that she felt that the annual expenditure on patriotic education, administered by the Defense Committee, could be more wisely handled. On April 12, *The New York Times* quoted her as saying: "No one could be more devoted to our institutions than I am nor more opposed to subversion but I don't believe in hysteria. There are lots of people with schizophrenia loose in the world but I am not one of them." She went on to explain that she felt a need for more open discussion in the organization with the view of developing a more constructive attitude than the present one. She said that as an educator she had discovered that youth readily responded to well-informed leaders but immediately rejected speakers who labeled others communists without knowing what communism really was.

Mrs. Becker stood on her record. Shortly before the election, *The New York Times* (April 12 and 17, 1935) divulged that she had endorsed *The Red Network*, even though it included an attack on Mrs. Roosevelt, Frances Perkins, Donald Richberg, and other important members of the New Deal administration. The *Times* continued that certain Daughters criticized her lack of taste in endorsing the volume, and that during the campaign, Mrs. Becker tried as much as possible to disassociate herself

from it, fearing that the connection might sway the vote in **Dr.**
**Gillentine's** favor. She need hardly have worried. At the time of
the tally she received 1,463 votes and **Dr.** Gillentine only 619.
Such an overwhelming majority swamped the hopes of delivering
the Society from its militant policy. Never again did any **DAR**
with liberal leanings contest the will of the hierarchy for election to an important office.

# X

A LITTLE CHILD SHALL LEAD THEM

In her acceptance speech, Mrs. Becker reminded the Daughters that "Differences of opinion are desirable, but differences of convictions on fundamental matters can only break up the Society." Florence Becker was petite, attractive, and very feminine in appearance, but she was a woman of decided "convictions." One of the firmest was that, in order to circumvent the infiltration of communists and fellow travelers into the school system, every teacher must be compelled to take an oath of allegiance to the Constitution before gaining employment. Before anyone had time to dispute the question, the Becker forces jockeyed the Daughters into line and immediately accelerated the DAR program to enact and enforce the teachers' loyalty oath in every state of the Union.

This statute had been on the books of a few states since the Reconstruction. However, after that period, interest in it remained dormant until the Red scare of the 1920s. In 1921, Colorado, Oklahoma, South Dakota, and Oregon took steps to guard their youth against communist corruption. West Virginia followed suit in 1923 and Florida in 1925. The DAR soon started to take a lively interest in the oath. Indiana Daughters began to work for the law in 1926 and succeeded in having it passed in 1929. Again with Daughters' help, Ohio adopted the legislation in 1930.

At the fortieth Congress in 1931, Mrs. Fred C. Morgan, chairman of the Committee on Legislation, announced that "exigencies" of the times demanded a teachers' pledge of allegiance law. To clarify confusion she pointed out that although some members were "skeptical" as to just why they should work for passage of the law in their own state, it was their duty to follow the policy that had been endorsed several years earlier by the National Society. In 1931, five states— Michigan, Montana, New Mexico, California, and Washington—jumped on the bandwagon. In Michigan, at least, happy, triumphant Daughters were photographed watching the governor sign the provision.

Even before Mrs. Morgan's prodding, the DAR's loyal protégé, the Children of the American Revolution, twice had gone on record with a precocious motion of their own reading:

> Whereas there are sinister influences being used in our schools to undermine love of the flag and our country, be it resolved that the CAR formulate a bill and present it to the United States Congress, making it necessary for all teachers to subscribe to the oath of allegiance to our country, or resign the certificate to teach.

By 1934, the movement had gained such momentum that a New Jersey Representative, Edward A. Kenney, actually introduced a bill into the House calling for national enforcement of the oath. It is unknown whether his bill was the one formulated by the alert Children, but Kenney claimed to be the spokesman for ninety-five organizations with more than 25,000,000 members. Even though Congress defeated the measure, pressure in individual states was so great that New York took action of its own a short time later.

Educators watched this trend with justified apprehension. Many belonged to the powerful National Educational Association and many more joined soon after July 4, 1934, when the Association set up the Commission on Teacher Tenure and Academic Freedom. Upon completion of an intensive survey, the NEA proposed to send trained investigators to trouble spots in response to the call of any beleaguered teacher who claimed dismissal on unfair charges.

When the Commission started its work, the DAR part in the crusade was being conducted almost entirely on a chapter and state level. Local action had been so successful that the National Society had not felt the necessity to make any strong public commitment. Thus, the organization escaped serious adverse criticism until Mrs. Becker's new policy clarified the evidence that all Daughters were merely following the line of a National directive.

In 1935, the year Florence Becker became President General,

Arizona, Georgia, Massachusetts, New Jersey, Texas, and Vermont enacted oath legislation. Bolstered by the expectancy of protection from their Association, certain educators decided it was time to resist, some members of the Harvard Faculty foremost among them.

On October 2, 1935, Dr. Kirtley F. Mather, a geology professor at Harvard, refused to take the pledge in accordance with the law Massachusetts had passed in June. Dr. Mather insisted that he would have no objection to the oath if everyone were required to take it but that he considered it an insult for the teaching profession to be singled out as if it alone harbored dangerous subversives.

On the same evening, President General Becker happened to be the guest of honor at a DAR state banquet in Springfield, Massachusetts. Close to the scene of action, she considered it imperative to utter a strong personal rebuke to Dr. Mather. In her speech, she declared: "If anyone teaching in public schools and institutions cannot take the oath of allegiance to the constitution of his state and country, he should not be instructing American youth."

Both statements reached the press almost simultaneously. Most papers hailed Kirtley Mather as a hero, and because of the size and reputation of the DAR, Mrs. Becker fitted neatly into the role of archvillainess.

Next day, Dr. Mather announced that he and a group of other Harvard liberals were forming a committee to fight for rescindment of the ruling. He and his friends kept the issue in the limelight by constant needling of the DAR. The historian Samuel E. Morison (who was a member of Mather's protest group) pointed out that when Harvard was founded oaths similar to those favored by Mrs. Becker and her Society were customary in all universities in Christendom. Harvard, however, held the proud record of never having imposed religious or political tests on her student body or her faculty.

The Daughters were quite inured to individual or group censure, but in the present case they underestimated the strength of their foe. Dr. Mather, his colleagues, and countless teachers who had previously considered it prudent to remain silent, were all members of the powerful National Educational Association. For the first time in its history the NSDAR suddenly came up against rugged, organized opposition. (For over thirty years since that time, the DAR and the NEA have continued to slug it out. The Daughters have won some rounds, the NEA others. At the moment, the NEA seems to be ahead.)

Dr. George S. Counts, of the teachers' college at Columbia, got in the first blow. Prior to the formal opening of the 1936 NEA Convention, which was held at St. Louis in February, Dr. Counts addressed 1,000 school administrators. He denounced William Randolph Hearst for trying to "control the curriculum of our schools," and the Detroit priest Father Coughlin, who, he said, was using his "sacred office to spread confusion, misunderstanding and falsehoods among the people." He claimed the Daughters were too ignorant of American history and American ideals to know what they were doing. He called their brand of patriotism "a combination of thinly veiled snobbery and the protection of privilege." They barely had time to recover from this onslaught when the American Federation of Teachers published a sober report in which Henry R. Linville divulged that the DAR, the American Legion, and Veterans of Foreign Wars were the chief promoters of the obnoxious loyalty laws.

The following August, Mrs. Becker retaliated by intensifying the campaign, by commanding all Daughters to strive for strict enforcement of loyalty laws in the approaching fall school term. She explained that it should be considered an honor to take the oath, not a reflection on character. At the same time, she insisted that anyone refusing to take the pledge voluntarily was guilty of insufficient faith in our form of government and should not be allowed "to mold the minds of future citizens." Persons harboring un-American sentiments must be weeded out of the school system and forced to find employment in some other profession. She said she was issuing her statement to correct false reports that the Daughters were trying to raise a Red scare by creating "the alarming impression that America's schools are packed with Communistic teachers" and hastened to add that the Society was not attempting to determine courses of studies. "These," she promised, "will be safe in the hands of loyal teachers."

On August 19, Louis M. Hacker, also of Columbia, disregarded Mrs. Becker's plea of innocence. At the convention of American Federation of Teachers in Philadelphia, he called the Daughters "busybodies" and "witch hunters" and warned that it was time to tell the ladies what their "ancestors fought for." Describing the American Revolution as "a popular uprising," he insisted that unions of the present day were "the true inheritors of this tradition."

The battle raged throughout 1936–1937, each protagonist making some headway. Then, on September 18, 1937, *The Nation* published an article by M. B. Schnapper called "D.A.R. in the Schoolroom."

Schnapper stated that with the exception of the American Legion, the DAR was running the most intensive campaign of all professional patriotic groups to deprive teachers of their academic freedom. He warned that under the leadership of President General Becker, the Society was speeding up its efforts to oust all teachers who opposed the DAR conception of American government. He also charged that even in communities where Daughters were only moderately snoopy, it was the foolish instructor who dared express ideas that could be misinterpreted or who was courageous enough to broach the topics of internationalism, social planning, or the Soviet Union with any objectivity.

Schnapper refuted Mrs. Becker's claim that the Society was innocent of an effort "to determine the course of study" and went on to cover in depth DAR attempts to censor public school textbooks. He reminded the public that a DAR, Mrs. R. M. Jacobs, had been one of the chief troublemakers in the sensational New York investigation of history textbooks in 1920–1922. He also divulged that, along with other superpatriots, New Jersey Daughters had given wholehearted support to a bill designed to legalize censorship of texts in that state and that a short time later, all over the country, Daughters had been avid fans of a series of syndicated Hearst articles that endeavored to show parents that "school histories now being taught their children had been revised and in some instances wholly rewritten in a new and proprietary spirit towards England."

Quoting from a 1934 report of the American Historical Association, Schnapper pointed out that many distinguished scholars had suffered because of DAR criticism. He said that chief among them was Professor David S. Muzzey, whose *American History* had been denounced by the ladies because "it gives to military history insufficient emphasis to make good soldiers out of our children." They had waged a spirited crusade against its use in the District of Columbia and had succeeded in removing it from the approved list in North Carolina because it "unjustly called slavery the chief cause of the Civil War."

A number of other noted authors had enjoyed similar harsh treatment, including Charles and Mary Beard, authors of *The Rise of American Civilization*. In each criticized book the Society had detected a tendency "to intentionally distort the traditions of American heroism and patriotism" and a desire to substitute "radical pacifist slogans calculated to stress internationalism in place of nationalism."

Out of the hundreds of books devoted to American history, Schnapper found that only two met with DAR approval. One was *The Story of the American People*, by Charles F. Horne, and the other was *The American Government Today*, whose author was Frederick J. Haskin, a journalist employed by the conservative Washington *Evening Star*.

Horne's book, which appeared in 1925, originally was commissioned by the American Legion in cooperation with the DAR and thirty-two other superpatriotic orders. Its author was cautioned to "preserve the legends . . . praise noble deeds . . . and emphasize effort and success, not failure." Horne did his utmost to follow instructions. His approved outline proposed that the history, designed for the seventh- and eighth-grade level, would be divided into two volumes, the first ending with the year 1789. In order to bring the War of 1812 alive to children, he called it the "Second War for Independence"; he spoke of the Spanish-American War as "a people's war" and bolstered nationalism by stating that in World War I "we were no feeble foe to match even the terrible German colossus."

Taking a visionary approach, Horne stressed that "a divine purpose" had controlled our destiny because, although the

United States is on "perhaps the oldest continent in the world," it lay unused until the time "civilization should prove worthy of it." Throughout the entire tome, America is constantly referred to as "the land of hope . . . a kind of paradise." The student was repeatedly reminded that "work brings its best reward" to those privileged to live in this "land of opportunity."

Reliable educators immediately tossed the work aside as worthless, but Schnapper disclosed that the DAR still was urging members to bring the history to the attention of schoolboards and recommend its adoption as a textbook. He also said that the Daughters were enthusiastic distributors of Haskin's mediocre book *The American Government Today.* In 1935 alone, through their efforts, 12,000 free copies had found their way into the libraries of CCC camps, the YMCA, the YWCA, and similar centers where it might come to the attention of American youth. (Although Schnapper seemed unaware of the fact, a 1935 DAR magazine announced that Haskin had given the NSDAR 12,000 of his books gratis for exactly this purpose.)

M. F. Grueninger, circulation manager of *The Nation*, was thoughtful enough to send the issue containing "D.A.R. in the Schoolroom" to the DAR magazine, which recently had acquired a new editor, Mrs. Frances Parkinson Keyes. A professional writer, Mrs. Keyes was prudent enough to keep her rebuttal mild. She said that upon taking up her duties in November she had hoped to be the "recipient of a few encouraging remarks," but that one of the first things to reach her desk was the abusive *Nation* article.

Mrs. Keyes' tone was doleful and somewhat humorous. Referring to the author she said "what a snapper he is." She wondered if the gentleman had ever heard of the fine accomplishments at the Tammassee DAR Industrial School in Tammassee, South Carolina, and the Kate Duncan Smith DAR School in Grant, Alabama, or of the partial-aid program given to other schools on the Society's "approved list." Mrs. Keyes left the question dangling, explaining only that a feature article by the national chairman of the Approved School Committee, Miss Katharine Matthies, would appear in the December issue of the DAR publication and that a marked copy would be dispatched promptly to Grueninger.

Careful examination of the list of DAR schools shows that all but two, Hillside School and Northland College, are in the Appalachian region, where, by the Society's own admission, they were founded to further the education of the "purest remaining Anglo-Saxon stock." South Carolina Daughters opened Tammassee on a modest scale in 1918 and the 1920 DAR Congress voted to adopt the school. Since then, the National Board has appropriated $5,000 a year to it, but the bulk of its support comes from state, chapter, or individual contributions. Kate Duncan Smith—generally called KDS—which has been a national DAR project since 1924, receives the same assistance. In each instance, the Society pays the salary of a maintenance staff and a few teachers, but most of the faculty are on the state payroll.

Tammassee has a campus of twenty-eight buildings, all of which were financed and are kept in repair by the Daughters. Methods of raising funds are often ingenious. In 1936, when the school needed a new laundry, equipment was obtained through a nationwide appeal for members to pool coupons of various household products that offered suitable premiums.

The original enrollment was only five girls, but in 1932 Tammassee became coeducational. Today it furnishes food and clothing, as well as education through the twelfth grade, to 215 boarders and 141 day pupils, all of whom are "needy mountain children." Special emphasis is laid on "homemaking, citizenship and Christian living." "Under constant supervision" girls do the household chores and boys are trained in shop and agriculture. Since 1965, boarders may attend high school in nearby Salem, where they can take advantage of a college preparatory course not included in the Tammassee curriculum.

KDS is a twelve-grade day school with an enrollment of 716. It has a campus of 29 buildings, all DAR owned. This institution also concentrates on mechanical and farm training for boys and home economics for girls. In 1964, it became accredited, and now approximately one-third of the graduating class is prepared for college. "Good sportsmanship" is featured at KDS and their basketball team, called the "Patriots," won the Alabama state championship for the 1964–1965 season. Students issue a monthly paper, which gives lively accounts of athletics, glee clubs, and sundry extracurricular activities, but ample space is saved for such articles as "Why Not Teach Love of Our Country?" and "Communism—A Threat to Our Democracy." The paper generally includes a photograph of the incumbent President General and/or a group of lesser Daughters while visiting the campus during the annual DAR School Pilgrimage.

"Approved schools" must also cater to "underprivileged children who otherwise would not have the opportunity for education" and to students of foreign parentage. In order to qualify as an "approved school," each must maintain "high scholastic standards" and teach "Patriotic American Principles." Fifteen institutions were assisted in 1937, but the number now has dwindled to seven. They are Berry College and Berry Academy, Mount Berry, Georgia; Blue Ridge School, St. George, Dyke, Virginia; Crossnore School, Inc., Crossnore, North Carolina; Hillside School, Inc., Marborough, Massachusetts; Hindman Settlement School, Inc., Hindman, Kentucky; Lincoln Memorial University, Harrogate, Tennessee; and Northland College, Ashland, Wisconsin.

Each of the lower schools is based on a domestic-science, farm-trade principle, and even the colleges stress self-help. The DAR concentration is on preparing citizens for a useful life, mainly in the homogeneous Appalachian locality. To many critics this hardly seems the necessary experience to qualify them to set up a strict criteria for instructors and instruction built around the needs of the complicated, heterogeneous universal public school system.

Nevertheless, since the society first began its crusade to drive the Reds out of American schools, its program has caused trained educators incessant headaches and often hardships. In spite of the tireless fieldwork of the National Education Association's commission on Teacher Tenure and Academic Freedom, which got under way in 1937, the drive for enactment and enforcement of loyalty oaths continued to preoccupy the DAR and many other superpatriotic groups. A 1941 article called

"The Trumpet Call" appeared in the DAR magazine. In it, the incumbent DAR defense chairman, Saidee E. Boyd, urged all chapters to do their duty and see to it that "persons in positions of public trust who are paid from public funds" be forced to take "the Oath of Allegiance to the Constitution of the United States." She also warned that textbooks must be examined and in the same article raised a cry against federal aid for public schools. She stated, "To the several states belong the responsibility and control over public education . . .," and added that any legislation designed to remove state power would be firmly opposed by the DAR. The DAR had first passed a resolution to this effect in 1940 and since then have been increasingly militant toward any bill that might allow our schools to become "part of the socialistic scheme that has our government building roads, setting the wage rate, buying surplus crops, and erecting hospitals."

World War II naturally diverted the attention of all patriotic groups from education but after the war the arrested campaign started again with a new fury. In 1947, the DAR President General, Mrs. Julius Y. Talmadge, issued this brisk command:

> Every Daughter of the American Revolution should constitute herself a committee of one to oppose by every means within her power the infiltration of communistic teachers in our schools and colleges and to combat the spreading of communistic poison in the minds of our young students.

The Daughters and their allies succeeded in getting five more states to pass drastic laws between 1950 and 1952, and their determined surveillance so intimidated teachers that many kept their views to themselves and complied with the demands of packed school boards rather than risk dismissal on the grounds of disloyalty. As a result of the findings of a questionnaire sent out in 1951, the NEA published a report claiming that such self-censorship by teachers was "today's most critical danger to the rights of students to learn."

After a 1952 Supreme Court ruling rejecting an Oklahoma Loyalty oath, the demand for the oath slowly abated. By this time both the Sons and the Daughters of the American Revolution were concentrating on familiar but now more fertile fields of endeavor. A 1951 report on activities of the Texas Daughters explained that in order to discover if children were being "taught the principles embraced by our forefathers" members were checking American history textbooks. It stated that in Texas "393 members have read textbooks and 1695 have visited history classes." Obviously, by one method or another, the DAR was in the schoolroom to stay.

# XI

One of the easiest ways to prick a Daughter's conscience is to mention civil rights. The conversation always leads to Marian Anderson, with the DAR member defending the Society for its denial of the use of Constitution Hall to the great Negro contralto on Easter Sunday, April 9, 1939. Although the incident occurred thirty years ago, the NSDAR is still haunted by a compulsion to justify the action, and in an effort to do so, a series of pamphlets reviewing the circumstances have been issued. The latest one, *Statement re Constitution Hall*, appeared in 1966.

It emphasizes the fact that until the early 1950s the city of Washington maintained strict segregation in schools, hospitals, restaurants, churches, playgrounds, theaters, and auditoriums. In self-vindication the Daughters offer the argument that they had no choice when they refused their stage to a Negro artist. They merely were acting in accordance with the prevailing municipal custom.

Miss Anderson's specific case is explored in depth. The pamphlet explains that on January 6 Charles C. Cohen, Chairman of the Howard University Concert Series, tried to book Constitution Hall for Marian Anderson on April 9. Fred E. Hand, manager of the hall, regretted that the date had been reserved by the National Symphony Orchestra.

Although the pamphlet does not mention it, some of the subsequent misunderstanding may have resulted from the fact that the symphony was scheduled for the afternoon whereas Cohen proposed an evening performance for Miss Anderson. It was a policy of the Society to limit the use of the auditorium to one daily attraction, but at the time, Hand failed to specify the rule as a reason for its unavailability. The regulation was not divulged until Congress Week when Mrs. Henry M. Robert, Jr., the incumbent President General, issued a formal statement to this effect. By then, however, the public was in no mood to listen to flimsy excuses and refused to believe that the Daughters had acted in good faith in any part of the struggle.

Although the pamphlet refrains from comment on this technicality, it stresses that no alternative date was requested by Cohen. It is also careful to point out that Miss Anderson's race did not enter into the original correspondence and that negotiations were reopened only after unsuccessful attempts had been made to book the Belasco, the National, Loew's, and the Rialto theaters for the concert.

Then Hand received a letter dated January 23, from Miss Anderson's agent, Sol Hurok, asking if the Society would be willing to "waive the restrictions in Miss Anderson's case." It remains unclear which restrictions may have been used as a point of reference. Since it is doubtful that Hand would have allowed himself to be drawn into a controversy on segregation, it must be supposed that the inquiry alluded to the dual-billing rule. In any case, Hand simply repeated the excuse of prior commitments and advised Hurok that any matters of policy were beyond his jurisdiction and had to be taken up with the President General.

There is no indication that Hurok made an effort to contact Mrs. Robert, but on February 7 the pamphlet says he wired Cohen: "Am informed Constitution Hall available April 8th and 10th. Take steps immediately to book Anderson either date." Finally the real issue behind the action, desegregation of public buildings in Washington, was in the open. The move forced Mrs. Robert into a public pronouncement. Her February 13 press release reads: "The rules governing the use of Constitution Hall are in accordance with the policy of theaters, auditoriums, hotels and public schools of the District of Columbia." Immediately Hand wrote Cohen: "The Hall is not available for a concert by Miss Anderson." To prove the legality of the decision the Daughters pleaded that Miss Anderson also was denied the use of the auditorium at the all-white Central High School for exactly the same reason.

A torrent of abusive criticism broke loose on these two principal offenders. *Statement re Constitution Hall* maintains a dignified silence on the subject. The reader is left with the impression that the Society and the District's Board of Education were martyrs in a controversy about a municipal custom over which they had no control.

In some ways this is true. In retrospect, the Marian Anderson "incident" is seen more clearly for what it actually was: the earliest organized civil-rights test case to dramatize the impropriety of the stringent segregationist rules then existing in the capital. It is quite possible that the civil-rights movement recognized the advantage of implicating the powerful DAR as a symbolic scapegoat. The Society's ultrareactionary reputation made the Daughters a perfect example for an injustice universally practiced. The Daughters' unpopularity in liberal circles assured loud publicity to the injustices of segregation.

At the moment, emotions ran so high that it was forgotten that no theater or auditorium would allow the concert. The DAR position might have found more sympathy if Hand had seen fit to qualify his decision or even if he had been more tactful.

Instead, his directness created such unanimous resentment that a mass meeting of 1,500 irate Washingtonians followed in the wake of Hand's statement. The "Marian Anderson Protest Committee" resulted from the meeting. The Daughters were in hot water. Not only were they denounced by the committee but indignant letters poured in from all over the country.

With public temper reaching a boiling point, on February 19 Cohen tried to hire Central High's auditorium for Miss Anderson. Dr. F. W. Ballou, superintendent of schools, refused to consider the application, and the Board of Education was picketed on the 20th. On the 27th, Mrs. Eleanor Roosevelt sent a wire of encouragement to the committee's secretary, James E. Scott. On the same day, she indicated that she planned to resign from an organization that she only had joined "upon request" and whose views she found contrary to her own. Although she refrained from naming the society, everyone took it for granted it was the DAR.

Reporters received little satisfaction when they rushed to 1776 D Street for verification of the news of Mrs. Roosevelt's letter. Mrs. Robert was out of town; her secretary was at home ill; and if Mrs. Roosevelt had written, it was supposed her letter must be among unopened mail piling up on the President General's desk. However, speaking from Boston, Mrs. Frank Leon Nason, DAR registrar general, said that if a resignation were forthcoming she was the proper person to receive it and she had not. Mrs. Robert broke her silence on March 1 from Phoenix, Arizona. She explained that any discussion of the topic "would be contrary to our policy . . . There are members admitted and some drop out, but we never discuss these matters. It simply is not done." Mrs. Roosevelt herself cleared up the mystery. In her March 6 Scripps-Howard column she finally acknowledged that it was the DAR she had had in mind and that she had resigned. Even then, Mrs. Nason refused to verify the receipt of her papers.

Even during the hapless tussle with the District's Board of Education, the DAR remained the focal point of the controversy. All week tensions mounted. A *New York Times* editorial wanted to know if the refusal to rent Constitution Hall to Miss Anderson was based on grounds of social or racial snobbery and hoped the astonishing action reflected only the opinion of a few irresponsible officers rather than the true organizational feelings.

The Reverend Elmore M. McKee, rector of a fashionable Episcopal church in New York, called the whole affair "quite pagan." His views appeared in the weekly church bulletin, and, joined by his curates, he requested his parish committee to give consideration to the deep issues represented in the incident. He advised them to second Heywood Broun's suggestion to arrange a Marian Anderson concert on a national hookup on Easter Sunday. At a luncheon in the Hotel Commodore, a thousand members of the American League for Peace and Democracy expressed their disapproval by prolonged hissing when old DAR enemy Bishop McConnell branded the Daughters "Mothers of Fascism."

The society also was bitterly criticized by prominent educators, politicians, and Miss Anderson's fellow artists. A telegram personally addressed to "Mrs. Henry M. Robert, Jr., DAR President," and signed by Deems Taylor, Charles K. Gilbert, Oliver La Farge, and a host of others, read in part:

"This action . . . subverts the clear meaning of the United States Constitution and particularly the Bill of Rights . . . and places your organization . . . in the camp of those who today seek to destroy democracy, justice and liberty . . ." Although perhaps she never had occasion to visit the premises in the past, the film star Sylvia Sidney stoutly maintained that she refused to "set foot" in the hall again unless the DAR apologized to Marian Anderson. When Jascha Heifetz arrived in Washington for a concert scheduled at Constitution Hall, he declared that he was ashamed to appear. This must have hurt, because the great violinist was a favorite of the Daughters.

New York's Mayor Fiorello La Guardia and Senator Robert F. Wagner kept up a harangue, and finally, on March 3, a mightier voice than theirs joined the hue and cry. It was no less a personage than Harold L. Ickes, Secretary of the Interior, who explained that as early as January 30 he had sent Mrs. Robert a personal letter to inquire if the original refusal had been based on racial regulations. He admitted receiving a reply from Mrs. Robert but did not divulge its contents. Leaving the matter open, he delicately emphasized his feeling of deep concern.

On the same day, under all this pressure, the Board of Education reversed its decision by a vote of 6 to 2 and said Miss Anderson could appear at Central High School provided assurance was given that the concession would set no precedent and that the board would not again be asked "to depart from the principle of a dual system of schools and school policies." When the sponsors found the conditions unacceptable Dr. Ballou withdrew the offer.

Shortly thereafter, the protest committee hinted that Miss Anderson might give an outdoor concert. On March 30 Secretary Ickes proclaimed that, as supervisor of memorials and parks, he was proud to offer Lincoln Memorial to Miss Anderson for a free half-hour recital at 5 P.M. on Easter Sunday.

An integrated audience of 70,000 jostled together to hear the distinguished artist, and the Blue Network carried her voice from coast to coast. The concert was without precedent.

It did more to quicken American sympathy for civil rights than any other single act since the Emancipation Proclamation.

The ignominious part the Daughters had played in the drama was emphasized even in this moment of triumph. In his introduction of Miss Anderson, Secretary Ickes reminded the audience: "There are those, even in this great capital of our democratic Republic, who are either too timid or too indifferent to lift the light that Jefferson and Lincoln carried."

The DAR rode out the storm in a dignified silence. Its forty-ninth Congress came less than two weeks after Miss Anderson's historic performance. Only on this belated occasion did Mrs. Robert divulge the rule prohibiting two attractions in one day at Constitution Hall. She said nothing more in defense of the DAR position except to reiterate that blame for existing segregation regulations must not rest on the Society but on the community. (A more logical explanation was offered by certain Howard University officials. They recalled that soon after the completion of Constitution Hall, a series of Roland Hayes concerts was being arranged. A "house rule" of the hall allowed Negroes to sit in the balcony, but Hayes insisted on an integrated audience. The management was considering making the concession, but some season subscribers offered such bitter objections that the concerts were canceled. To avoid future embarrassing complications the "White Artists Only" law went into effect.)

In her speech to the DAR congress, Mrs. Robert mentioned no names, not even that of Miss Anderson. She referred to the situation as the "incident." The word still retains this special meaning in the vocabulary of present-day members.

Mrs. Roosevelt's resignation caused almost as much public stir as the "incident" itself. A Gallup poll showed that 67 percent of the country approved of her reasons for leaving the organization. Again Daughters were tight-lipped to outsiders, but among themselves they were bitter and vocal. Some felt it was technically impossible for a life member to resign. Others said they did not care if she did; they were glad to be rid of her. They sniffed that, at the time of Mrs. Roosevelt's admission, the Society's genealogists had chosen to ignore the embarrassing discovery that every one of her Revolutionary ancestors was collateral.

That year the White House reception was held as usual, but Mrs. Roosevelt was out of town. Giving as an excuse a year-old promise to help celebrate a grandson's birthday in Seattle, Washington, she had arranged for certain Cabinet wives to appear as substitute hostesses. Nevertheless, her absence was so conspicuous that a society columnist of the *Washington Times-Herald* tittered: "So Mrs. Roosevelt is going to Seattle for the DAR Congress."

The guests went through the affair with ladylike endurance, but, when a routine resolution of thanks for the reception came before them the next day, the angry Daughters showed their true feelings. After the resolution was read, Mrs. Robert called for "Ayes." No "Nays" were called for, and one ruffled delegate rose to ask why. The President General stiffly reminded her that "courtesy" measures customarily were passed by a unanimous vote. After a frigid pause, a second disgruntled Daughter asked point blank if Mrs. Roosevelt had made personal arrangements for the reception. She received a hasty assurance that a lengthy correspondence had ensued between the First Lady and the DAR leader. Here the flurry ended. "Peace and harmony" was restored to the Society by parliamentary procedure. A steady hand at the helm saved the Daughters from further ridicule.

Marian Anderson finally did sing at Constitution Hall, on January 7, 1943. Moreover, she appeared at the request of the organization. The DAR was sponsoring a series of concerts to aid war victims, and Miss Anderson was invited to perform for the benefit of China Relief. She agreed, providing the "Jim Crow" seating arrangement was abandoned for the evening and not resumed in the future. The Board accepted the first condition but rejected the second. Miss Anderson decided not to press the latter point, and for the first time in Washington's history, Negroes enjoyed complete integration in a place of public entertainment. However, an important technicality undercut the force of this event. Since a benefit is not subject to ordinary management rules, the concession to Miss Anderson had no effect in deleting the "White Artists Only" clause from professional contracts.

The Marian Anderson–DAR controversy is still vivid in the memory of many Americans, but it often is forgotten that the question of segregation again made headlines during the 1945–1946 season of booking engagements for Constitution Hall. This time the first disappointed artist was Hazel Scott, who was married to Republican Adam Clayton Powell, Jr., during the summer of 1945. On October 1 her booking agent announced that Miss Scott had been denied the use of Constitution Hall for a concert on October 20.

Having learned the wisdom of tact through bitter experience, Fred E. Hand made a prompt apology. He added that although Constitution Hall was definitely out of the question, he would be glad to help the pianist find a suitable auditorium. He revealed that he had rendered the same service satisfactorily for Paul Robeson on a previous occasion.

Both Miss Scott and her agent spurned the offer. Her new husband was so injured by the treatment of his wife that he wrote to President Harry S Truman, demanding immediate action against the DAR for practicing discrimination. He sent another letter to Mrs. Truman, urging her not to attend a DAR tea scheduled for October 11.

On that day a *New York Times* editorial disclosed the contents of Powell's letter to Truman and the President's reply. In it, Truman compared the DAR policy to Nazism but said he was unable to interfere because the Society was a private enterprise. The editorial was careful to point out that Truman's statement was not entirely correct. It explained that the Daughters of the American Revolution originally had been incorporated by an act of Congress as a tax-exempt organization. One of its purposes was to "secure for all mankind the blessings of liberty." The charter gave the Society certain privileges not enjoyed by other organizations, among them the right to store its collections at the Smithsonian or the National Gallery if room could not be found for them elsewhere. Under the circumstances, the *Times* continued, the DAR should not regard itself as an exclusive social club but as a public institution with a public moral responsibility. At all times it should be ready to use its property in the best interests of the American people. The conclusion of the editorial was that, by banning Negro artists, the Society was belying the ideals specified in its charter.

Later the press revealed Mrs. Truman's personal reply to Representative Powell. In it, she also had "deplored" the regulation barring the appearance of Miss Scott but rejected the congressman's suggestion to be absent from the tea. She said it would be improper because she had accepted the invitation prior to any trouble.

Mrs. Truman was known to be a Daughter, and some critics felt that her loyalty to the Society exceeded her concern for civil rights. Powell denounced her decision, calling it weak in comparison to Mrs. Roosevelt's stand during the Marian Anderson case, and at a Harlem rally, he openly criticized the President as well by saying: "I don't see how anyone can compare the action of the DAR with Nazism and then let his wife sit down and have tea with the Hitlers."

The rally was held under the auspices of the "People's D.A.R." an organization formed by Powell only two days after the fateful DAR tea party. Its initials stood for "Drive Against Reactionaryism." The group's first act was to send a telegram to President Truman demanding that tax exemption be denied the Society.

It became apparent that the new protagonists were in deadly earnest and threatened to suck the life blood out of the DAR. By October 18, two bills had been introduced in the House to withdraw treasured privileges from the DAR. Representative Emanuel Celler, New York Democrat, offered a sweeping measure to revoke its charter. A more moderate bill was proposed by Mrs. Helen Gahagan Douglas, Democratic representative of California. She wanted to withhold tax exemption on Constitution Hall unless the Daughters rented it without regard to "race, creed, color or national origin." Although Mrs. Douglas probably meant a fair real-estate tax on the entire building, the piece of legislation was somewhat ill advised because the Society did pay taxes on receipts from hiring the hall to outsiders. Mrs. Charles Carroll Haig, DAR Treasurer General, was able to confuse the issue by stating that for the year ending March 31, 1945, the organization had been responsible for $6,346.92 in taxes. The amount seemed like a mere pittance on such a valuable piece of property, but it was enough to weaken the effect of Mrs. Douglas' proposal.

During the House debate the atmosphere was rowdy. Representative John Rankin thundered that the attack on the DAR was communist inspired. He was shouted down by Congressman Coffee of Washington, who insisted it was a disgrace to draw the color line in a tax-free building. Coffee's stirring speech was greeted by wild applause from the galleries.

Nationwide resentment against the stubborn DAR stand ran so high that one New Jersey judge actually forbade the Daughters to distribute DAR *Manuals* to new citizens in his Trenton naturalization court. In Waterbury, Connecticut, a senior-high-school girl refused a Good Citizen's Pilgrimage Award, saying she wanted no award sponsored by a Society that barred Miss Anderson and Miss Scott from its premises. On January 16, 1946, *The New York Times* announced again on the editorial page the rejection of a DAR American history prize by an elementary school pupil.

Within the Society itself there also was evidence of discontent. The National Board disdained to comment, but it could not be hidden that "peace and harmony" was sadly lacking in the rank and file. As early as mid-October, Dr. Emanuel Chapman, chairman of the Committee of Catholics for Human Rights, urged Catholic Daughters to protest and resign if the leaders did not change their attitude. During the same month, the LeRoy Chapter in New York adopted a resolution opposing the stand of the National Society, and many other chapters followed suit. The Polly Wyckoff Chapter, oldest of two units in Bergen County, New Jersey, was more explicit. It made a public disavowal of any necessity for the organization to abide by "prevailing customs" in the District of Columbia. Its protest pointed out that DAR headquarters was not a local Washington city possession but belonged to women all over the country who should rise above stupid racial prejudice.

After Mrs. Truman's first statement to Powell, she remained

quietly on the sidelines, showing no aspiration to assume Mrs. Roosevelt's role in the current uproar. Instead, Connecticut's Congresswoman Clare Boothe Luce was the public personage to seize Mrs. Roosevelt's banner. As a member of the Putnam Hill Chapter of Greenwich, she sent a telegram from Washington urging her local group to form a resolution opposing the denial of the hall to Hazel Scott and threatened to resign if they failed to do so.

In spite of the prospect of losing such an illustrious member, the ladies of Putnam Hill gathered together on November 1, with a record attendance of three times the size of an ordinary meeting, and voted 48–2 to abide by the executive ruling of March 23, 1932, which had made the "white artists only" clause effective. Although they admitted that Negroes had performed at their own chapter house, they felt it imperative to sustain the stand of the National Board. The Putnam Hill decision was a good indication that the Board had started to deploy the faithful to hold the line against "troublemakers."

Rudely repudiated by her home group, Mrs. Luce moderated her original vow to resign and began to look for a Connecticut chapter with compatible views. On November 29, she transferred membership to a Fairfield group that had filed a strong protest. If the Daughters mistook her change of heart as a gesture of obeisance to the will of the hierarchy, they were soon to have a rude awakening. Congresswoman Luce simply was biding her time.

The Hazel Scott "incident" dragged to a dreary, frustrating close. With no shining victory such as the Marian Anderson concert at Lincoln Memorial, both bills limiting the privileges of the DAR had died in the House. The Board showed no inclination to relax its decision; nevertheless, discontent still ran high within the Society. It again flared up on the eve of George Washington's birthday, 1946, when Howard Taubman disclosed in *The New York Times* that Eddie Condon's jazz band was the latest victim of the restriction. In this case, color was not mentioned at all. Fred Hand had another convenient rule up his sleeve. He said:

This auditorium, owned by the Daughters of the American Revolution, operates under a policy which is most restrictive as to the type of attraction we may play. One of these restrictions prevents us playing any jazz bands, not because of the attraction itself, but because of the type of audience which attends and which in some cases may be very destructive.

During negotiations, Taubman said that Condon's agent, Jerome H. Cargill, had offered to post a $100,000 bond. Hand refused to listen. Cargill pointed out that Condon had had five concerts at Carnegie Hall and had toured the country, playing at places like Boston's Symphony Hall, without rowdyism. He also pointed out that sixteen members of the band were white. However, these inducements didn't alter Hand's decision. He regretted that it was impossible to let Condon use Constitution Hall.

Suddenly the Daughters' most dissatisfied member, Mrs. Luce, had the chance she was waiting for. On the evening of February 21, she went on the air to make a nationwide appeal for all Daughters to join in a united effort to eliminate the "White Artist Only" clause. She insisted that there were absolutely no grounds for the plea that Washington statutes forced the insertion of the ruling into the Society's by-laws. In a witty and brilliant speech she laid the blame for the continuance of the clause directly on the incumbent President General, Mrs. Julius Y. Talmadge.

This was the same Mrs. Talmadge who had tried to keep the youth of the south uncontaminated by Mrs. Mead's pacifist lectures. Affectionately known as the "Georgia Peach" within the Society, Mrs. Talmadge was the first southerner to be elected to the high office. The coincidence played right into Mrs. Luce's hand. With tongue in cheek, she baited the leader by saying:

See here, Mrs. Talmadge of Athens, Georgia, you are a fine woman and a gracious lady, but whether you will admit it or not, in your deep concern for white faces you are paradoxically enough giving our D.A.R. a couple of black eyes by insisting on this clause in our Constitution Hall contract.

Mrs. Talmadge disdained to answer the barrage. There matters rested until April 4, when Mrs. Luce announced the formation of the DAR Committee Against Racial Discrimination in Constitution Hall. It consisted of herself and nine other Daughters, all of whom emphatically refused to consider withdrawal from the society as a means of protest. The Committee had an "impartial non-DAR" secretary, Dr. Marianna Chesterton-Mangle, who was a writer and lecturer on interracial problems.

It immediately contacted all Daughters who had expressed disapproval of the ban, asking them also not to resign but, instead, to sponsor protests in their various chapters. In this way, the opposition hoped to show sufficient strength to force the issue before the fifty-fifth Congress, which, because of the Society's wartime exodus from Washington, would convene on May 20 in Atlantic City. The committee also suggested that whenever possible dissenters should try to be selected as delegates or at least make sure that delegates representing them shared the same views.

Mrs. Talmadge was on tour, visiting various state conventions, and could not be reached for comment. "Silence is golden" seemed to be the unanimous password of the organization. When approached, a New York official was frigid. In her opinion, the clause was a matter of discussion for the national officers alone. Later it was discovered that as early as October 1945 Mrs. Talmadge had sent a circular letter to 3,000 chapters directing members to refrain from public comment.

The situation was further complicated by a refusal to allow the Tuskegee Institute Choir use of the hall on June 1. When Mrs. Luce heard of the new affront, she immediately sent a telegram to Mrs. Talmadge, urging the Board to reconsider the request "lest once more DAR's all over the country are forced to apologize." Mrs. Talmadge finally was harassed into words. In a return wire, she declared that the case for the Tuskegee Choir was being hindered rather than helped by the "so-called" committee, which she said was "illegal and masquerading under false pretenses" of fighting for integration. She insisted its real purpose was to incite revolt against the President General and the National Board.

Mrs. Luce was not the only one to recognize the value of surprises. As the time for Congress approached, Mrs. Talmadge suddenly announced that the Tuskegee Choir would sing at Constitution Hall on June 3 and that there would be no charge for the hall or for the services of DAR employees. The proceeds of the concert would be contributed to the United Negro College Fund, a philanthropic project benefiting thirty-three Negro institutions. "This is a most worthy undertaking and we will help in every way to make it a splendid financial success," Mrs. Talmadge concluded.

To the uninformed, Mrs. Talmadge might have seemed to be waving a white flag, but Mrs. Luce and her committee recognized the benevolent gesture for what it was. The real issue had been by-passed. The Marian Anderson recital for China Relief had shown that benefits did nothing whatever to erase the words "white artists only" from contracts in professional leases, and the Luce committee was determined to continue the fight to have the clause eliminated.

Dr. Chesterton-Mangle the committee's secretary called the benefit a maneuver to relieve the pressure of threatened action and to quiet further public censure. In spite of the feint, she said a resolution had been submitted to strike out the offending clause. Its author was Mrs. Denny Vann, another committee member, who belonged to the original protest group, the Polly Wyckoff Chapter. Dr. Chesterton-Mangle revealed that even if a loophole were found to table Mrs. Vann's resolution, hundreds of other chapters had filed similar petitions.

Mrs. Talmadge admitted the receipt of Mrs. Vann's resolution but announced that it would not be reported; that, in fact, the coming Congress planned no action on the clause. Mrs. Talmadge had devised a clever scheme to evade the issue. On the opening day of Congress, she informed delegates that the Board had appointed a special committee to investigate the matter of leases. At the same time, she made it perfectly clear that although the Board was willing to consider the recommendations of its chosen committee, it would retain absolute power over the final decision on acceptability of rental applicants.

Charging that the present fight was motivated by "politics and publicity," Mrs. Talmadge declared that banned artists had reaped a million dollars' worth of free advertising out of the controversy. She bitterly attacked "the little band of women" who had taken it upon themselves to challenge the wisdom of the leaders of the Society.

Above all, she accused Congresswoman Luce of stirring up racial and sectional discord by her February 21 speech, which, as she reminded the Daughters, had been read into the *Congressional Record*. She quoted at length from the address, stressing the "couple of black eyes" section. Playing for sympathy, she said the personal attack on her place of birth demonstrated to what lengths the antagonists would go in order to create dissension within the ranks.

Eager reporters flocked to Atlantic City. To their disappointment, Mrs. Luce failed to attend the Congress, but she soon showed a marked ability to manipulate the course of events from a distance. Her first move was to send a telegram to the Resolutions Committee. Issuing a demand for the clause to come to the vote, Mrs. Luce reminded committee members that she knew quite well how a reactionary chairman and a small minority could pigeonhole or defeat a measure.

She had every right to be wary. Mrs. Grace Lincoln Hall Brosseau was chairman of the 1946 Resolutions Committee. In an interview on opening day, she heaped disdain on her adversaries by saying, "When a person who has never been to a DAR meeting in her life forms a group of dissenters, they don't even rate." While never underestimating her opponent's talents, Mrs. Brosseau was sure she had parliamentary means at her disposal to quell the revolt.

She was relying on a hard, fast rule that prohibited the establishment of any organization committee without the full sanction of the Society. Working on this premise, Mrs. Brosseau lost little time at the business session in introducing a resolution declaring that the Luce committee was illegal, was unconstitutional, and had to be dissolved. A chorus of deafening "Ayes" left no doubt about the mood of most delegates. The sound hardly had died away before Mrs. Brosseau offered a second resolution, calling for a show of "implicit confidence" in the ability of the National Board to reach a "wise solution" to any controversial question that might arise. Again came a roar of "Ayes" followed by wild applause.

In spite of Dr. Chesterton-Mangle's optimism, the dissenters had not succeeded in capturing many seats, nor had they managed to exert much influence on the delegates sent to represent them.

No petitions similar to Mrs. Vann's were forthcoming, but in spite of the sheeplike acquiescence to the will of the hierarchy, Mrs. Vann refused to withdraw her motion and insisted on staying at Congress to see if it would be reported. In derision, Mrs. Brosseau pointed out that the resolution in question was "just a side issue now," but Mrs. Vann was brave enough to stand her ground.

The next day, Mrs. Luce released a statement explaining that her committee could not be dissolved since it was not official. Its letterhead plainly read that it was made up of a "voluntary group of members of the DAR." As such, the Congress had no jurisdiction over its actions. This again gave Mrs. Vann a legitimate claim to force the reading of her resolution.

Mrs. Brosseau was flustered. She fumed, "We are not going to take orders from Clare Luce." Illogically, she insisted that if some other member—a State Regent, for instance—had introduced the measure it would have gone through "like a breeze." She recalled that as a fellow member of Mrs. Luce in the Putnam Hill Chapter, she had attended the meeting that had repudiated the congresswoman, and Mrs. Luce's threat to resign had made little impression on the gathering. Everyone seemed willing for her to go ahead and get out if she wanted to.

Mrs. Brosseau claimed that the Board had received numerous letters from Negroes who upheld the DAR stand and insisted that the present fight was hurting their cause. However, when asked, she failed to give the names of any correspondents.

Pressed for the reason why she refused to report the measure, her only excuse was that too many other important matters deserved consideration.

No matter how much Mrs. Brosseau might try to hedge, the fact remained that the committee had been clever enough to force the hand of the Board. On the final day, shortly before adjournment and after some backstage maneuvering, Mrs. Vann finally was permitted to come to the platform and read the committee's proposal. It was greeted by jeers and uncontrolled laughter, but, much to the surprise and disappointment of the 4,000 members assembled, Mrs. Vann had the last word. As soon as she finished reading the resolution, she withdrew it, depriving the delegates of the satisfaction of voting it down. After the meeting she admitted that she knew she would take a "fearful licking" if a vote were taken, but she expressed complete satisfaction in having the motion aired in public.

Not long thereafter, the Society lost two distinguished members. Not only did Mrs. Luce resign, but also Republican Congresswoman Frances Bolton, a multimillionairess who compared her erstwhile fellow members to Lot's wife, who was turned to salt for looking backward. "Unless the organization promotes active work for better national and international conditions, then fiddle de doo with the DAR."

# XII
## CAT'S CRADLE

Because of their negative attitude toward every New Deal measure, the Daughters were awarded few plaudits by the Roosevelt administration during World War II. Assured of colossal appropriations, the armed forces had no special missions for the Society to perform. The DAR were forced to accept the role of plain civilians.

Nevertheless, they subscribed over $200 million in War Bonds, financed a large fleet of Bloodmobiles to collect much-needed plasma, filled at least 197,000 "buddy bags" for GIs overseas, donated generous gifts to individual branches of the services—including a steel-encased electric Hammond organ to an airplane carrier—and even lent their "home" to the Red Cross, their old rival and neighbor. From 1943 to 1947 the Daughters went into four years of voluntary exile, meeting first in Chicago, then Cincinnati, then New York, and finally Atlantic City.

Some members felt that the organization's charter might be revoked if a DAR Congress was not held in Washington for two consecutive years. It was deemed prudent to consult the President before reaching a decision. Roosevelt hastily brushed aside the possibility of any penalty. Giving them his blessing, he declared that the Society was rendering the nation a great patriotic service by relieving congestion in the capital.

Roosevelt's praise was one of the few acts of official recognition they were to receive until 1945, when the State Department invited the Society to send "observers" to watch the United Nations draw up and sign its original charter. Two delighted Daughters attended the historic San Francisco conference. They were President General Talmadge and Honorary President General Becker, the former loyalty-oath champion, who again was serving as chairman of the National Defense Committee.

Both ladies stressed the honor of being given the assignment. Forty-two national organizations had been invited to send repre-

sentatives, but the NSDAR was the only woman's patriotic association among them. The compliment seemed to have restored a
much-needed luster to DAR prestige.

At the 1946 Atlantic City Congress the unpleasant Constitution Hall "incidents" were forgotten long enough for both ladies
to give their impressions of the memorable occasion. Because of
commitments to visit western chapters, Mrs. Talmadge had attended only the opening sessions. However, she described the
meeting as "impressive and thrilling," calling it the most "satisfying experience" of her year. Mrs. Becker, who "observed"
during the entire three-month period, also claimed the occasion
as "one in a lifetime . . . thought-provoking . . . stimulating."

Their expression of enthusiasm seemed to indicate that
Daughters might be more in sympathy with the United Nations
concept of international relations than they had been with the
League of Nations. However, in spite of Mrs. Becker's lavish
praise for the conference, her speech, as it continued, developed
a more qualified tone. She pointed out that under its charter the
UN was set up as international machinery to make and keep
peace through cooperation between national governments in the
continuing Council of Nations and that there was a grave differ-
ence between this idea and that of world government, which
would destroy national sovereignty. She warned members to
beware of speakers who were beginning to flood the country
with the insidious propaganda that a new world government or
world union was the only possible means of keeping peace. The
NSDAR was vigorously opposed to the latter program, she declared, and no Daughter should join any organization favoring
aspects of one-world planning.

The 1946 UN resolution reflected Mrs. Becker's caution.
While the DAR pledged support to the new body, it put itself
squarely on record for more "affirmative education to prevent
confusion of the United Nations plan for world responsibility
with any plan for world government involving world citizenship, universal currency, free trade, and the dominance of the
United States by any other nation." World government implied
that a world court could make rulings on our domestic affairs.

The DAR opposition to the United Nations is based on a deep-seated fear of this danger.

To the intense relief of the Society, the Senate also recognized the potential threat of handing over limitless power to an international organization. It sanctioned America's entry into the UN only after the insertion of the Connally Reservation (or Amendment). The amendment, limiting the jurisdiction of a world court over internal matters except "as determined by the United States," was hailed by the DAR as the "six classic words" that would save the country from a sinister fate.

The Daughters hastened to emphasize the fact that elected state representatives, not the executive arm of the government, was the legal treaty-making body. They reminded other Americans that this was the greatest blessing of our constitutional rights and implored them to restrain the administrative branch from usurping legislative power as it had been trying to do ever since the advent of the New Deal.

The Daughters' exile ended in 1947, and they finally returned to Washington. Mrs. Talmadge chose the title of "The Eagle Wings" for her homecoming message. Resolutions passed that year showed that, although satisfied with the apparent protection of the Connally Reservation, the Daughters were going through a period of watchful waiting. At the first suggestion of a new attempt to subject this country to international control, they were ready to bare their talons.

In 1948 world federalists held an international conference. They decided that in order to become an effective force the United Nations had to be transformed into a federal world government and strongly recommended an immediate amendment of the UN charter to increase its authority. This meant that the Connally Reservation was endangered.

This was not the first time world federalists had expressed these views, nor would it be the last. Most Americans had become so inured to similar pronouncements that the recommendation received scant attention outside DAR circles. Sympathy for the movement was so weak in the United States that in 1950 President Truman came out firmly against participation in any international plan; the State Department gave the Senate explicit advice to draft no favorable resolutions, and Cordell Hull, former Secretary of State, predicted that, even if drafted, the resolution would be allowed to die in committee.

However, the Daughters were taking no chances on the possibility of a national referendum. They went into action as soon as world government proposals were taken under advisement by individual states. On August 8, 1949, Mrs. Roscoe C. O'Byrne, the new DAR leader, announced that the NSDAR intended to lead many other organizations in a drive to thwart the "one-worlders' " plot. Mrs. O'Byrne failed to name the "other organizations" and neglected to make clear by what right the Society assumed leadership. It is generally supposed that the Daughters worked mostly on their own and became so involved in the tremendous task that finally they took full credit for safeguarding America's sovereignty almost single-handed.

The campaign continued into the term of the next President General, Mrs. James B. Patton of Columbus, Ohio, widow of a prosperous lumber dealer, who intensified the effort. In New York, where the federalist movement was expected to find some favor, a torrent of protest letters and telegrams poured into the state legislature, and because of them, the bill never reached the floor in Albany. In 1951, when anti world-government bills had been adopted by most states, a DAR resolution commended the "valiant work" of the Society for being instrumental in turning the tide in twenty-two of them.

That year, and for several more to come, the Daughters gave a routine nod of approval to the UN. However, they also passed five resolutions indicating disapproval of specific aspects of the organization. Two resolutions concerned the supremacy of the American flag within the jurisdiction of our country. One of these, a pet since 1948, urged legislation to assure the Stars and Stripes its "place of honor" over the new UN emblem. The other vowed to resist a movement "to supplant the pledge of allegiance to the United States flag with a universal pledge of allegiance and the U.S. National Anthem with a UN anthem." They also voiced the first strong opposition to the Covenant of Human Rights and the Genocide Treaty though neither one had been ratified by the Senate and both seem unlikely to find favor in the predictable future.

The covenant states that no one shall be subjected to cruel and inhuman treatment; all are equal before law and, without discrimination, entitled to equal protection. The Genocide Treaty proposes that acts of individual and group destruction, such as those perpetrated by Hitler, are a crime under international law in peace and war alike.

UN supporters hail both measures as the most humanitarian regulations conceived in modern times. The Daughters call the covenant an attempt by a "few to dictate one set of rights for all people of the world regardless of background, traditions, achievements and belief." Their deep-seated objection is that a communist conception of human rights replaces the Christian one; state, rather than God, acts as the determinant.

The Daughters feel that we don't need the Genocide Treaty because "we have no laws that approve these inhuman principles" of mass murder—that, in fact, "these actions are against the moral and civil laws of this country." Above all, the treaty sustains their fear of Americans being tried in a court higher than our own. Particular exception is taken to Article II, section b, which deals with "bodily or mental harm" done to members of national, ethnic, racial, or religious groups. The word "mental" is fraught with danger. DAR literature constantly reminds members that an injured party could press charges of "mental harm" against a person who refused to hire him, or fired him, or would not let him join an organization (public or private). The so-called "culprit" could be punished under Article II, section b. The judgment would be out of the hands of the United States, placed in those of the genocide convention, and the trial would take place in any corner of the globe where the genocide court happened to be sitting. DAR arguments against the Genocide Treaty generally end by posing the Kafkaesque question. "How would 'you' like to be tried in some foreign land just because someone accused 'you' of doing harm to some ethnic group?"

The fifth and most important resolve in 1951 was a demand for stricter legislative control over all global agreements and treaties to ensure the supremacy of both state and national

American laws. This was a direct reflection of a bill recently introduced into the Senate by John W. Bricker and Harry F. Byrd, which had suddenly awakened Americans to a new peril that even the Connally Reservation could not restrain. The Constitution plainly states that treaty commitments made by the executive branch of the government need not be ratified by Congress and are binding unless ruled unconstitutional by the Supreme Court. In the past, most executive treaties had concerned only territorial fishing rights or boundary lines, but the power could be interpreted to encompass UN treaties concerned with political, economic, and social rights. It was the contention of the senators that unless the Constitution was amended to limit treaty power, our national sovereignty could be eroded by being made subject to UN rulings without the consent of the people.

The Bricker-Byrd disclosures caused such a hubbub in patriotic circles that the Sons of the American Revolution immediately repudiated the United Nations. Both Bricker and Byrd were loyal Sons. A 1953 DAR magazine lists other SAR senators of the eighty-third Congress who were: Homer E. Capehart, Price Daniel, James H. Duff, Carl Hayden; Bourke B. Hickenlooper, Estes Kefauver, William F. Knowland, Edward Martin, A. S. "Mike" Monroney, Wayne Morse, Richard B. Russell, Leverett Saltonstall, and Robert A. Taft. There were also twenty-one members in the House, including Franklin D. Roosevelt, Jr.

Although the Daughters did not take a decisive step as soon as the Sons, from that time forward they also sounded a perennial alarm about the inherent risk of the United States remaining within the United Nations.

The Daughters have been far from successful in arousing the fears of the general American public, but the incessant repetition of GET THE US OUT OF THE UN AND THE UN OUT OF THE US—a slogan they picked up from the Sons—has earned them more adverse criticism than any of their other activities in the cold-war period.

Budget-minded Daughters are constantly concerned about the financial arrangements of the United Nations. They urge Congress to tighten the national purse strings and criticize both houses for allowing the administrative arm of the government to squander taxpayers' money on a number of UN agencies from which America derives no benefit though it pays the lion's share for their support. They see this as a wanton drain of our great resources and part of a gigantic Russian plot to so weaken us that a communist-dominated UN will have us at its mercy.

This is one of the many reasons the DAR finds fault with all UN agencies. The first to arouse their wrath was UNESCO. Republican Representative John T. Wood of Idaho was primarily responsible for bringing its imperfections to the Daughters' attention. On October 18, 1951, he read from the floor of the House a newsletter published by an obscure organization called the American Flag Committee. The newsletter attacked all UNESCO literature and claimed that a set of nine pamphlets called *Towards World Understanding* was particularly obnoxious because the series directed teachers to eliminate educational methods and classroom material designed to foster a natural love for and loyalty to the United States of America. Half a million reprints of Congressman Wood's speech were in circulation by the spring of 1952 and as late as 1963, two-cent copies were still on sale in the lobby of Constitution Hall.

The 1952 DAR Congress pushed a steamroller of forty-five resolutions through the business session. One, surprisingly, opposed drafting women into the armed services or industry because this would "lead to the breakdown of family life and the moral structure of the nation." Another, demanding a joint congressional investigation of our gold supply at Fort Knox, inspired former President Truman to suggest that if the Daughters were so interested in the gold count why didn't they go to Kentucky and conduct it themselves?

Other motions offered fierce defiance to liberal domestic issues of tax increase, socialized medicine, and federal school aid, but the bulk of the resolutions concentrated on the management of the United Nations. Resolution 25 voted that no United States funds should be appropriated to UN agencies without previous study and consent of Congress. Resolution 13 condemned *Towards World Understanding* and demanded instant withdrawal of these pamphlets from the public schools. The

Society pointed out that since the series had been printed "largely at the expense of the American taxpayer," it was disgraceful for it to discourage a belief in nationalism among youthful citizens.

The tone of the Congress prompted Mrs. Eleanor Roosevelt's remark that although she knew there were many fine women in the DAR, she believed the era was "too dangerous for any group to pass resolutions without careful study."

The criticism did not seem to ruffle the Daughters. They were basking in the triumph of a July 1952 Department of Defense pronouncement on proper display of the international flag. The ruling specified that the emblem had a rightful place over the UN's New York headquarters at all times, but elsewhere it could be flown only on special occasions and in no case should it ever be larger than, raised to a higher altitude than, or placed in a position superior to the Stars and Stripes. The regulation was identical to the DAR flag resolution, which had been on the books since 1948, and the National Board took full credit for the department's action.

Soon after, Congressman Wood called to the nation's attention another "strange and alien rag" that was desecrating American soil. At the opening of the North Atlantic Treaty Organization's naval installations in Norfolk, Virginia, the NATO banner waved supreme above a semicircle of member nations. This was a blatant violation of the new rule.

President General Patton started "voluminous correspondence and arguments" with the NATO commander, Admiral Lynde D. McCormick, USN. Admiral McCormick insisted that the American flag always was treated with proper respect, but Mrs. Patton had no faith in his protestations. Finally, on August 15, 1953, she and her successor, President General Gertrude S. Carraway (the only unmarried woman ever to become a DAR leader), made a special sortie to Norfolk to "observe" if the admiral was complying with the law. To their intense relief they found the NATO flag relegated to its own headquarters; even "the central flagpole from which it had previously flown had been taken down entirely and the hole where it had stood was filled with cement." Returning to the DAR Washington "home,"

Mrs. Patton said: "Thus, AGAIN a stand of the Daughters of the American Revolution in behalf of 'Due Glory for Old Glory' has been FULLY VINDICATED."

Flag ritual settled, the Daughters once more turned to what they considered the encroachments of the UN. The resolutions of the 1953 Congress were so ill tempered that, at last, a few delegates tried to halt the querulous policy. Mrs. Philip R. Peck, from Glens Falls, New York, was the most eloquent speaker for the opposition. She pointed out that although the National Society professed to support the United Nations, its attitude was always critical or lukewarm in praise. She said that to her knowledge no resolution ever had been submitted that commended a single UN action, and she ended by imploring the Daughters to become a constructive rather than a negative force.

Debate on both sides of the question was unusually open, but it was rudely cut off when Mrs. Frank Leetch of Washington, D.C. declared that the UN would "fall on its face" if America withdrew its financial support. Another Washingtonian, Mrs. Ernest W. Howard, quickly asked why we should care whether the foreign countries liked us or not, adding, "As long as we hold the purse strings they'll love us to death."

In 1955 the DAR repudiated the "atoms for peace" plan, which would pool all atomic energy under United Nations' guardianship. They passed a sweeping resolution declaring that the pool would give "an international oligarchy" a monopoly on atomic energy, enabling it "to hold all nations of the world in terror." Worst of all, it would create "immeasurable potentials for the destruction of the United States by its openly avowed enemies."

President Eisenhower had originated the control plan and considered its adoption imperative. In December 1953, he had made a personal appearance to present his ideas before the UN General Assembly. His proposal met with worldwide acclaim, but almost immediately the NSDAR voiced its official disapproval. In retaliation to the stubborn stand on atoms for peace and other measures favored by the President, the Eisenhowers broke a date to attend the 1955 DAR Congress.

Regardless of ill will toward much of Eisenhower's policy, the

Daughters remained loyal to the Commander in Chief after their own fashion. When the President's health became a political issue in the 1956 campaign, DAR genealogists made a careful search of their records and revealed that for five generations both his male and female progenitors had averaged a seventy-four-year lifespan. This evidence was publicized as an indication of Eisenhower's own life expectancy in spite of his heart condition. Even though Mrs. Eisenhower had become an inactive Daughter when her husband had assumed office, both she and the President seemed unimpressed by this show of goodwill and remained aloof from the activities of the organization after the 1955 Congress.

Not all delegates agreed with the platform adopted in 1955. Mrs. Roswell Tripp of Washington, Connecticut, rose to suggest that before further condemnation of the United Nations, the Society should send accredited "observers" to prove or disprove rumors about its activities. Mrs. Howard sprang up to exclaim that any such action was beneath the dignity of "this great organization." "Let us do our own personal observing," she cried, "and do as our forefathers did when they went out with their clubs or what have you."

Only a few courageous members gave public expression to their disapproval of the Society's official UN stand but the National Board must have been sensitive to the mounting pressure of internal discontent. In 1956, they made a feeble attempt to placate dissenters. Mrs. T. B. Throckmorton, who had been Resolutions chairman for six years, suddenly called her first press conference. During the interview she complained that the NSDAR had been misunderstood on its 1955 atoms for peace resolution. ("We aren't against pooling our atomic know-how with other nations," she said, "if other nations would do likewise.") Then she confessed that she was a "little unhappy" because even "some of our own membership and church women" seemed to be under the illusion that the organization was completely anti-UN. She promised that a resolution would be brought up this year to clarify the official position on the controversial question.

However, at the business session, the liberal minority was

given little satisfaction. Only threadbare proposals appeared on the agenda. One called on the United Nations to "abide by the objectives set forth in its Charter and desist from participation in any plan, project, agency or principle which would *intervene in our internal affairs, interfere with our domestic legislation, or spread doctrines contrary to our American philosophies and way of life.*" Another, the clarifying one, pledged support to the international body in "its ORIGINAL purpose"—sovereign nations voluntarily working together for world peace and understanding. Other 1956 resolutions made it plain that the Daughters were not retreating. This was the first Congress to denounce UNICEF Christmas cards. UNESCO was again a burning issue.

Over the years superpatriots had provoked a number of UNESCO investigations, which had been conducted by the Senate Appropriations Committee, the Chamber of Commerce, and the House Foreign Affairs Committee. None had offered substantial proof of a UNESCO effort to convert American children to one-worldism. Nevertheless, pressure continued, and the probe finally culminated in an Eisenhower appointment of three distinguished Americans to "explore" the agency. The President's representatives found that neither directly nor indirectly was UNESCO encouraging "the substitution of loyalty to and love for super-national authority for loyalty to and love for one's own country as has been alleged in some quarters." They made the flat statement: "UNESCO does not attempt to interfere in the American school system."

In spite of this evidence, the Daughters remained adamant. Even the word of Ray Murphy, former commander of the American Legion, failed to make an impression. After a thorough study, with the aid of a committee, Murphy disclosed that the principal charges against UNESCO could be traced back to the American Flag Committee. He emphasized that this was nothing more than "a one-man organization, virtual successor to the Nationalist Action League which was designated by the president of the United States as 'fascist.' " Murphy's report was presented at the 1955 Legion convention. Legionnaires tossed aside his revelations and passed a motion demanding immediate elimination of all UNESCO material from American schools.

Although Daughters must have had easy access to the Murphy material, they chose to ignore it and the 1956 DAR Congress gave warm commendation to the Legion's 1955 resolution and took similar strong action. They also branded their old enemy the NEA as chief perpetrator in flooding the country with the offensive literature. In this light, Mrs. Throckmorton's press conference protestations were only lip music.

Matters reached a climax when the January 1957 issue of the DAR magazine carried an editorial entitled "Shall We Withdraw?" The article charged that Stalin had been responsible for a postwar world organization and had refused to sign the 1941 Anglo-Russian Mutual Assistance Pact unless Britain agreed to the formation of such an organization. We had become enmeshed in the Russian plot through the undue influence of traitors like Alger Hiss and Harry Dexter White.

The article continued that the only casualty of America's leaving the UN "would be the death of a few naïve and unrealistic ideals held by starry-eyed people in the face of unassailable facts." It proposed that the United Nations' New York real estate could be returned to its original donors and helpfully suggested that the organization could meet in Paris, or, as an afterthought, perhaps the vacant League of Nations buildings in Geneva might be useful. It continued:

> In time, we should be able to establish a framework for economical and political collaboration between free peoples, in which each nation could better its own position by its own efforts, rather than submit to the domination of one of the great powers. Leadership of free peoples is our logical role, rather than our present appeasement and open collaboration with Russia, her satellites and the rising group of neutrals. So long as we are a member of the United Nations we will of necessity assist Russia to her expansion of power. The first step towards resisting her expansion and helping others to save themselves, is to leave the United Nations to Russia, who conceived and created it for her own evil purposes.

In case any member had been careless enough to miss the article in the magazine, "Shall We Withdraw?" was distributed in pamphlet form at the 1957 Congress. It was used as a basis for a resolution, with a qualifying provision. If Red China were admitted to the international body the Daughters called for the United States' withdrawal. Only twenty members were brave enough to stand up in opposition. That year the habitual motion for limited UN support was not mentioned. When asked why it was omitted, Mrs. T. B. Throckmorton, still chairman of the Resolutions Committee, said that no one had submitted such a resolution. She then added that naturally past resolutions remained in force unless repealed.

In 1958, the Society took the final step and made a formal request that the United States Congress withdraw from the United Nations for the following alarming reasons: 1. An anti-Christian philosophy motivates the UN that is hostile to fundamental American principles. 2. Lack of determination in solving the problems of Korea, Hungary, and the Middle East offers proof that the body is a declining factor in maintaining "international peace and security." 3. On numerous occasions the UN has been guilty of abusing diplomatic immunity by harboring international espionage agents. 4. All too often it allows itself to be used as a sounding board for attacks on the capitalist system. 5. While this country foots one-third of the bill, the UN has been developed in such a way that a bloc of small nations can outvote the United States in the General Assembly. 6. By using treaty law to enforce social, industrial, and trade conventions, the UN has the power to shape domestic laws in such a way as to jeopardize rights guaranteed citizens by the Constitution and the Bill of Rights. 7. Without the consent of the taxpayer, American funds are being used to develop a socialized one-world state through United Nations technical assistance programs.

With this ultimatum, the National Board drew the DAR curtain which has been as inflexible in obstructing the view of most members as if it were made of iron or bamboo.

On June 4, 1959, Henry Cabot Lodge, then United States ambassador to the UN, revealed that in 1958 he had written a detailed rebuttal to the DAR charges against the United Nations and offered to appear at their Congress that year to clear up their "virtually total misapprehensions." He repeated the offer in

1959. Both letters were silently tabled, and Lodge was never asked to appear on the DAR platform. In 1959, Democratic Senator Herman Talmadge of Georgia was guest keynote speaker, and his fiery comments on states rights won generous applause. (Although he and former DAR leader Mrs. Julius Y. Talmadge come from the same state and have the same surname, they are not related.)

That year the DAR made its strongest denouncement of UNICEF, its Halloween Trick or Treat project, and its Christmas cards because a substantial portion of its funds went to Russia and her satellites. Earlier legislative investigations had proven beyond doubt that less than 3 percent of all aid from this organization found its way behind the Iron Curtain. On May 8, 1959, *Commonweal* disclosed that the executive director of UNICEF had asked to be allowed to attend the recent DAR Congress and present the true facts about his agency, but as in the case of Ambassador Lodge, the request had been ignored. Mrs. Eleanor Roosevelt sighed and said, "If the good ladies of the D.A.R. really studied UNICEF and did something to help it, they would discover that this U.N. agency is doing a great deal for the children of the world." However, "the good ladies" refused to listen. At best, they sniffed, UNICEF was only doing what church missionaries should and could do better.

The attack seemed so outrageous to a large group of Daughters that the newly elected leader, Mrs. Ashmead White, promised to introduce a more constructive note into the Society's official pronouncements. Nevertheless, by December she seemed to have forgotten her good intentions. That month the DAR magazine published an article called "UNICEF—Cradle of Socialism," which subsequently was reprinted in pamphlet form. It was written by Mrs. Wilson King Barnes, whom Mrs. White had chosen as her national defense director. Mrs. Barnes indulged in some curious flights of fancy.

She declared, for example, that October was becoming a month of triumph for the foes of patriots: It already contained United Nations Day on the 24th, which she gravely suspected "One Worlders" hoped would gradually replace Independence Day as the nation's most important nonreligious holiday. Now

UNICEF was taking over Halloween. To her, it was preposterous for schoolchildren to be encouraged to go from house to house collecting funds for the UN agency "instead of engaging in the usual fun-making and pranks" previously associated with October 31.

Even blacker criticism was directed toward the UNICEF Christmas card series. Mrs. Barnes claimed that the cards were part of "a broader Communist plan to destroy *all* religious beliefs and customs."

This was not the first attempt of the Daughters to regulate Christmas greetings because they failed to symbolize a spirit traditionally associated with the holy day by good Christians. The Hallmark Art Award had felt the sting of their displeasure for giving its 1952 $2,000 prize to Anton Refregier "for a weirdly designed tree with a [Picasso] dove in suspension above it." Brentano's Book Stores, Inc., had been censured in 1953 for their new line of "mischievous" greeting cards that depicted "Santa Claus with a big glass of brandy." Even the Museum of Modern Art was unable to escape criticism when it sold a card picturing "a starved-looking deer, half-skinned with his 'innards' showing like those of a dollar alarm clock." The general trend toward irreverence was shocking enough, but the UNICEF series was particularly outrageous because it offered absolute proof that the United Nations was bent on turning December 25 into "a 'One World Peace Festival' instead of the Birthday of Christ." Otherwise, why sponsor cards utterly devoid of the holy Christmas spirit? The Daughters offered a plan to counteract the destructive force turned loose by UNICEF. A 1962 six-page single-spaced pamphlet called *Facts About UNICEF* carried an announcement that the Society was selling "little noteheads for correspondence." On the front they read: "Greetings —please Don't Send Me a UNICEF Card" and on the back was a list of UNICEF artists and their affiliations with communist-front organizations. The price was modest: 50 for $1.00, 500 for $7.50, and $10 per 1000, prepaid.

*Facts About UNICEF* also acted as a helpful guide to flush out not only subversive painters but also members of the agency's executive board and a number of other people who, in some way, had assisted in the charitable work. On page 4 appeared a "Key to References." The "Key" will be printed in full:

A—        means "affiliation"
C—        Publications of Circuit Riders
          110 Government Place,
          Cincinnati 2, Ohio
                e—6,000 Educators $6.00
                m—2109 Methodist Ministers Vol. 1, $1.00
                p—614 Presby. Ministers $2.00
                r—Recognize Red China $1.00
                u—Unitarian Clergymen and Rabbis $5.00
Cal.—      Report of the Senate Fact-Finding Subcommittee on Un-American Activities. Year of issue follows each reference
CE—        California Senate Investigating Committee on Education. Figure following refers to Report No.
CR—        Congressional Record
F—         means organization is officially cited as a communist-front
FL—        Firing Line, American Legion publication
HCUA*—House Committee on Un-American Activities
IX*—       Appendix—Part IX, Communist-Front Organizations by Committee on Un-American Activities
RC—        Red Channels by Counterattack
SISS*—     Senate Internal Security Sub-Committee
TE*—       Special Committee to Investigate Tax-Exempt Foundations and Comparable Organizations, 83rd Congress, Second Session
WW—        Who's Who in America

*Example:*   2A in HCUA, means there are 2 affiliations listed in the index of the House Committee on Un-American Activities.
           6A in CR means that 6 affiliations are listed in the book "Recognize Red China" by Circuit Riders.

* Government Depository Public Libraries have these reports, with the possible exception of Appendix Part IX, a 1905-page report. Microfilm of this report available from Washington Summary for $10.00.

Thus, every Daughter quickly could evaluate the "risk" of 99 dangerous characters. Ludwig Bemelmans, who had contributed one of his paintings in 1959, was condemned for 1A in IX. Dr. Ralph J. Bunche, described as a UN official who had accepted a UNICEF youth citation, had 7A in HCUA, 4A in IX, 1A in TE, and 1A in SISS after his name. Elsa Maxwell (2A in HCUA) and Fannie Hurst (more than 12A in HCUA and IX) had both donated paintings to UNICEF. Danny Kaye had committed the sin of promoting the agency through entertainment and was found to have 2A in HCUA; Cal. 48 and Cal. 49. It could be discovered that Edward R. Murrow had 1A in TE and was suspicious because he was a signer of an undated UNICEF letter in 1961. Of course Mrs. Roosevelt was listed as having more than 50A in IX, HCUA, and TE. It was certainly common knowledge that Pablo Picasso was an admitted communist but he was included anyway, as was Marc Chagall—for 3A in HCUA. Dr. Ralph W. Sockman, a representative of the National Council of Churches who spoke in behalf of UN agencies was given the full treatment. He had 11A in Cm, 19A in Cr, 2A in HCUA, 2A in WW 1948, 1954–1955, 1A in IX, 1A in SISS, 2A in Cal. 48. Incidentally, Dr. Sockman was the only one whose name was followed by a *Who's Who* reference.

Mrs. Jacqueline Kennedy publicly announced that she planned to buy UNICEF Christmas cards in spite of all the DAR warnings. The pamphlet seemed to consider her statement unworthy of mention; instead it stressed the fact that Mrs. Khrushchev had never bought a UNICEF card in her life although Russian was one of the languages in which the greetings were printed.

In 1962, the seventy-first Congress passed the strongest anti-UNESCO measure to date, accusing the agency of an attempt to gain "entire control of all public, private and religious institutions of learning of whatever faith" in this country by using federal aid to education for its own aims. The hysteria of the National Board was becoming so offensive to an increasing number of Daughters that on April 17, the eve of the seventy-first Congress, a star member sent in her resignation. It was Mrs.

Ernest Ives, sister of the incumbent UN ambassador, Adlai E. Stevenson. Mrs. Ives admitted to the *Washington Evening Star* that it was a wrench to leave the Society since her mother had been one of the most beloved of all DAR Presidents General. However, she said her conscience would not permit her to remain in any organization where the official policy was so entirely at odds with the national one.

The next year, 1963, the blanket anti-UN resolution was presented and accepted. This was the year when Mrs. Dennis E. Kent and about a hundred other Daughters were brave enough to defy the hierarchy, which was later described by Mrs. Kent as "a tiny band of purposeful people" determined to distort the original aims of the Society.

No loophole was left for the discussion of individual agencies like UNESCO and UNICEF. Reporters and the liberal element among the membership naturally assumed that the wording of the 1963 UN motion was a clever maneuver to squelch further public display of internal disapproval of the Board's position on the most controversial aspects of the question. The NSDAR had a very different explanation. It said that since the limited test-ban treaty was under consideration in the United States Congress at the moment, the Board had felt it their duty to emphasize the dangers of allowing the UN to gain control over our armed forces. For this reason it was imperative to focus full attention on the perilous nature of the international organization, as a whole, rather than continuing to deal with the evils of its separate units.

The divergence of opinion between the leaders and the minority "radical" wing offers certain aspects for speculation. At least to their own satisfaction, the hierarchy vindicated themselves for dropping the hot subject of individual UN agencies. On the other hand, the dissenters also won a certain victory. For several years after 1963 no major resolution on the United Nations was brought up at a DAR Congress, and the Society no longer indulges in its former public criticism. However, every good Daughter is well aware of the DAR barnyard secret. As Mrs. Throckmorton pointed out in 1956, any resolution remains effective in the Society's policy unless it is formally rescinded.

# XIII

Few DAR critics noticed that the perennial harangue about
UNESCO was part of a broader plan to remodel education. The
tussle with the powerful National Education Association over
loyalty oaths had taught the Sons and Daughters a bitter lesson.
In the new campaign of the 1950s and 1960s they streamlined
their tactics. They shied away from harassing teachers and, instead, concentrated on publishers, who often were found to be
vulnerable to civic pressure.

Early in the cold-war period the two organizations quietly
began to gather impressive "facts" about "dangerous" textbooks.
Supplemented by literature from other groups and individual
"authorities," the alarming disclosures were circulated to a sympathetic audience in provincial cities and towns where members
and nonmembers alike shared a pride in being the conservative
backbone of the nation and considered it their duty to guard
youth from communist indoctrination.

It was a mistake to underestimate the influence of the "dod-
dering antediluvians" over affairs at this grass-roots level, where
they were apt to be among the "best people." Their word carried weight with friends and neighbors—the butcher, baker,
hairdresser, barber, and druggist. Fellow citizens unaffiliated
with the Societies but having respect for them were willing to
listen.

Since members of patriotic groups seldom aimed above a
statewide inquiry and often found it expedient to speak as individuals rather than identify themselves with an organization, the
program got results and received little of the national publicity
it deserved. In a hit-and-run type of Indian warfare, the attack
went on year after year in various sections of the country. Horrified communities heard the serious charges against certain textbooks for the first time and were incited to raise a spontaneous
outcry for public investigations of the offending volumes.

The textbook industry had no mighty NEA to rush to its aid

and air the issue. Publishers are victims of the profit system and cutthroat competition in the textbook field. Appearing before wrathful school boards to defend editorial policy, a publisher's representative sometimes was forced to make concessions in order to keep his firm's books on a state's preferred list. It is economically impossible to print a variety of editions to mollify local whims. Therefore, each textual deletion made to placate the prejudices of one state affects the whole nation. When enraged Texans, led by Daughters and John Birchers, demanded the removal of Albert Einstein's name from certain books, a sales representative of one house refused, sadly remarking, "We can't change history." Unfortunately, however, other publishers were often less courageous.

The Sons' and Daughters' new technique scored its first success in 1947 in California, where they played a significant role in bringing about a senatorial investigation of textbooks. At the 1948 DAR Congress, California Daughters proudly announced that they had spent $500 to help precipitate the inquiry; Sons were even more deeply involved.

The campaign was begun by local patriots who denounced *Building America* as a key to "a series of subversive textbooks." In actual fact, *Building America* was the universally accepted teacher's guide published by NEA, and the California superintendent of schools retorted that he would be willing to stake his professional career on its innocence. After a thorough study, the PTA corroborated his statement. The state's Library Association on Intellectual Freedom declared that *Building America* "provided valuable extension on the basic textbooks in social science" and accused its critics of having "an aversion to unpleasant facts and pictures, even though they may be true."

On the surface the attack may have looked like another round in the traditional battle with the NEA, but it was far more encompassing. Not only was the association's magazine put under scrutiny, but irate citizens raised enough clamor to instigate a legislative review of all the instructional material used in California. They managed to have one edition of *Building America* suppressed, and numerous textbooks suggested in the teacher's guide were placed under suspicion. This was the beginning of a battle which has raged in the state for many years. Elated by success in one area, in 1949 the Sons published a fifty-four-page booklet called *A Bill of Grievances* which soon received national attention. Although much of the information was out of date in 1962, the *Bill* was still regarded by amateur censors as valuable basic research. Its importance lay in the fact that it spelled out the real direction of a new campaign that, hiding under the cloak of anti-communism, actually was an attack on progressive education.

What the *Bill* did was to fan an inherent distrust among conservatives for all new-fangled theories that were overtaking the rigid rote of the "3 Rs" type of learning. The crux of its argument was embedded in the warning that our schools were at the mercy of a powerful clique of misguided eggheads who had cornered a monopoly on writing accredited textbooks and advised the average taxpayer to look into just what kind of training American children were getting.

The authors, many of them Columbia trained, were not accused of being out and out communists. The implication was that an author was unfit to mold young minds if he was "gullible" enough to support a communist front organization and, perhaps unconsciously, become "indoctrinated" with theories foreign to the American way of life. The *Bill* stressed that *Building America* recommended writers belonging to 113 front organizations but it soon became evident that the NEA teacher's guide was being used as a springboard from which to dive for bigger game.

The Sons' barrage concentrated on Colombia's Dr. Harold O. Rugg, a disciple of John Dewey, and a pioneer in gaining national acceptance for progressive theories. Rugg had devised an entirely new approach to the study of social science. By combining history, government and social problems he awakened interest in the subject at the elementary school level. His books which began to appear in 1932 were so stimulating that they immediately became bestsellers. Dr. Rugg's annual sales had risen to 300,000 in 1940 when "Treason in the Textbooks" appeared in the American Legion Magazine. The article attacked Rugg and several other Dewey exponents. An accompanying cartoon showed frightened children cowering before a leering schoolmaster who dribbled slime from his hands on four volumes labeled "Constitution," "Religion," "U.S. History," and "U.S. Heroes." The caption read: " 'The Frontier Thinkers' are trying to sell our youth the idea that the American Way of Life has failed." "Frontier thinkers" was the term commonly used to describe "Deweyites."

The assault was so successful that four years later Rugg's sales had dwindled to 21,000 books a year. His name had become synonymous with the evil progressive system and the Sons only had to mention it to rekindle a feeling of antagonism. Elaborating the charges, one DAR defense brochure charged that progressive education was a "plan of collectivists at Columbia Teachers' College, New York City, to propagate alien ideologies through public schools from coast to coast."

However, in the first stages of the campaign, the Daughters did not aspire to compete with the Sons on a national scale. They were content to confine their activities to their home fronts. A report of the 1950 Congress shows that 691 chapters were complimented for independent "surveys" of histories. One Indiana chapter received special praise for inducing its school board to install a three-man layman committee to judge texts. West Virginia Sons and Daughters were highly commended for exerting pressure to replace obnoxious volumes with proper ones.

The movement was particularly strong in the south. Perhaps the most ambitious DAR venture of the period was in Texas, where the State Regent set up a committee to "evaluate public school texts." A questionnaire was sent to all Lone Star State Daughters, asking if their local schools were switching to the left. How many "One World" books were used? Had school libraries been checked? Were they gaining the support of their town paper and radio station in alerting the public on dangerous "subversive" educational trends?

Each Daughter also received the committee's list of seventy volumes to be watched for at the community level. Only one was rated as "very good," two more "good," and another "fairly good." All the rest slid down from "not recommended" to "really a bad one." Four encyclopedias met with disapproval because of the generous space devoted to Russia: *Collier's* was "fairly good," *World Book* and *Britannica* were dismissed as "not satisfactory," and *Americana* was damned as "bad."

In that year, Texas Daughters began agitation to ban Frank Abbott Magruder's *American Government*. Daughters in some parts of the country may have thought the overall Texas program rather extreme, but they agreed with Texans on the charges against Magruder.

Various editions of this high-school classic had been used in all forty-eight states for twenty-five years. Not a breath of criticism had touched it until 1949, when suddenly it was discovered that Dr. Magruder's conception of democracy led "straight from Rousseau, through Marx, to totalitarianism." Most Daughters had read the alarming exposé in the first issue of a new quarterly newsletter, the *Editorial Reviewer*. Its publisher, Mrs. Lucille Cardin Crain, was one of a host of "authorities" on education who came into vogue during the cold-war period. Although responsible educators pointed out that Mrs. Crain had no college degree and that the *Reviewer's* report was full of glaring inaccuracies, she soon had a large claque of loyal admirers.

Fulton Lewis, Jr., a favorite DAR commentator, found Mrs. Crain's arguments so persuasive that he noted the analysis of *American Government* on several broadcasts, adding his own warning: "And that's the book that has been in use in high schools all over the nation, possibly by your youngster." Archconservative papers like the Chicago *Tribune* constantly urged readers to subscribe to Mrs. Crain's newsletter. The generous publicity prompted outraged parents everywhere to call for the removal of Magruder's book from study courses. Many of them never even bothered to open *American Government* to ascertain the validity of the charges. By 1950, it actually was banned in Richland, Washington; Little Rock, Arkansas; Lafayette, Indiana; Houston, Texas; and the entire state of Georgia.

Trying to block the Georgia action, the Atlanta *Constitution* reminded the public that many prominent state officials, including Governor Talmadge, had been taught from the book and

defied the school board to prove "it had made subversives, social-
ists, or radicals of them." However, the former President General of the DAR Mrs. Julius Y. Talmadge was now a powerful
member of the board. Displaying haughty disdain for the newspaper's appeal to reason, she replied that the Magruder book
contained "controversial material." Issues of this nature had no
place in a Georgia classroom, she declared, and her colleagues
stood firmly behind her. Oddly enough, board members showed
no concern for the purity of children in other states. Georgia's
30,000 copies of the odious volume were offered for sale to
out-of-state schools.

Two years later Mrs. Talmadge and the board finally agreed
to reinstate the history if certain offensive passages were deleted.
Special emphasis was placed on all remarks complimentary to
the United Nations. Dr. Magruder himself was dead and his
publishers complied with the state's demands.

The revised edition returned to Little Rock and Houston
about the same time it regained favor in Georgia. The bitter
controversy abruptly ended all over the Union.

A number of other books were under scrutiny and, in at least
one instance, twenty-five firms joined forces and were able to
halt the interference of amateur censors. In Alabama, a law became effective on January 1, 1954, that required every text used
in the state to have a publisher's affidavit that the author—and
any writer whose work was recommended for supplementary
reading—had never advocated Marxism or belonged to a communist-front organization. "Defense Notes" in a 1954 DAR
magazine warmly congratulated the state on its sound judgment,
but numerous people were horrified by the new ruling. The
Alabama Polytechnic Institute estimated that to comply with the
act 28 million names would have to be investigated. Publishers
took this issue to court, and eventually the law was thrown out
as a violation of the Fourteenth Amendment.

President General Carraway (1953–1956) injected a more
constructive note into the DAR educational policy. Although
Daughters remained firm against UNESCO material and stepped
up opposition to federal school aid, they eased up on schoolbook
censorship.

The Society announced at the 1954 Congress that an ambitious national program had been launched to encourage love of American history among children from the fifth through the eighth grades. As an incentive, DAR prizes were awarded to winners of essay contests and to pupils earning top grades in the subject.

Miss Carraway's successor, Mrs. Frederic Alquin Groves, continued the project. Nevertheless, in the first year of her administration, the Society became involved in an unpleasant scandal that quite overshadowed any advances they might be making in a positive direction.

On February 10, 1957, the *Denver Post* reported that Mrs. Charlotte Rush had refused to allow a Mexican boy to carry the American flag in a Lincoln's birthday pageant to be staged by the DAR at a correctional institution, the Colorado State Industrial School. The principal announced cancellation of the entertainment by "mutual consent." The governor, swamped with protests, closed all state buildings to DAR programs, and naturally the news gained wide coverage.

In an effort to counteract the flood of criticism, on February 11, Mrs. Groves publicly stated that Mrs. Rush's action was absolutely contrary to all DAR principles. She also started wheels rolling behind the scenes. Later in the day, acting on a directive from the National Board, Mrs. Rush issued a public apology. She admitted that she had spoken "carelessly" and that she personally, not the Society, was at fault. That same evening, after a hasty meeting of the Denver chapter, State Regent Mrs. Richard P. Carlson revealed that Mrs. Rush had "vacated" her post as chairman of the Patriotic Education Committee.

Lengthy explanatory telegrams went to every DAR officer. State press chairmen received by wire official releases to be issued to their local press. The National Public Relations Department sent 300 letters to newspapers and answered each unfavorable editorial.

A month later the most curious "true story" in the history of the NSDAR was released to all chapters from headquarters. The memorandum disclosed that, in a recent interview with the *Denver Post*, Mrs. Rush suddenly recalled that the event had not occurred in 1957 as supposed but in 1950 and that the circumstances had been grossly misinterpreted. According to Mrs. Rush's belated explanation, an American boy assigned to carry the flag had lacked proper enthusiasm while a little Mexican begged for the honor. She said she had tried to shame the American into doing his duty by saying: "I wouldn't let a Mexican carry Old Glory, would you?" That's all there was to it; it was merely an "appeal to a child to carry his own flag."

At the 1957 Congress President General Groves made a point of jogging the memory of delegates. "May I again remind you that this is an incident that happened in 1950, not 1957?" she insisted. "May I also remind you that we have every reason for pride in the accomplishments of our National Society? We have a magnificent record of service." Later, at a New York luncheon, apparently still worried about the incident, she admonished members to "watch their words."

In spite of her concern for the DAR public image, the next year Mrs. Groves gave whole-hearted support to a second, and far more serious, stage of the textbook battle. Alerted by the defense chairman, Mrs. Ray L. Erb, the Daughters began to investigate courses being taught at the primary and secondary level. The new campaign included almost every subject and made the Sons' earlier attempts look innocuous.

*Brainwashing in the High Schools*, by E. Merrill Root, may be regarded as the flint that rekindled book-burning fires among the Daughters. Root's book, published in 1958, was advertised as an objective analysis of eleven American histories, used in about 10,000 schools. However, it also was a sounding board for the author's strong, superpatriotic opinions on states rights, the dangers of fluoridation, government regulation of business, foreign aid, and the welfare state. Older antecedence groups, the Birch Society and new rightist organizations gave loud endorsement to Root's theories on education.

Root believed that the United States was losing the cold war because books like the ones he had examined were "brainwashing" students by distorting historical facts and offering collective ideas instead. Ignoring statistics that showed that eighteen of the twenty-one "turncoats" in the Korean War were high-school dropouts, he insisted that the questionable texts were responsible for the ease with which American soldiers in communist prison camps were converted to Marxist doctrines. *Brainwashing in the High Schools* was promptly dismissed by reliable authorities. In commenting on Root's evaluations, Paul Simon, newspaper publisher and Illinois legislator, described them as an attempt to "measure subversion by the inch." Indeed Root often put a text in the "brainwashing" class if the description of a liberal president contained more lines than that of a conservative one or if fewer pages were devoted to reactionary eras than progressive ones. In spite of this approach, his book received a number of surprisingly good reviews in such reputable papers as *The Wall Street Journal* and the Cincinnati *Inquirer*.

In November 1958, soon after Root's book first appeared, Daughters throughout the country quietly began to compile their own list of objectionable primary and secondary textbooks. Alert Connecticut reporters learned that the state's DAR Defense Chairman, Miss Barbara F. Allen of Norwich, had procured a list of texts from her local school superintendent. When asked for comment, Miss Allen replied that she was not at liberty to explain at the moment; she simply was "carrying out instructions of our national headquarters in Washington." The National Board issues no press releases on documents prepared for members and interested outsiders so, except for Miss Allen's cryptic statement, the *DAR Textbook Study 1958–1959* slipped, unnoticed, into wide circulation in the spring.

The twenty-page pamphlet was admittedly patterned after the SAR *A Bill of Grievances*, which was praised as a survey par excellence to determine if children were being "taught love of God and Country or being corrupted to accept socialism and materialism." However, the Daughters covered a broader field than either the Sons or Root, who both had confined their comments to slanted histories and geographies "disguised as social science." According to its author, who remained anonymous, the DAR *Study* was a comprehensive sampling of educational material. A taint of subversion was detected in everything from music to chemistry.

Out of 214 texts examined, only 49 met "minimum DAR standards"; a number of these were accepted with reservations. A 9-page preamble covered 88 offensive volumes in some detail. It was followed by three lists, the first of which awarded a short descriptive paragraph to each approved book; in the second, 177 offensive ones were tabulated merely by title, author, and publisher; the third gave Root's total list and boosted sales of his book by mentioning the price and the full address of his publisher. The preamble explained that the reasons for the rejection of most "unsatisfactory" texts were too complicated to be included in the present report. Upon request, the reader could obtain specific reviews from DAR headquarters.

The *Study* used a stern criterion. Any author was taboo if he treated "our Christian heritage warily" or if he was "guardedly patriotic." An undercurrent of "economic determinism" was so prevalent in questionable texts that the reviewer suspected "some central force" was at work. In the social sciences, for instance, impressionable students never were warned about dangers of a welfare state, and although the First and Fifth Amendments frequently came into discussion, there was a total lack of interest in the Tenth, "which guarantees the several states against Federal encroachment."

The preamble dealt with individual courses. It suggested that even science could be "God-conscious and God-centered" and cited Sister M. Aquinas' *Man in God's World* as a fine example. Pointing out that this could be purchased in paperback at one-tenth the price of less worthy material, the science section ended: "Books of such reverent knowledge would vastly improve the moral behavior of any student."

In literature, anthologies often were dismissed because they included too many "sordid and shocking stories for which the young reader is not prepared." One gave a "gruesome description" of an ant army in the Amazon jungle that first attacked the eyes of victims "so they will flounder around helplessly."

"A woman with a Master's Degree in Mathematics" found an arithmetic book wanting because, among other faults, it used long forms of federal tax in examples. Another textbook pampered students by supplying square-root tables, depriving them of much-needed mental exercise. The *Study* moralized: "Such indulgence is not likely to develop scientists of tough fiber and persistent habits."

Most music books ignored "the heavy responsibilities of the managerial and professional classes" and promoted class struggle by concentrating on "work tunes" and "folk songs." One, making full use of time-tested native and national airs, was found delightful until it was discovered that "brothers" was substituted for "darkies" in "Way Down Upon the Swanee River." The violation was called "an intolerable form of censorship."

The *Study* objected to all youth opinion polls and life-adjustment courses. Theodore Dreiser's *An American Tragedy* was considered dangerous reading because a prayer for teachers appeared on page 29 in which the author implored them to stop putting "conformity to old customs above curiosity about new ideas." The inclusion of John Hersey's *Hiroshima* and other "fear" texts as recommended reading was stressed as an example of an attempt of pacifists to indoctrinate "future voters" with the belief that world government offered the only solution to the threat of atomic warfare. Nearly sixty writers were guilty of this sin, including Margaret Mead, Ruth Benedict, Alan Lomax, William C. Menninger, Lincoln Steffens, and Burl Ives.

The physical make-up of modern textbooks also displeased Daughters. Many were so heavy they had to be braced "on a table in order to turn the pages comfortably." A dim view was taken of gay, light-colored bindings, which "soiled twice as fast as the more practical browns and maroons." Readers were reminded of "the use to which the boy Lincoln put a dingy copy of 'Pilgrim's Progress' or 'The Bible.' "

To the Daughters the most vital discovery of their survey was that, because of determined opposition by patriotic and veterans' groups, the popularity of certain authors such as Rugg and Muzzey had faded but their viewpoint was still being promoted by dozens of disciples under the slogan of "THE FUSED DISCIPLINES." The "fusion text," they found, was a hopeless jumble of history, geography, civics, and personal guidance that served to confuse pupils rather than give a proper basic education. The preamble ended with a suggestion of five activities. The first four told the same old story: interested parties should check local books with the DAR list; let their views be known to school authorities; find out if their system was dominated by "fusion texts" and, if so, influence community leaders to insist on the reinstatement of "satisfactory" courses. The fifth introduced a new note. It proposed that "good" books be donated to schools and libraries—"or at least give them to your young friends and relatives to combat what they are learning."

Soon after the appearance of the *Study*, bitter controversies began to erupt in California, New York, Michigan, Ohio, Illinois, Oklahoma, North Carolina, Georgia, Alabama, Arkansas, Virginia, Mississippi, and Texas. It would seem that Daughters were carrying out instructions. In December 1959, the American Library Committee warned: "Of all the programs by organized groups, the DAR textbook investigation, at both national and state level, was the most specific and . . . the most threatening." By 1961, the American Book Publishers Council reported that school texts and recommended reading in school libraries were under the fire of amateur critics in eighteen states. Among the initiated self-appointed censors the DAR *Study* was almost always exhibit A. Root's book and pamphlets of America's Future, Inc., ranked next in importance. (America's Future was a booming patrioteer outfit that had launched *Operation Textbook* in 1958. Lucille Cardin Crain was head of the new department and Root one of its star reviewers. He and two other "eminent authorities" on education enlisted by Mrs. Crain were also on the editorial staff of *American Opinion*, the Birch Society publication.)

The *Textbook Study* created excitement far beyond DAR circles. An attack on books used in the schools of Meriden, Connecticut, was based on the DAR study. Ed Casey, one of its initiators, liked to gather inside "dope" on communism. Finding the DAR *National Defender* an excellent source, he became a regular subscriber and, as a matter of routine, received his copy of the *Study* in 1960. Shocked by the pamphlet's disclosures, Casey instantly decided to check all the social studies courses used in Meriden.

Since it was a laborious task, he took a friend, Fred Dobson into his confidence, and together they obtained lists of texts from the Maloney and Platt high schools. They discovered that fourteen of the twenty-nine books were condemned in the *Study* and only two appraised as satisfactory. It seemed unscholarly to rely on the DAR report alone, so Casey asked the National Defense Chairman, Mrs. Wilson K. Barnes, for additional reliable source material. Mail soon was pouring into his postbox; it included the *Bill of Grievances*, bulky reports from the Florida Coalition of Patriotic Societies and the Parents for Better Education in Los Angeles, even old American Legion statements and resolutions were considered useful. Most of their information was lifted bodily from the DAR, *Brainwashing in the High Schools*, and an avalanche of America's Future pamphlets.

For a year, only their immediate families were aware of the Casey and Dobson project. Finally they were ready to present their findings in a thirty-page document. They paid to have 200 copies mimeographed, sending them to school boards, newspapers, libraries, "and to some other people" where "they would do the most good."

The Meriden *Record* hastened to come to the defense of the authors attacked in this document. Its reporters telephoned historians and political scientists in Connecticut colleges to get their reaction, and the paper announced the unanimous indignation of leading educators for unjust charges brought against people like Pearl Buck, Norman Cousins, and Henry S. Commager among others.

The Meriden school board also expressed prompt disapproval. Its chairman, Morton H. Greenblatt, found Casey and Dobson lacking in "experience and qualifications" and charged, "They have taken canned reports prepared by others far removed from Meriden." Nevertheless, egged on by countless sympathizers, the team by-passed the school board and demanded a hearing by the Meriden Board of Education, which had absolute authority over the choice of the city's textbooks. The hearing was set for December 17, 1961.

The people of Meriden were of two opposing opinions on the matter. Even the local DAR chapters couldn't agree. The Susan

Carrington Clarke Chapter rushed to aid Casey-Dobson forces while the Ruth Hart Chapter, disdainful and aloof, prepared a critical statement that they failed to release only "in obedience to the direction of the national organization." A former regent, Mrs. Helen Rader, was not so faint-hearted and told the press that the two men had done more "to subvert a free society than the combined contents of the fourteen unsatisfactory textbooks."

Meanwhile, Casey-Dobson hopes ran high. They anticipated a red-carpet atmosphere for the investigation because E. Merrill Root, now living in Rhode Island, had agreed to be their star witness. He backed down at the last moment, pleading that age made him reluctant to drive over icy roads. The cancellation obviously unnerved the critics but it was too late to gain a postponement. Trying to hide their disappointment, they entered the hearing room hauling a bulging book rack of anti-textbook literature and trailed by more than a dozen supporters.

Dobson was the first speaker, but instead of dealing with textbooks, he complained that the meeting was part of a "Red-fascist timetable" rigged to "smear" him and his associate. Greenblatt snapped that this was irrelevant and asked him to keep to the subject. Dobson crumbled and Casey took over. Composed and aggressive, he insisted that their charges were well documented and supported by unquestionable authorities like the DAR and E. Merrill Root. When asked why he had written the report, he cried that he was prompted by "Being a good patriotic American."

The next witness was Emmett Rutland, a high-school teacher from Stratford who described himself as education chairman of the Anti-Communist Committee of Connecticut. He also emphasized DAR standards as the best available for judging texts.

When the defense ended, sober educators attacked Casey and Dobson's arguments so effectively that the books under question were vindicated and retained in the Meriden curriculum. Sanford H. Wendover, the Meriden *Journal*'s conservative editor, wrote an obituary for the case. Over the weekend he had read nine of the fourteen books under fire and found nothing objectionable. In fact, he declared them to be "much better than the textbooks on American history and government we studied when we were in school."

Jack Nelson and Gene Roberts, Jr., authors of *The Censors and the Schools*, interviewed DAR defense chairman, Mrs. Barnes, on March 7, 1962. They wanted to know by what criteria books were evaluated; were the Daughters reviewers, educators, experts on communism; and, specifically, who had leveled charges?

Mrs. Barnes pointed out that she became chairman after the *Study* was completed and the she, personally, had not worked much on textbooks. "Every chairman has her own hobbies," she confided.

She did concede that she had "told those men in Meriden" how much the Daughters appreciated their efforts. She also admitted that during her administration the three-year-old *Study* had received wide distribution and that daily requests were still coming in. She refused to divulge the number in current circulation or where the requests came from. Informing the young men that DAR files were not open to the public or the press, she ended the interview with the suggestion that a visit to America's Future would be rewarding. "They're going at the textbooks tooth and toenail and doing a mighty fine job," she declared.

The DAR pamphlet had been prepared under the supervision of Mrs. Ray L. Erb, President General Groves' Defense Chairman. When her term expired she began to write the *Report to the Nation*, an American Coalition of Patriotic Societies publication. It will be remembered that the coalition was started by Fred K. Marvin in 1929 and that, after his death, the flamboyant Mrs. Sherman Walker became executive secretary. Although the Board makes frequent denials of affiliation with any outside organization this intertwining chain is another example of prominent members who frequently accept key posts in groups other than their own and definitely exert influence on sister members.

Mrs. Erb continued her purge of allegedly subversive texts in *Report to the Nation* and probably retained numerous DAR fans. Furthermore, Mrs. Erb now reached a far larger public since the coalition claims to consist of 125 conservative orders

with approximately 4 million members. In the haggle over textbooks, certain local leaders took a cue from Mrs. Erb's tactics
and broadened their influence by joining with outside groups.
Mrs. Harry Artz Alexander of Mississippi and Mrs. A. A.
Forrester of Texas are notable examples.

Soon after the distribution of the DAR *Study* in 1959, Mrs.
Alexander, Mississippi's DAR defense chairman, entered the
arena with a list of forty-four "unsatisfactory" books. On the
strength of her findings, she made a spirited demand for the
State Textbook Purchasing Board to appoint laymen to screening committees that formerly had consisted of only teachers.
The DAR proposal was seconded by its old ally the American
Legion and even more vigorously by two out and out segregationist groups: the White Citizens Council and the Mississippi
Farm Bureau Federation. Together they raised such a hubbub
that a legislative investigation resulted. When it met in Jackson,
a large bloc of DAR were on hand to offer assistance; so were
two White Citizens officials; and Myers E. Lowman, director of
the Circuit Riders, came all the way from Cincinnati to attend
the hearing. (Lowman was a familiar figure to southern educators. Since 1954 several states had hired him as an underground
agent to fight desegregation.)

Mississippi legislators trimmed the DAR list to twenty-seven
questionable volumes but admitted they were in a quandary because they felt unqualified as book examiners. They then announced that they had been "fortunate in securing the services
of Mr. E. Merrill Root . . . who was confidentially recommended . . . by an unimpeachable source." No one seemed to
recall that Root's last appearance in the state had been in 1957 at
Biloxi, where he acted not as an educator but as a member of the
Resolutions Committee during a convention of the Congress of
Freedom, Inc. The congress placed the NAACP on the "enemy"
list because it was "not an organization of Negroes, but of Jews
and left wingers that would drive a wedge between Negroes and
whites of the South and do untold harm to both races."

In the south, of course, Root had no fear of icy roads, so he
was happy to return to Mississippi. Asking only a modest fee of

$400 for two weeks' work, he labeled twelve of the books good, twelve bad, and three mediocre. His report was accepted without reservations by the committee, which added the advice that mediocre and bad books "should be eliminated from further use."

Root showed a remarkable sensitivity to the ideology of his audience. Speaking of one text, he conceded its authors a right to the opinion that schools should be a "melting pot" of varying economic, cultural, and racial backgrounds. However, he had the forethought to add "if they do it in wise ways AND WITHOUT FORCED INTEGRATION, it will be good."

Following the committee's report, the 1960 Mississippi legislature took under advisement a bill backed by the DAR. It proposed to remove selection of book-committee members from the jurisdiction of the superintendent of education and place it in the hands of the governor, who at the time was Ross Barnett. Admitting that he had "a lot of confidence" in the DAR and other organizations fighting for the bill, Barnett made a personal appeal for the House to vote in favor of the act "to clean up" textbooks so children would be "properly informed of the Southern and true American way of life." Although opposition was bitter, a law finally gave the governor the power to appoint four of the seven members in each of the state's eight screening boards. A triumphant Mrs. Alexander told reporters that screening committees often used DAR evaluation advice and that several of the governor's new appointees were Daughters. (Two other Barnett choices were the president of the Farm Bureau and a political science professor in a Mississippi college who was a frequent speaker at White Citizens Council meetings.)

According to Nelson and Roberts, Mrs. Alexander's success in her own state brought her wider fame. In February 1962, along with Circuit Rider Lowman and several Birchers, she was on the "faculty" of Reverend Billy James Hargis' "National Anti-Communist Leadership School," which held a seminar in Tulsa, Oklahoma. On the printed program Mrs. Alexander was billed as a "dynamic leader in eliminating Communist-authored textbooks from Mississippi schools." The 178 people who each had paid a hundred-dollar tuition fee went home to 25 states bearing Mrs. Alexander's ringing message to check textbooks and weed out "subversion" in their own schools.

Mrs. Alexander's zeal often had carried her far beyond the limits of the DAR. As soon as she had accomplished her purpose in Mississippi, she rushed to Texas, where the biggest book battle in the country was brewing. She was a tireless guest speaker before groups like the Amarillo Conservative Club, and her remarks were most helpful in whipping up enthusiasm for a statewide investigation.

One of the largest markets in the world, Texas spends from $6 million to $10 million on books a year. A state committee approves five books for every course, any one of which may be chosen by local boards. The approved list remains effective from six to nine years, so publishers are sometimes quite anxious to please the Texas Education Agency.

In 1961, the DAR and Texans for America served notice on the selection committee of the Texas Education Agency that choice of books would have to meet their approval before adoption. Texans for America had been organized by J. Evetts Haley, an extremely wealthy rancher who described himself as just a plain cowboy. His impassioned style and distrust of everything from Roosevelt's New Deal to the Supreme Court decision on desegregation of schools made him a spellbinder capable of unifying a solid front of DAR, SAR, Legionnaires, the Birch Society, and numerous lesser rightist groups. The local DAR Defense Chairman, Mrs. A. A. Forrester, was a former schoolteacher and an ardent Haleyite. Her enthusiasm for the Texans swept Daughters into the role of the chief supporters of the organization.

Haley claimed that until children "were old enough to understand both sides of a question they should be taught only the American side . . ." Another theory of his was that public-school guidance and counseling threaten "to become a gigantic mental health program for the suppression of the individuality of every child to make him a cog in a socialistic society . . . selected for him in advance by hand-picked servants of the Super State." According to him no history could measure up if it was favorable toward school and farm subsidies, income tax, labor unions, the UN, and, naturally, integration. He complained of one text because it contained four pictures of George Washington that made him look "as if George Gobel posed for the painting."

Except for the *Texas Observer*, a scrappy, liberal Austin weekly, only two dailies in the state sent reporters to cover the meeting of the textbook committee on October 5, 1961. Robert Sherrill, representing the *Observer*, commented, "The press heard the fanatics' full voice, but heard hardly a chirp from the publishers," whom he criticized for showing "an eagerness to sail with the wind of strongest opinion."

Despite the confusion in the overcrowded assembly room, the committee adopted fifty books including twenty-seven on the Texans for America's blacklist. The dailies blithely dismissed the matter as a smashing defeat for Haleyites, but the persistent *Observer* emphasized that Texas Education Agency records would show otherwise. Sherrill based his analysis on the fact that the committee had rejected twelve books opposed by the Texans and four of the five criticized by Daughters. Further, in obeisance to censors' pressure, substantial changes in numerous approved books had been suggested.

The agency's files did not reflect all the alterations. There was no public record of oral, closed-door discussions between publishers and the committee. Modifications were not actually ordered, only recommended, but as a secretary in the education commissioner's office remarked, "The competition is so fierce, you know, that the textbook publishers are anxious to make any changes the committee recommends."

The official TEA document showed that whole passages in numerous books were discarded or changed to comply with Texas standards. One example of the substantial alterations in the Silver Burdett Company's geography, *The American Continents*, is sufficient to show how a text can be transformed through censorship efforts.

*Original version*: "Because it needs to trade, and because it needs military help, the United States needs the friendship of countries throughout the world. But, to keep its friends, a country must help them, too."

*Changed to*: "The United States trades with countries in all parts of the world. We are also providing military help to many nations. In addition, the United States aids many countries in other ways."

The *Observer*'s prediction was correct. This was only the beginning of the battle. At the instigation of Mrs. Forrester, Representative Bob Bass got a bill through the Texas House that set up a committee to travel around the state to hear charges against books. Its chairman was W. T. Dungan, a dairy farmer whose only other claim to fame as a lawmaker was an unsuccessful attempt to make every teacher in Texas swear to a belief in the Supreme Being.

No matter where the committee met, the room was bursting with Daughters, Sons, Legionnaires, Birchers, and Haleyites always ready to offer advice and busily distributing literature varying from the 1958–1959 DAR *Study* to pamphlets of the National Anti-Communist League and the Watch Washington Club of Columbus, Ohio. Local witnesses came in droves, lugging armloads and suitcases full of improper material.

One lady in Amarillo planted a small American flag in front of her as she took to the stand to testify that "triumphant heroism" was absent in history books. She particularly objected to one because it failed to tell the story of "our lovely Statue of Liberty" and printed only one photograph of it taken from the rear. However, most of the criticism centered on "filth" found in public libraries. One Midland, Texas, housewife, a member of the Cornish Baptist Church, found *Andersonville* so repulsive that she was too modest to read the passages in public and brought her minister along "to do her dirty work." He quickly took over and a hush fell as his booming voice read: "Page 20. 'God damn the Yankees. God damn the Yankees. God damn the Yankees. Amen!' Ought to have left out that 'Amen.' " He continued without interruption until he got to page 185, which said, "Hey, go stick a weasel up your ass." Suddenly a sweating fat man jumped up. Eyes bulging, he shouted, "Preacher! That's enough! I'm a Baptist preacher myself, and I can't stand any more!"

Needless to say, *Andersonville* was ripped off the shelves in many Texas libraries. Because of similar criticism, so were numerous other minor classics like Aldous Huxley's *Brave New World*, Thomas Wolfe's *Of Time and the River* and Oliver La Farge's *Laughing Boy*. Four Pulitzer Prize winners were among the prime offenders.

Dungan continued his rampage throughout the year. He predicted his report would shock the 1963 legislature into passing laws that would ensure procedures of adopting texts that emphasize "our glowing and throbbing history of hearts and souls inspired by wonderful American principles and traditions . . ." Despite his promises, the investigation fizzled out with no decisive action and never again reached the wholesale intensity predominant in this period. According to Edwin W. Davis, associate secretary for special studies in the NEA's Commission on Professional Rights and Responsibilities, there have been no recent eruptions of censorship in Texas other than the usual controversies that take place and are settled at a local level.

Meanwhile, the ardor for the textbook purge seems to have subsided in the NSDAR. Although the *Study* was still a popular item in the lobby of Constitution Hall in 1963, Davis reported in 1968 that there have been "very few DAR outbursts . . . in the last five years." He added, "In fairness to the DAR, an occasional NEA staff member or a fine acquaintance of the staff is found to be a member of the DAR and many of these DAR members have come to us for assistance in correcting or changing the DAR textbook reviewing program . . ." He ends by expressing the feeling that "these fine members have been able to influence the offices and policy makers of the DAR Defense Committee toward more constructive patriotic endeavors."

Viewing their own resolutions, it would seem that the Daughters' crusade for better education has been siphoned into a new channel. Since the 1962 and 1963 Supreme Court decisions, they have concentrated on putting God back into the public schools.

# XIV

## BLEST BE THE TIE THAT BINDS

The hierarchy often displays an alarming naïveté about the effect their words have on the outside world. Although during her entire term, President General Mrs. Robert V. H. Duncan constantly implored Daughters to tell "the true DAR story," and reminded them that thoughtless remarks of members harmed the organization's image, yet one of her own statements at the seventy-second Congress was exactly the sort of thing that reflected on the good name of the Society.

At the opening session, on April 15, 1963, Mrs. Duncan read the customary presidential letter from John F. Kennedy. It was quite a departure from the one of the previous year, in which he delivered a tart lecture on the meaning of democracy. This time President Kennedy praised the DAR's constructive activities, dwelling on its schools for underprivileged, important restoration work, and maintenance of Constitution Hall as a museum and cultural center "for all the people." In these worthy endeavors, he said, the Society helped make the spirit of '76 a vital force. Now he called for its aid in "the great struggle to close the remaining gaps in the American dream of equality and brotherhood. . . . For some of our people, the promise of the Revolution is not yet known—poverty, illiteracy and racial prejudice block its fulfillment in their lives."

Marion Duncan is a Virginian. She was a Moncure. She has charm, and her sweet southern voice softened the underlying criticism during the reading. Nevertheless, when her thank-you note to the President was released to the press on Tuesday, it revealed she had not missed the barbed implication.

She wrote that she "was very pleased with the message," then was unwise enough to continue:

As a matter of information you may be interested to know that the National Society, DAR, does not have—and has never had—any policy on integration or segregation as such . . . However, lest there be a misapprehension, it is true that the National Society has stood and does stand for States' rights as set forth in the Constitution.

This was the strongest statement a President General had made on the controversial issue since the Marian Anderson "incident." To make sure the public would get full benefit of the DAR's reactionary views, Mrs. Duncan's reply was boxed beside a resume of President Kennedy's letter on April 16th, in Washington's *Evening Star*. Papers carrying the story reached the stands just as Mrs. Duncan was going into the Mayflower, where she was to be guest of honor at a Maryland state luncheon. She was the principal speaker, but her words received no coverage because, on this occasion, reporters found Honorary President General Carraway's remarks on taxation more newsworthy.

Miss Carraway said Daughters must take every precaution to erase the idea that "we are a political organization. We are not political," she insisted. "We are an educational, patriotic and historical organization and get our tax exemption status on that basis." She warned that an investigation was being made of tax-free groups in the District and that the DAR was one that might be questioned. She reminded members, "Our buildings are worth $10 million and we can't afford to pay real estate taxes on that."

In May of 1963, when Mrs. Dennis E. Kent accused the hierarchy of thrusting the DAR into the vanguard of right-wing opposition to liberal legislation, her statement made national headlines. The leaders seemed to consider it below their dignity to answer her charges. They maintained their accustomed silence to criticism until Senator Maurine B. Neuberger of Oregon took up the issue.

On June 24, 1963, Mrs. Neuberger challenged Bill 159, which called for the printing and mailing of the DAR annual report at government expense. She questioned the propriety of the measure since the report contained not only the good deeds of the organization but also their resolutions, which she characterized as "ill-tempered complaints."

Quoting Mrs. Kent's statement in its entirety, the senator said that, after reading the material herself, she found Mrs. Kent's attitude justified. In substance, the resolutions ranged from a cry that " 'the Domestic Peace Corps would delay the entrance of the youth of this Nation into the field of free enterprise' to the doctrinaire restatement of the John Birch Society's conspiratorial view of recent American history." Mrs. Neuberger claimed:

> No arm of government escapes the wrath of the Daughters: Congress is tarred with the brush of "progressive encroachment upon the constitutional rights of the several States of the Union with serious impairment of their vested rights, liberties, and control of their institutions." The Federal courts are "usurping the rights and powers of the legislatures of the several states." And the administration, through "subservience" to the United Nations has "permitted communism to become entrenched 90 miles off our shore in Cuba" . . . I find it particularly offensive that we, by publishing this report as a Senate document, should thereby give the color of official approval to these flagrantly partisan views.

She said she had no intention of blocking the bill, because the appropriation ($3,000) was too slight to warrant attention. She merely wanted to show that the DAR was "symptomatic" of a growing number of organizations that enjoyed an illegal tax-free status by posing as apolitical, religious, or educational groups while, in reality, they were right-wing political propaganda mills. The senator explained that she had directed a letter to Mortimer M. Caplin, then commissioner of internal revenue, requesting his department to reexamine the advisability of exemption for any order—right or left—that was disseminating political doctrines.

If action were taken, Mrs. Neuberger's proposal posed a far more serious threat than the one foreseen by Miss Carraway. On top of the $10 million piece of Washington real estate, a 1967 Treasurer General's report gave current DAR assets as $1,772,218. This is a modest estimate. That year, the *Washington Post* pointed out that while over half the sum is invested in government bonds, DAR's holdings in twenty-one blue-chip stocks are appreciably greater than listed because figures are based on a 1957 level or at cost if purchased later. For instance, the report quotes 365 shares of General Motors at $6,057, whereas this block had a market value of $29,200 in 1967.

This capital is not touched when their property needs refurbishing. Then, the Daughters take out a homeowner's loan, which is paid off by members' pledges. Because of the educational character of the Society, all individual contributions are tax deductible; so are the sizable bequests in the wills of many generous Daughters.

Woe to anyone who tries to tamper with the Society's purse strings. An NBC Huntley-Brinkley newscast of October 8, 1963, announced:

> . . . Mrs. Neuberger . . . since her speech . . . says she's come under the most ferocious attack . . . poisonous and abusive . . . and has been called everything, including a Communist.
> So it appears the DAR has not been so angry since President Franklin D. Roosevelt made a speech to them . . . and began it with the salutation: "Fellow Immigrants" . . .

The newscast was covering a second address in October in which Mrs. Neuberger sought to defend and clarify her position on improper tax exemption. She began by describing vicious *Life Line* broadcasts sponsored by H. L. Hunt, which accused her of going after the DAR simply because she personally disagreed with the Society's policy and gave a few samples of the vitriolic, anonymous mail received from people aroused by June speech. The senator also disclosed that on the day following her original speech, she had received a letter from Mrs. Duncan, which clearly showed that the DAR leader failed to understand the true meaning of the charges. Mrs. Duncan wrote:

> So far as the term "politicking" is concerned, I am surprised at its use and am at something of a loss to know just what is meant inasmuch as the national society maintains no lobby at National, State, or local government levels, contributes to no political party or candidates in any way, initiates no legislation, and does not—as do a number of

organizations—even in its own internal setup have any legislative chairmen. Yes, the DAR, being interested in the preservation and maintenance of our constitutional Republic, does urge its members as individual good American citizens to be informed and to exercise the privilege of the franchise and vote, but how one votes is entirely up to the individual.

Mrs. Neuberger commented that the word "politicking" was Mrs. Duncan's, not her own, but it was exactly what she had in mind. Asking permission to elucidate more fully on objectionable DAR tactics, she explained that shortly before her October speech, a DAR in good standing had sent her a copy of a bulletin distributed by the National Defense Committee to the various chairmen of that committee in local chapters. It strongly urged all members to contact their senators in opposition to the test-ban treaty. The circular stated in part:

> The great danger of this treaty is that the United States may be mousetrapped into unilateral disarmament, while the Soviet Union makes itself invincible. Instead of being a victory for the administration, as it is now represented, it may well turn out to be a great catastrophe for all of America.

The senator pointed out that simultaneously SANE had proselytized members and friends to support the bill. SANE had no government subsidy or tax exemption and, in Mrs. Neuberger's opinion, neither should the Daughters if they insisted on meddling in national affairs.

Although Mrs. Duncan made no further comment, the senator's warning had a profound effect on the Society. In 1965 there was a noticeable change from negative to positive wording in all resolutions. One example occurred when the Senate was commended for refusing to ratify the Genocide Treaty instead of receiving another command not to do so. Opposition to the Supreme Court's directive on legislative reapportionment was expressed by calling for state legislatures to continue the checks and balances provided by the Constitution. Reporters were reminded that no resolution denouncing communism had appeared since 1962. Although policy undoubtedly remained the same, controversial issues were soft-pedaled in the annual platform.

An important reason for the change may have been that in 1964 *Life Line* and about two dozen other rightist propaganda groups lost their tax-exemption status. Another stimulus for the DAR to mend its ways was its increasing unpopularity with the younger generation. Eighteen-year-olds had been eligible for membership from the beginning, but few seemed to be coming into the organization in recent years. Since 1963, the National Board has made an all-out effort to woo women between eighteen and thirty-five.

There is nothing new in the drive. As long ago as 1936, the aging Mrs. George Thacher Guernsey told the Daughters they were getting old and that, if they wished to survive in a changing world, they must have new blood to swell the ranks. With characteristic candor, she cautioned, "There are too many Junior Leaguers, university women and sorority girls who have not 'followed mother' into our society, for the simple reason that somewhere along the line we have become too 'sot in our ways.' "

In the past, the DAR never had made an open bid for recruits. Now, Mrs. Guernsey's words prompted the organization to set up the Junior Membership Committee. As an incentive, the Society let it be known that Juniors need not assume the heavy financial responsibilities of older members. Perhaps the best incentives would have been to soften policy and to offer youth a real voice in affairs and an opportunity for "intelligent activity," but these were not noticeably explored.

The DAR realized that women of the age group it wished to attract often were career girls or young wives, and Juniors were encouraged to hold occasional evening meetings of their own where patriotism could be merged with pleasant tables of bridge. However, Juniors were expected to attend the regular meetings of their elders whenever possible, and, above all, they must follow the National line, which, at the time of Mrs. Guernsey's warning, was dominated by Mrs. Becker's loyalty-oath crusade.

The campaign got off to a slow start. It did not gain sufficient momentum for the organization to give precise figures until 1947.

Each edition of the DAR handbook emphasizes "Lack of Junior Membership," as the "chief DAR weakness." Every President General has tried in her own fashion to rectify the alarming situation. In 1956, Miss Carraway offered an award to the DAR mother with the most daughters in the Society. Mrs. Margaret Clifford Jameson of Cynthiana, Kentucky, won with an enrollment of ten. An Illinois mother had nine, one from Iowa had eight, and a South Carolina matron seven. Still, today, large family memberships are the exception rather than the rule.

Another Carraway innovation was an annual honor roll, on which chapters won a gold star for meeting ten requirements. Emphasis was placed on the importance of enticing at least one Junior into each unit. Some 1,776 girls joined in 1956, and the historically significant number seemed a good omen since it brought Juniors up to 10,061. It had taken two decades of hard work, however, to push the category into five figures.

Because of counteracting factors, reports on membership growth often are misleading. For instance, there were 184,373 Daughters in 1963. Mrs. Duncan's breakdown of statistics showed 6,667 new enrollments, among them 1,364—or 26 percent—Juniors and 717 reinstatements. On the other hand, she had to announce 3,394 deaths, 3,954 resignations, and 960 drop-outs for nonpayment of dues, so the Society had lost rather than gained ground.

Her tally represented a slight slip from a 1957 high of 185,977. Mrs. Duncan's predecessor, Mrs. Ashmead White, attributed the decline to the inability of certain members to meet a dollar rise in annual dues, but it might be possible that the UN stand was at least somewhat responsible for the drop.

After 1963, when the Duncan administration started to follow a more constructive line, Society membership again began a slow upward climb. Gains were so slight that after the 1963 membership breakdown Mrs. Duncan had a tendency to quote a nice round sum of 185,000 when giving figures for publication. The next leader, Mrs. William H. Sullivan, Jr., of Scarsdale, New York, continued the custom until 1968, when, in her final report, she was able to proclaim that the Society had 188,093 Daughters, 33 percent of them Juniors—including Mrs. Nancy Woodruff Adler, who had been Miss Rheingold of 1955.

Nevertheless, compared to earlier growth, expansion has been slow in the past thirty-eight years. It is estimated that about 2 million women are eligible to become Daughters. Undoubtedly the Society's reputed inflexibility discourages many from joining. Also, aside from its reputation for meddlesome negativism, the DAR's brand of patriotism has been called droll and passé by a generation geared to protest marches and their concomitants.

When Mary Desha cried, "With a Washington, a Jefferson and an Adams, a Star Spangled Banner and a brass band we will sweep the nation," she awakened enthusiasm in contemporaries who, like herself, enjoyed parades, fireworks, and Sunday-school outings. Mrs. Cabell's emphasis on "social prestige" appealed to many ambitious young women who today would find it easier to meet the "right" people by becoming members and attending the openings of the Museum of Modern Art. These are a few of the reasons the DAR has lost luster. Quite simply, joining an organization of this sort has ceased to be the "thing" to do.

Jacqueline Kennedy notably exemplifies the change in attitude. She is eligible through her father, John Bouvier III, who belonged to both the Sons of the American Revolution and the Society of the Cincinnati. He was a glamorous figure on the New York scene during the 1920s, but he still considered it perfectly natural to join two patriotic organizations based on antecedence.

Not only is Mrs. Kennedy not a Daughter, she is the only First Lady in history to refuse the DAR the courtesy of at least one afternoon reception. When asked to give the function, soon after her husband took office, she announced that the White House was a private residence and used by its occupants in the afternoon. She added that the ladies were welcome to come during regular morning visiting hours.

The suggestion was rejected with frigid official silence, but it is rumored that many a Daughter skipped a morning session of

Congress to see just what "she" had done in "her" much-publicized restoration of the mansion. Another rumor is that on one occasion the National Board had the satisfaction of reciprocity in the feud. When Mrs. Kennedy began her refurbishing project, she asked for the gift or loan of a portrait of Andrew Jackson that hangs in the Tennessee Room in DAR headquarters and a gilt Bellanger chair directly below it. The chair belonged to James Monroe and its mate, as well as a matching table, are still at the White House, so the request, particularly for the Bellanger piece, seems reasonable. However, the Board refused on the grounds that it had no legal authority to dispose, even for a short period, of articles lent or willed to the DAR museum. It is said that the incident intensified Mrs. Kennedy's criticism of the Daughters. They were still on her mind when she was interviewed during a 1962 visit to faraway Pakistan. A *New York Herald Tribune* correspondent quoted her as calling members of the Society "old and lonely women."

DAR relationships with Lady Bird Johnson were much more cordial. She did not resume the custom of the exhausting reception, which entailed shaking hands with some 4,000 delegates. Instead, she gave an annual tea for the highest officials while lesser members roamed at will through the public sections of the premises.

The first year, at exactly 4 P.M., about 200 top-drawer Daughters filed into the Blue Room, where Mrs. Johnson waited to greet them. Mrs. Duncan, the first to be welcomed, gave the President's wife a white orchid, identical to the one she was wearing, and two pairs of long kid gloves—one white, the other bone color. Mrs. Johnson held the orchid in her hand throughout the visit and expressed delight when she opened the gloves. One guest murmured that they had been selected because they were "so utilitarian."

Lynda Bird and her college roommate also attended the party. At first they stood on the sidelines, humming and keeping time with the Marine Corps Band, which enlivened the affair with sprightly tunes like "Hello Dolly." Then, during refreshments, they mingled freely with the company.

It must be a disappointment to the Society that Mrs. Johnson is not qualified to join, but her daughters are eligible through their father. By happy coincidence, the President's claim to Revolutionary ancestry comes through the same line as that of Mary Desha. In 1965, the Daughters' Silver Jubilee year, Mrs. Duncan made an open bid for Lynda Bird and Luci Baines. She arrived at the White House tea carrying two genealogies, consisting of 160 typewritten pages. Each girl's name was embossed in gold on the cover of her copy. Unfortunately, neither prospect was on hand, but their mother gracefully accepted the gifts for them. During the presentation, Mrs. Duncan remarked that the seventy-five-year-old organization was "growing younger every day" and made a pointed reference to the increase of Juniors. To date Lynda Bird and Luci Baines are not among them.

Mrs. Sullivan became President General in 1965 and immediately intensified the effort to give the DAR a new look. She made progress in spite of odds. In her early fifties and still slim, Mrs. Sullivan had all the charm and beauty of early officers. She was the first President General in years to own a newsworthy wardrobe. At her initial reception after election, she appeared in a stunning Hattie Carnegie creation, and even her informal attire attracted constant attenton.

Mrs. Sullivan earned the nickname of an "air-conditioned president" by installing a much-needed cooling system in Constitution Hall, but admirers say she deserved the title for many other reasons. She was the first DAR leader ever to visit troops overseas and she wore slacks on the flight to Vietnam. Somebody yelled, "Hey, there's Mom!" and DAR stock went up 100 percent when she laughed and joined the boys in lively banter. Another Sullivan accomplishment was to present the Society in a favorable light during a grilling on David Susskind's program. She also diminished the cloud of racial prejudice hanging over the DAR when she greeted the guest of honor at the opening session of her final 1968 Congress: Walter Washington, first Negro mayor in the District. His wife—Dr. Bennetta B. Washington, director of Women's Job Corps Centers, who accompanied him—also was introduced from the platform.

Mrs. Sullivan's primary concern was to exhibit members as

pleasant people, not "cantankerous old ladies in tennis shoes."
Nevertheless, two unfortunate events within her term got more
publicity than all her constructive work to erase the negative
picture of the organization.

One blast of wholesale raillery came in 1965 when every news
medium took up the story that the Daughters had chastised the
Treo Company, Inc., for putting out a new line of Pop Art
girdles. A half-page ad in the August 22 *New York Times Magazine* pictured a glamorous model caught in the act of donning a
pullover. Her only other article of clothing was Pop-Pants embellished with two eyes, tears splashing out of the left one. This
probably did not shock Mrs. W. Carl Crittenden, national chairman of the DAR Flag Committee, but the filmstrip on the left
side of the ad most certainly did. Second from the top was an
odious garment made of bold vertical red and white stripes supported by a white waistband exhibiting eight brash blue stars. It
was called the "Stars 'n' Stripes" girdle. Mrs. Crittenden hastily
consulted President General Sullivan. Over the telephone, they
agreed it was mockery to name a girdle after "Old Glory." Mrs.
Crittenden dispatched a prompt letter to the manufacturer in
which she condemned the "shocking caricature" of the national
emblem and demanded its instant removal from the Treo line.
"Patriotism should be encouraged by proper respect to the Stars
and Stripes, the symbol of this great country and the many
opportunities enjoyed here," she reminded the merchandisers.
She said that she believed all patriotic citizens would join the
DAR in agreeing that it was deplorable "to downgrade our flag
in this fashion."

On August 24, immediately upon receipt of her letter, Treo
called a board meeting. Next day, Harry L. Gross, secretary-
treasurer of the company, released a public apology. "We, of
course, had never called the garment a flag. We called it bunting, among ourselves," he explained. He admitted that about
3,000 Stars 'n' Stripes girdles were in circulation and that it was
too early to estimate retail sales. However, he said the rest had
been recalled because "the D.A.R. or any other organized group
can spread comment that would be detrimental to us." When
asked what would happen to the offending garments, Gross

sighed: "We'll burn the damned things or send them to some foreign country where our flag isn't involved." Then, as an afterthought, he added: "Maybe we can give them away as charity gifts to people in other parts of the world." Daughters made no further comment. Perhaps Treo's decision was too reminiscent of Mrs. Talmadge's willingness to let Georgia sell 30,000 copies of Magruder's *American Government* to any other school system in the Union after it was deemed unfit for home consumption.

The second event occurred in May 1967, when President General Sullivan refused to rent Constitution Hall to Joan Baez on the grounds that she had no right to withhold part of her income tax as a protest against the Vietnam war. Several months later, Miss Baez countered by obtaining permission to give a free concert at Sylvan Theater, an outdoor, government-owned stage situated between the Washington Monument and the tidal basin. The concert was scheduled for August 14. Mrs. Sullivan wrote a personal letter to Secretary of the Interior Stewart L. Udall in a final effort to ban the performance. Her protest read:

> I respectfully request that Joan Baez be denied the privilege of using property supported by Federal taxes, since it has been reported in the press that she refused to pay a portion of her own legal Federal taxes because of disagreement with Government policy concerning the Vietnam war.

On the Saturday before the concert Mrs. Sullivan confirmed her request when interviewed by *The New York Times*, then she added that the DAR stood firmly behind the government's Vietnam policy and felt support should be given to our boys who were dying there. A spokesman for the department indicated that Secretary Udall was not shown the letter since it was not the department's policy to inquire into the political views of artists granted the use of the stage.

Wearing a short bright orange dress, the pacifist folk singer prefaced her concert by thanking the DAR for all the publicity. She twitted the Society throughout the evening, to the immense amusement of her fans. She called the DAR protest "petty and silly" and said, "The main point where the D.A.R. and I differ is that they feel the nation comes above all. The whole problem is that 123 nations feel the same way." Then she asserted that the Daughters were "acting out the same kind of fear we all make mistakes by."

In a special *Times* report, B. Drummond Ayres, Jr. recalled the similarity of the circumstances to those of the Marian Anderson "incident." Miss Anderson, upon her retirement in 1965, had shown more charity than Miss Baez. When asked how she felt about the DAR after so long a time, she replied that she had forgiven them years ago. "You lose a lot of time hating people," she added.

In 1968, Patriots' Day was on Friday, and the DAR Congress was scheduled to convene on the preceding Monday, April 15. The delegates turned out in full force because this again was a DAR election year. Neither candidate possessed Mrs. Sullivan's youthful flair or photogenic features, but Mrs. John J. Ragan, the loser, seemed to be more concerned with continuing to modernize the DAR image than was her successful opponent, Mrs. Erwin F. Seimes.

Mrs. Ragan, a Washingtonian, is a retired Treasury Department employee. In her campaign she made a noticeable effort to gear the Society to current trends and promised, if elected, to give Junior members of college age more leadership responsibility. On the other hand, Mrs. Seimes, of Delaware, who is also a retired career woman, vowed strict adherence to DAR principles of law, order, and morality. While electioneering she was careful to explain that her views were nonpolitical, but she emphasized that "we should not be allowed to have too much civil disobedience" and expressed strong approval of the official ban on Joan Baez's concert at Constitution Hall "because of her direct opposition to the things we stand for."

Two former—and very militant—defense chairmen were prominent on her slate. Mrs. Wilson K. Barnes (whose pet project had been to harass UNICEF) was running for Organizing Secretary General, and Mrs. Herbert S. Jones, who acted under Mrs. Duncan, was up as First Vice President General.

Mrs. Jones was the author of the circular letter on the test-ban treaty to which Senator Neuberger objected. Even after it became the Duncan policy to muffle the reactionary tone in public, Mrs. Jones' articles in the DAR monthly show that she continued to give the Daughters fiery old-guard tirades for private consumption.

The Seventy-seventh Congress was in no mood for liberalism. For the first time since 1965, DAR motions were sufficiently bombastic to merit detailed press coverage. Elizabeth Shelton, a *Washington Post* staff writer, devoted an entire article to the 1968 platform under the heading "DAR Follows Hard Line on Resolutions."

Nullification of the United Nations charter had crept back into the agenda. The proposal for a three-day weekend to celebrate national holidays was opposed because it resembled "compulsory controls over leisure time and recreation imposed by authoritarian governments." Urban renewal was sharply criticized since it could lead to a "monolithically unified Nation." Out of the fourteen resolutions adopted, the strongest was the one on lawlessness. It noted that "unless a firm policy of law enforcement is followed, mob violence, insurrection and anarchy may well destroy our Nation" and demanded that federal, state, and local governments "use every available means necessary to end violence and crime and to restore order and justice . . ."

Someone wanted to add a clause stating the assassinations and riot deaths were evidence of threats to domestic tranquillity. It failed to be seconded when another delegate objected to Dr. Martin Luther King's name being included in the assassination category. "Assassination," she insisted, "is reserved for heads of state."

Mrs. Ragan and her progressive program were defeated. On the last day, after the installation of President General Seimes, another Congress ended with the traditional custom of Daughters clasping hands and singing the hymn "Blest Be the Tie That Binds."

All day long the staff, systematically but quietly, had been putting the building to bed for another year. By about 3:30 on the afternoon of April 19, lobby concessionnaires had almost finished packing their wares. Only "Ask Mr. Foster" remained open to give final travel aid to a belated inquirer. In the vestibule, a distributor collected last-minute orders for the *Washington Post* while his assistant snapped newspapers out of the wire rack in front of the building. Finally, an employee jiggled the door of the auditorium from the outside to make sure it was locked.

The scarcity of taxis was pathetic evidence of the end of festivities. Fickle drivers, enticed by new conventions, left the last stragglers to hail in vain at the scene of their recent glories. One delegate strolled over to the small formal garden where the monument dedicated to the founders stands. Executed by the DAR Mrs. Gertrude Vanderbilt Whitney in 1929, it is a statue of a woman with outstretched arms. On a tablet behind her are carved these words:

|  |  |
|---|---|
| TO THE WOMEN WHOSE | THE NATIONAL SOCIETY |
| PATRIOTIC FORESIGHT | DAUGHTERS OF THE |
| MADE POSSIBLE | AMERICAN REVOLUTION |
|  | OCTOBER XI MDCCCXC |

Below, each under a spinning wheel–distaff seal, are the four names: Mary Desha, Eugenia Washington, Ellen Hardin Walworth and Mary Smith Lockwood.

A huge wreath in front of the statue commemorates members who died in the previous year. It had been placed there during the traditional service on the Sunday afternoon before the opening of every Congress. It is an impressive ceremony. As the President General reads the names of the deceased one by one, a page steps forward to tuck a white carnation into the theretofore unadorned greenery.

Now, at the end of the 1968 Congress, as the Daughter stood in front of the memorial, the flowers were withered and yellowing and an old caretaker came to remove them. For a moment he hesitated but finally, knowing that the job must be done, he asked her gently if she would like a flower. In silence, she took one.

He was gone. The wreath was gone. Maple seed pods floated

down like tears of mute salutation. Bowing her head, she walked
down the box-lined path leading from the shrine. Suddenly she
saw one rebellious blade of grass shooting up through the heavy
gravel. How had it managed to survive the poisonous spray of
the gardeners? She stooped and yanked it up. It did not seem
to occur to her that, in a way, she was destroying a minor
miracle; that the blade of grass might represent the resistance
of youthful brave innocence. Perhaps another year, another
year. . . .

# BIBLIOGRAPHY

## BOOKS

Addams, Jane, *Newer Ideals of Peace.* New York, 1911.
——, *Patriotism and Pacifism in Wartime.* New York, 1917.
Allen, Frederick Lewis, *Only Yesterday: An Informal History of the Nineteen-Twenties.* New York, 1931.
Barrington, Lewis, *Historic Restorations of the Daughters of the American Revolution.* New York, 1941.
Beer, Thomas, *The Mauve Decade.* Garden City, N.Y., 1926.
Bell, Daniel, ed., *The Radical Right: Expanded and Updated.* New York, 1954.
Bendiner, Robert, *Just Around the Corner: A Highly Selective History of the Thirties.* New York, 1967.
Buel, Elizabeth Barney, *Report on War Work: DAR in Connecticut 1914–1918.* Meriden, Conn., 1920.
Curti, Merle, *The Roots of American Loyalty.* New York, 1946.
——, *Peace or War, The American Struggle.* New York, 1936.
*Cyclopedia of American Biography.*
Darling, Flora Adams, *Founding and Organization of the Daughters of the American Revolution and the Daughters of the Revolution.* Philadelphia, Pa., 1901.
Davis, Wallace Evan, *Patriotism on Parade.* Cambridge, Mass., 1955.
Devens, R. M., *Our First Century.* Mass., 1881.
Engelbrecht, H. C. and Hanighen, F. C., *Merchants of Death.* New York, 1934.
Ferguson, Charles W., *Fifty Million Americans.* New York, 1937.
Gabriel, Ralph H., *The Course of American Democratic Thought.* New York, 1940.
Hapgood, Norman, *Professional Patrioteers.* New York, 1927.
Hofstadter, Richard, *Anti-intellectualism in American Life.* New York, 1963.

234      *Bibliography*

Kempton, Murray, *Part of Our Time.* New York, 1955.
Lockwood, Mary S. and Sherwood, Emily Lee, *Story of the Records DAR.* Washington, D.C., 1906.
Lockwood, Mary S., *Historic Homes in Washington.* New York, 1889.
Nelson, Jack and Roberts, Gene, Jr., *The Censors and the Schools.* Boston, 1963.
Pierce, Bessie Louise, *Public Opinion and the Teaching of History in the U.S.* New York, 1926.
———, *Citizens Organizations and the Civic Training of Youth.* New York, 1933.
Strayer, Martha, *The DAR: An Informal History.* Washington, D.C., 1958.
Sullivan, Mark, *Our Times: The United States 1900–1925,* Vols. I-IV. New York, 1933.
Webb, William Seward, *Historical Notes on Organization, Sons of the American Revolution.* New York, 1890.
Wector, Dixon, *The Saga of American Society.* New York, 1937.

PERIODICALS

Aikman, Lonnelle, "The DAR Story." *National Geographic Magazine* (November, 1951).
*American Historical Magazine* (1939–1946).
*American Monthly* (1892–1912).
Bailie, Helen Tufts, "Dishonoring the DAR." *The Nation* (September 25, 1929).
"Blacklist Party." *The Nation* (May 23, 1928).
Catt, Carrie Chapman, "An Open Letter to the DAR." *The Woman Citizen* (July, 1927).
Cline, Leonard, "The War on the Peace Seekers." *The New Republic* (July 2 and 9, 1924).
Coolidge, Calvin, "Enemies of the Republic." *The Delineator* (June, July, August, 1921).
*Daughters of the American Revolution Magazine* (1913–1939, 1946–1968).
Dutton, Margaret Payne, "The DAR Sees Red." *The Forum* (1936).

Eastman, Elaine Goodale, "Are DAR Women Exploited?" *The Christian Century* (September 11, 1929).

Faulkner, Harold Underwood, "Perverted American History." *Harpers Monthly* (1926).

Gibbs, Angelica, "Madam President General Mrs. O'Byrne." *Life* (November 17, 1947).

Howard, Sidney, "Our Professional Patriots." *The New Republic* (August 20, 1924; September 3, 10, 17, 24, 1924; October 1, 8, 15, 1924).

Kenney, Hon. Edward A., "Educators Should Take Oath." *National Republic* (June, 1934).

Morse, J. Mitchell, "Daughters of the Counter Revolution." *The Nation* (June 1, 1946).

*The Nation.* (July 4 and 18, 1928).

*National Defender*, The DAR National Defense Committee.

Schnapper, M. B., "DAR in the Schoolroom." *The Nation* (September 18, 1937).

Smith, Helena Huntington, "Mrs. Brosseau and the DAR." *Outlook and Independent* (March 20, 1929).

Villard, Oswald Garrison, "What the Blue Menace Means." *Harper's Magazine* (October, 1928).

## PAMPHLETS

Buel, Elizabeth E. Barney, *Socialist Propaganda in the United States*. Connecticut DAR, 1925.

*DAR Buildings in the Nation's Capital*, 1951.

*DAR Handbook*, 1960.

*DAR Schools*, 1966.

Desha, Mary, *Circular of the Columbian liberty bell committee*. Washington?, 1893?

Gorden, Rosalie M., *What's Happened to Our Schools?* America's Future, Inc., 1956.

*Handbook of the National Society of the Children of the American Revolution*, 3rd edition. 1961.

"In Regard to Criticisms of the Schools and Problems of Concern to." *State of the Nation Bulletin No. 6*, Commission on Professional Rights and Responsibilities, National Education Association (December, 1967).

*In Washington, Diamond Anniversary 1890–1965.* 1965.
*Is That Lineage Right?* 1958.
McCausland, Elizabeth, *"The Blue Menace." Reprint of The Springfield Republic* (March 19–27, 1928).
*Ritual.* National Society Daughters of the American Revolution, 1961.
*What the Daughters Do,* 22nd edition. 1963.


VARIOUS PAMPHLETS PUBLISHED BY
The DAR NATIONAL DEFENSE COMMITTEE.

*Facts About UNICEF.* April, 1962.
Jones, Sara R. (Mrs. Henry S.), *United Nations Resolutions: DAR Endorsement to Repudiation 1946–1963.*
*Marxism in Christmas Cards.*
*Textbook Study 1958–1959.*

# Index

244  *Index*